Iowa Barn Quilt

Coloring Book

John H. Lettau

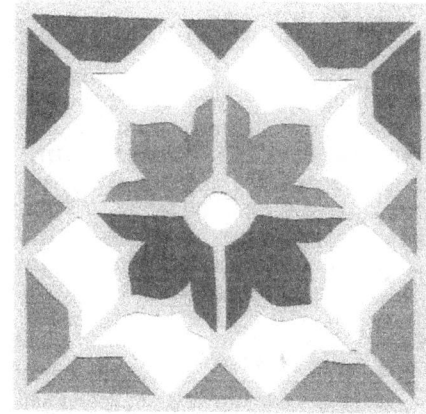

9th Infantry Division

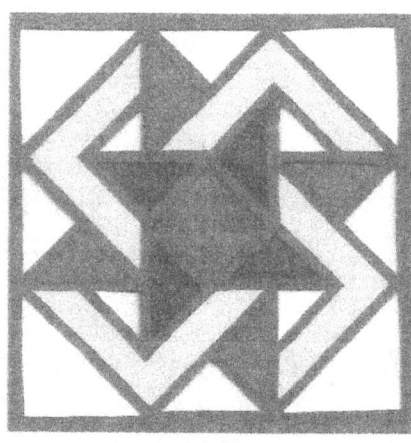

An Iowa Sun

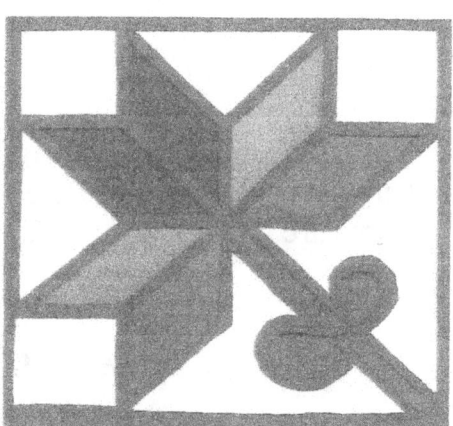

Single Lily

Barn Quilts of Delaware County Iowa

Cover Quilts
Cross & Crown...Yankee Puzzle
Season's Joy...Prosperity

2016 Copyright John Lettau & Shawna Lettau

Delaware County Iowa Barn Quilt Project

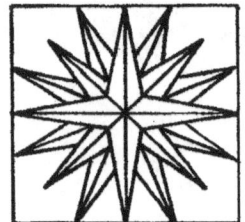 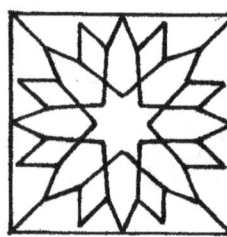 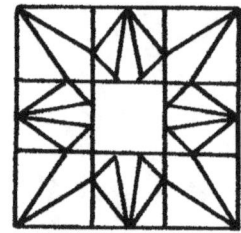 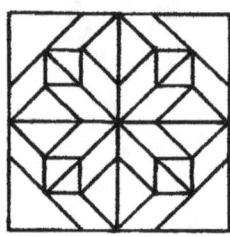 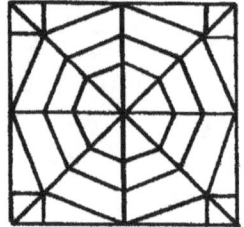

A drive through Delaware County is very colorful today because many brilliant "quilt blocks," called barn quilts, are on display on barns throughout the area. Five sample barns quilt patterns located in the county are pictured above...Mariner's Star, Starry Compass, Wisconsin Star, Rolling Star, and Homecoming.

The Barn Quilts of Delaware County was started by the Manchester Area Chamber of Commerce and the Quiltmaker's Shoppe and currently have over 75 barn quilts mounted and on display and more in the works.

The Barn Quilts of Delaware County is organized to educate, promote and celebrate the unique agricultural heritage of Delaware County through the visual combination of barns and quilts. Barns are vital to the economic well-being of the rural community, and the comfort of hand-made quilts provide warmth, beauty, and an outlet for individual artistic expression

Barn Quilts of Delaware County Objectives

1. Making it a fun project.
2. Bring tourists to Delaware County.
3. Bring smiles to the faces of travelers.
4. Build pride in the area.
5. Highlight the rural countryside.

What is a Barn Quilt?

A barn quilt is made by painting a barn quilt pattern on two 4' by 8'sheets of ¾ inch plywood then mounting them on barn to form an eight foot square. Two coats of primer are applied to both sides of the boards and the edges. After the pattern is drawn out Frog (painter's) tape is applied. Three coats of each color are applied, with each coat being allowed to dry overnight. After the quilt is finished, it is allowed to dry for at least two weeks before it is put upon a barn.

Barn Quilts of Delaware County Information

Books-Maps-Tours
Manchester Area Chamber of Commerce
The Quiltmaker's Shoppe in Manchester

On the next page find a listing of the 48 Delaware County barn quilts in this coloring book.

Barn Quilts of Delaware County Iowa

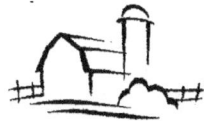

Woohoo	Hwy 3	Colesburg
Weather Vane	Firefly Rd	Manchester
Circling Swallows	210th Ave	Manchester
Father's Choice	190th Ave	Manchester
Cross & Crown	Linn-Delaware Rd	Coggon
An Iowa Sun	Hwy 13	Manchester
Grandmother's Choice	150th Ave	Manchester
Prairie Queen	Thunder Rd	Hopkinton
Yankee Puzzle	Quarter Rd	Hopkinton
Kansas	195th St	Manchester
Kaleidoscope	132nd St	Dundee
Twisting Star	275th St	Delhi
Double Star	110th Ave	Masonville
Hole in the Barn Door	137th St	Dundee
Mountain Star	Franklin St	Delhi
Ohio Star	150th Ave	Manchester
North Star	275th St	Delhi
Wisconsin Star	Hwy 38	Hopkinton
Mother's Fancy	310th Ave	Hopkinton
Colonial Garden	218thSt	Earlville
Blazing Star	Jet Rd	Greeley
Season's Joy	320th Ave	Worthington
Railroad Crossing	275th St	Delhi
Summer Blooms	150th Ave	Ryan
Double T	195th St	Manchester
Broken Band	182nd St	Dryersville
Union Star	315th St	Hopkinton
Rolling Star	200th Ave	Hopkinton
Mariner's Star	330th St	Goggon
9th Infancy Division	Hwy 13	Ryan
Four Tulips	310th St	Ryan
Lasting Bloom	210th Ave	Manchester
Star of Lahoma	315th St	Hopkinton
Starry Compass	110th Ave	Dundee
Bright Side	Thunder Rd	Hopkinton
Turning Star	330th Ave	Coggon
Single Lily	110th Ave	Masonville
Homeward Star	165th St	Manchester
Card Basket	160th Ave	Strawberry Point
The Long Pointed Star	248th St	Manchester
1094 Star	230th Ave	Hopkinton
Old Grey Goose	120th Ave	Dundee
Prosperity	Quarter Rd	Hopkinton
Home Again	Stiles	Manchester
Lucky Star	Hwy 38	Delhi
Homecoming	230th Ave	Delhi
Eyes of Blue	310th St	Hopkinton
Country Pride	190th Ave	Manchester

Barn Quilt Woohoo
Delaware County Iowa

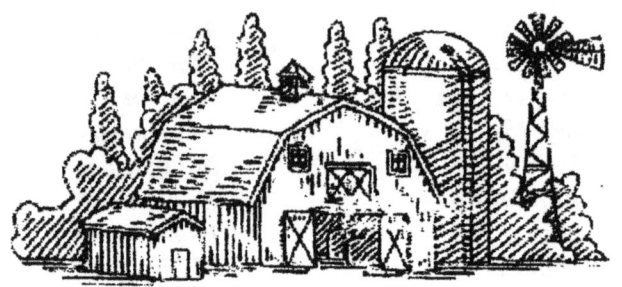

Barn Quilt Location
Hwy 3
Colesburg, Iowa

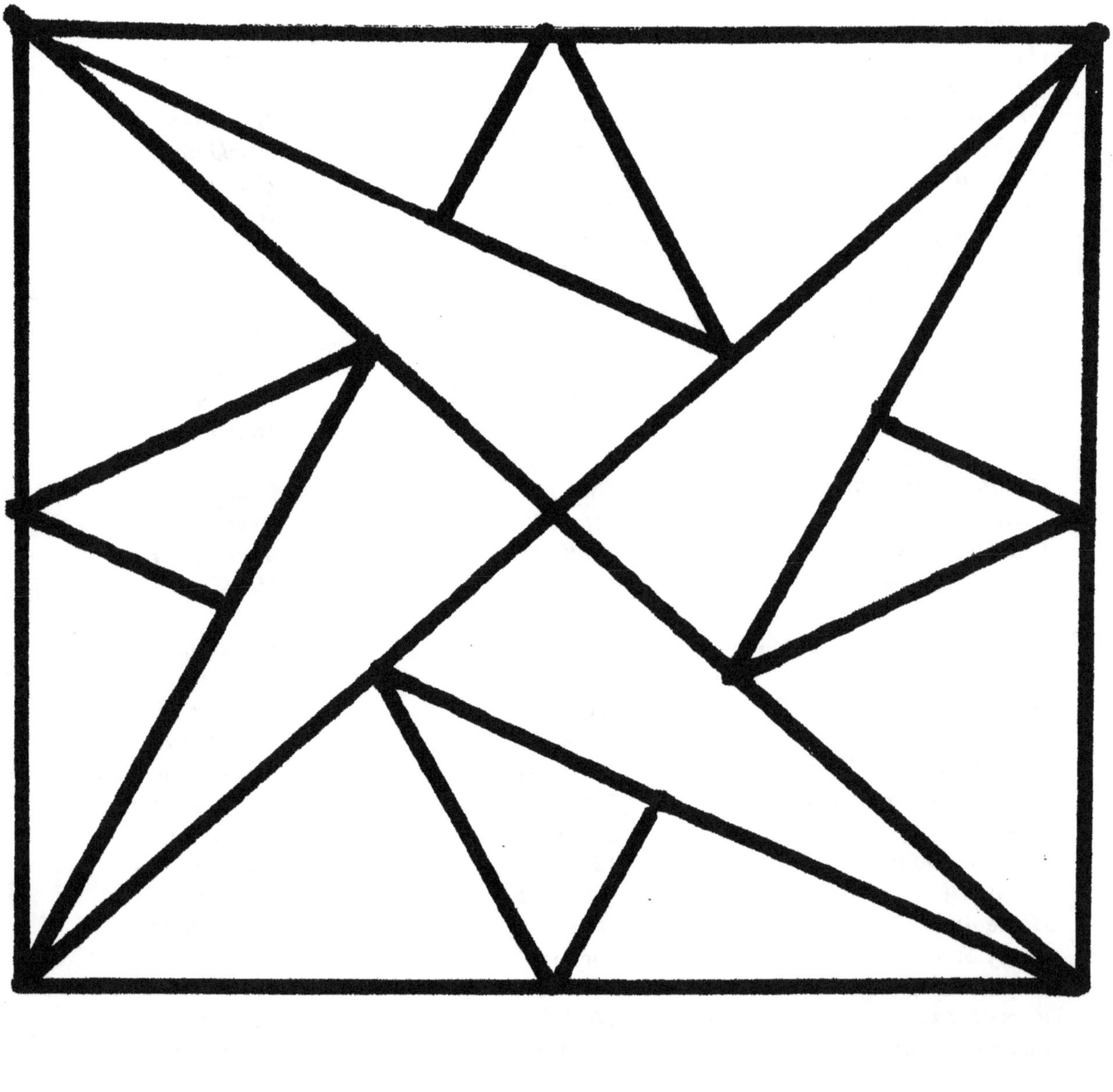

Barn Quilt Woohoo

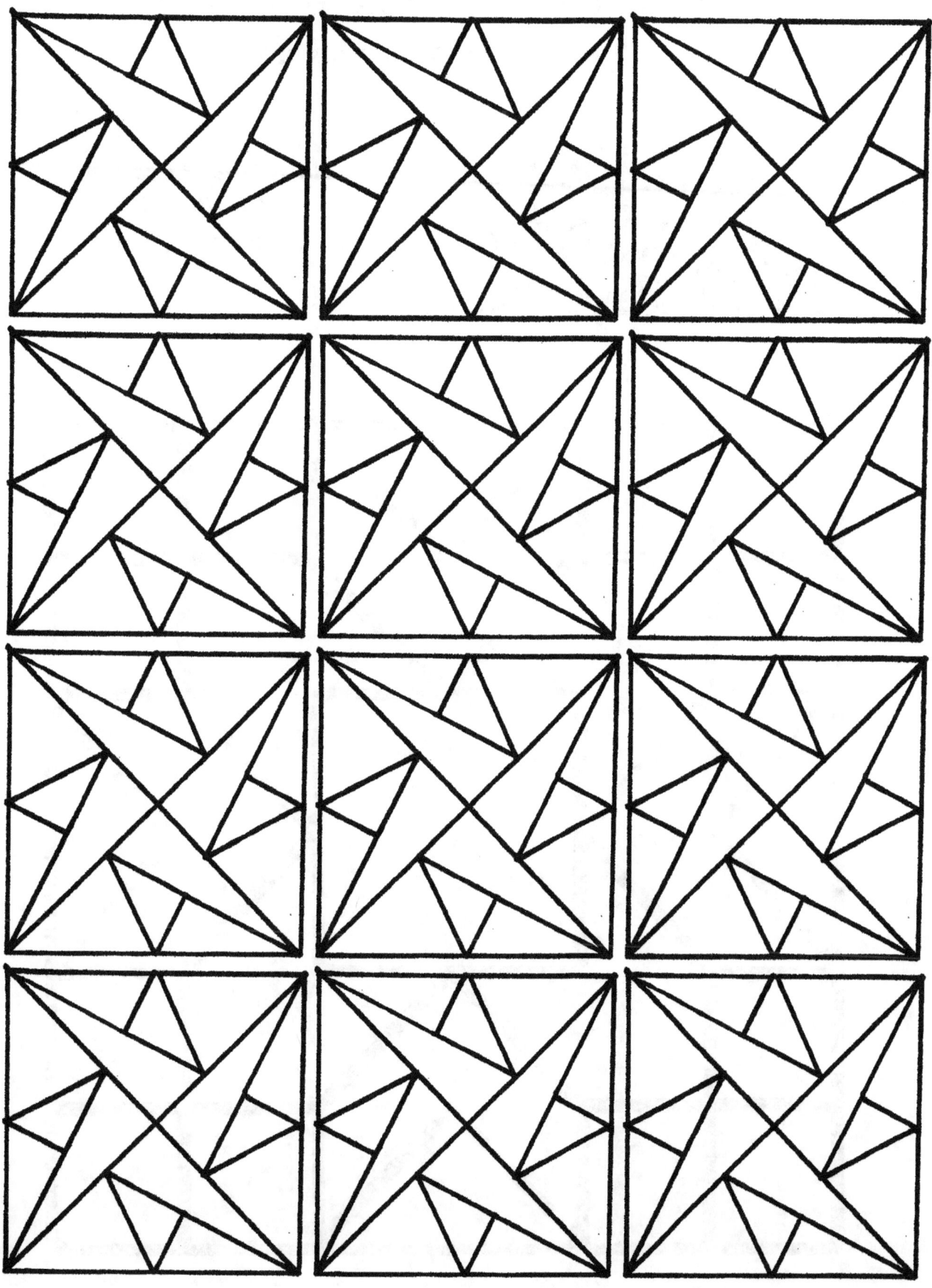

Barn Quilt Weather Vane
Delaware County Iowa

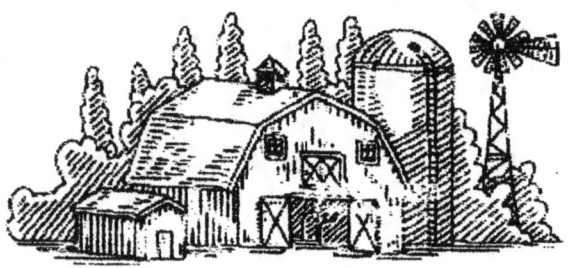

Barn Quilt Location
Firefly Rd
Manchester, Iowa

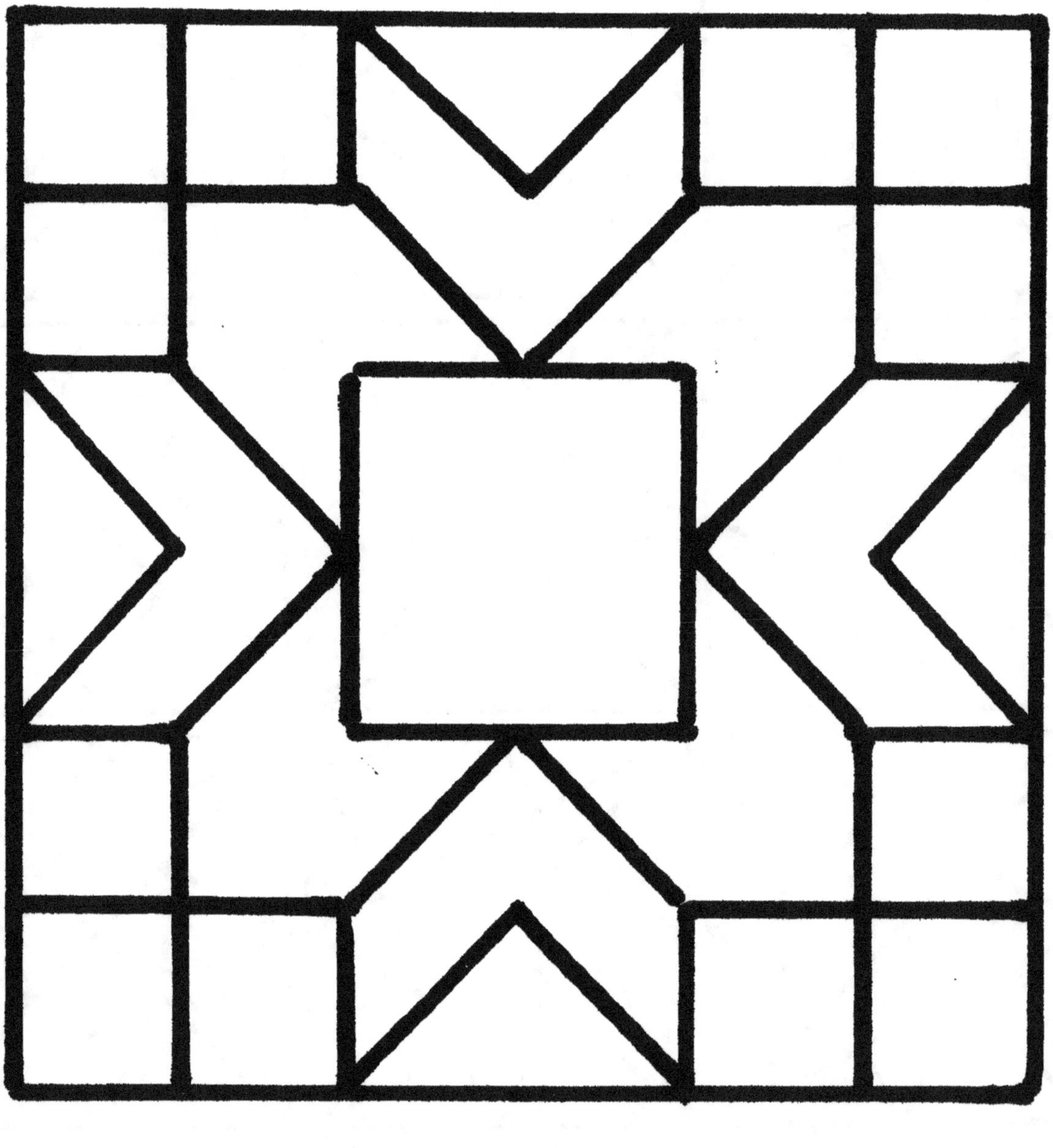

Barn Quilt Weather Vane

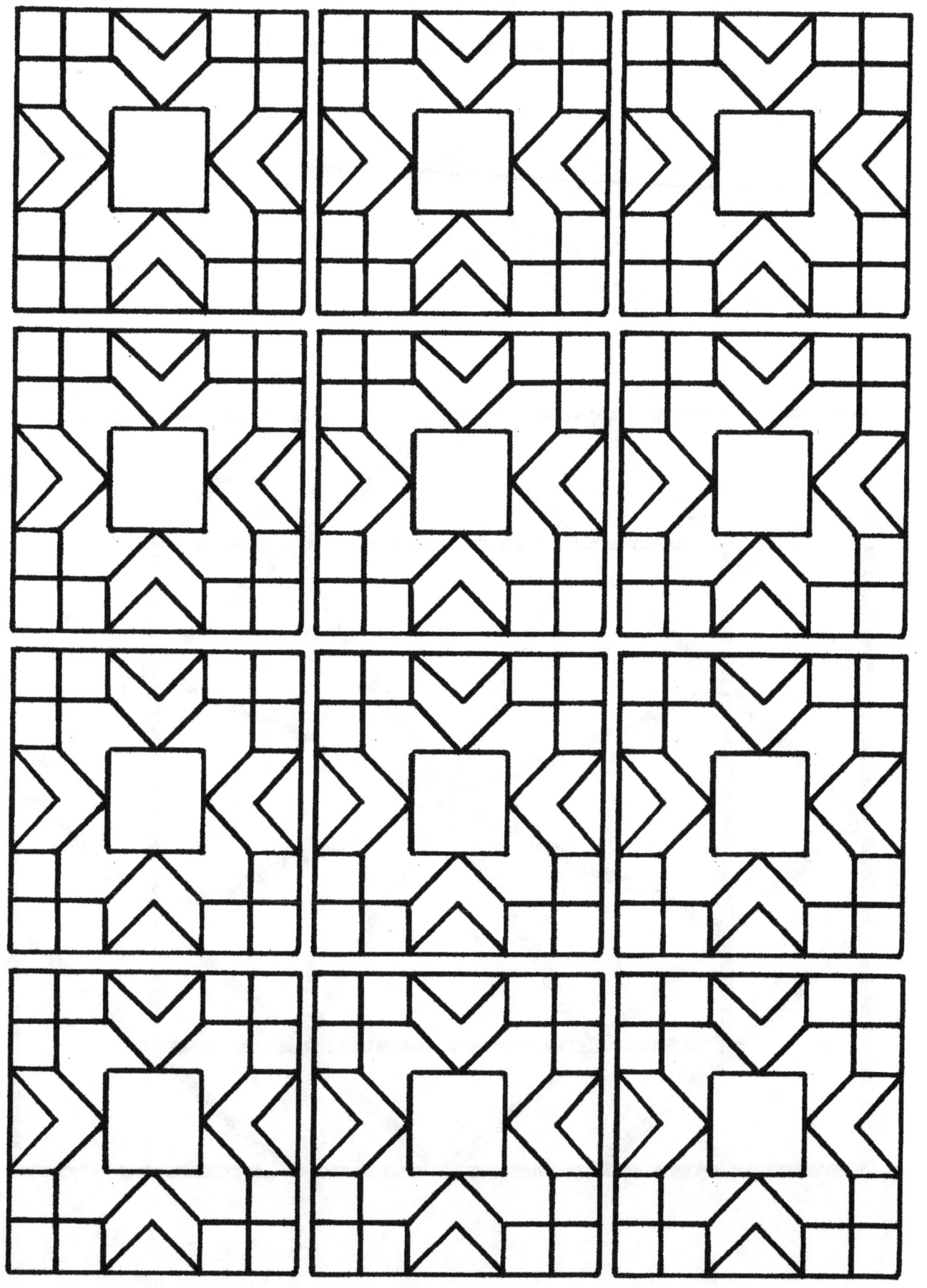

Barn Quilt Circling Swallows
Delaware County Iowa

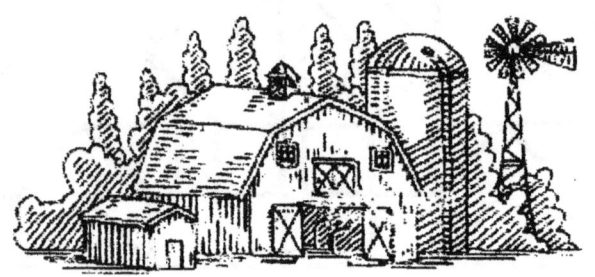

Barn Quilt Location
210th Ave
Manchester, Iowa

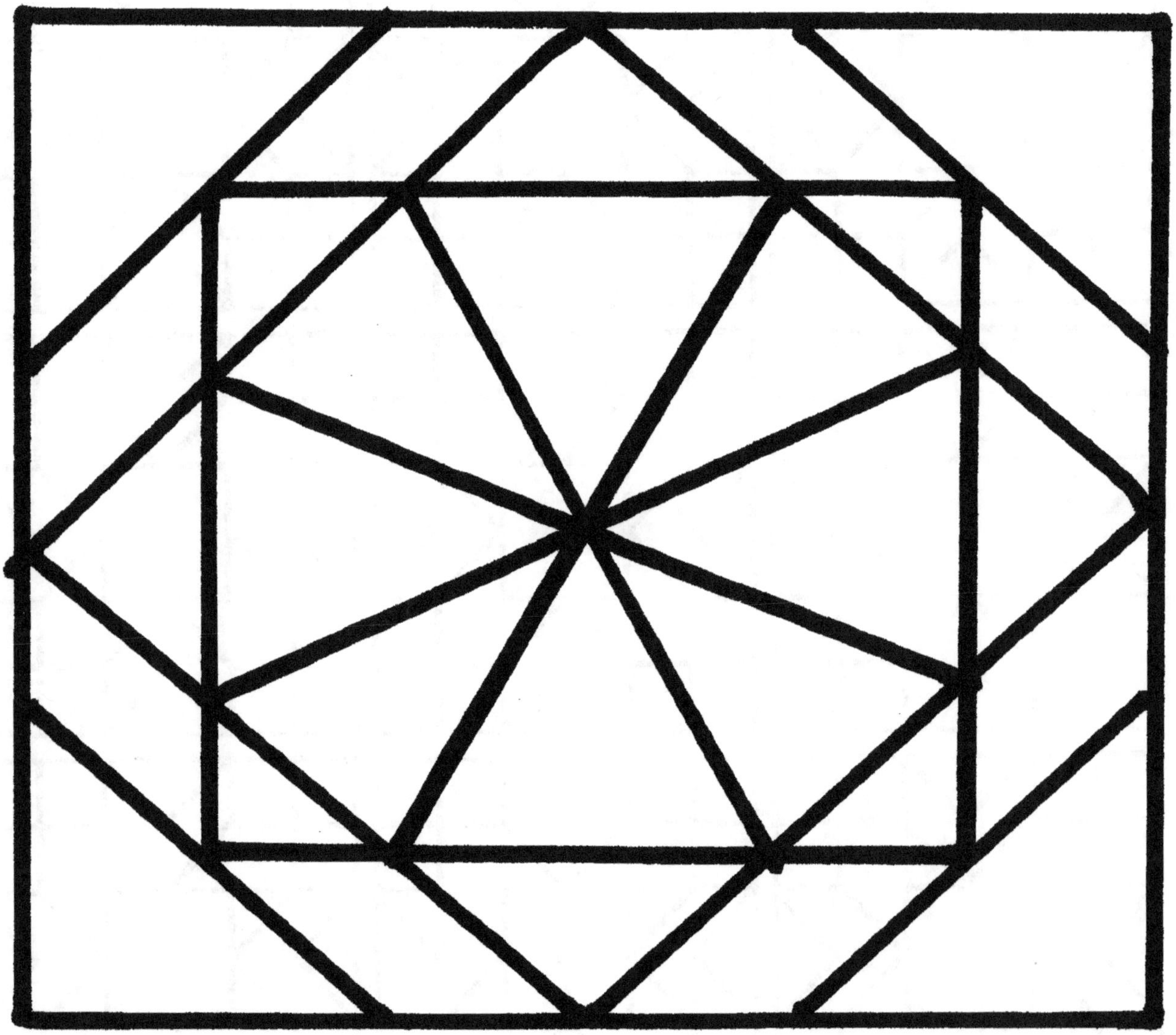

Barn Quilt Circling Swallows

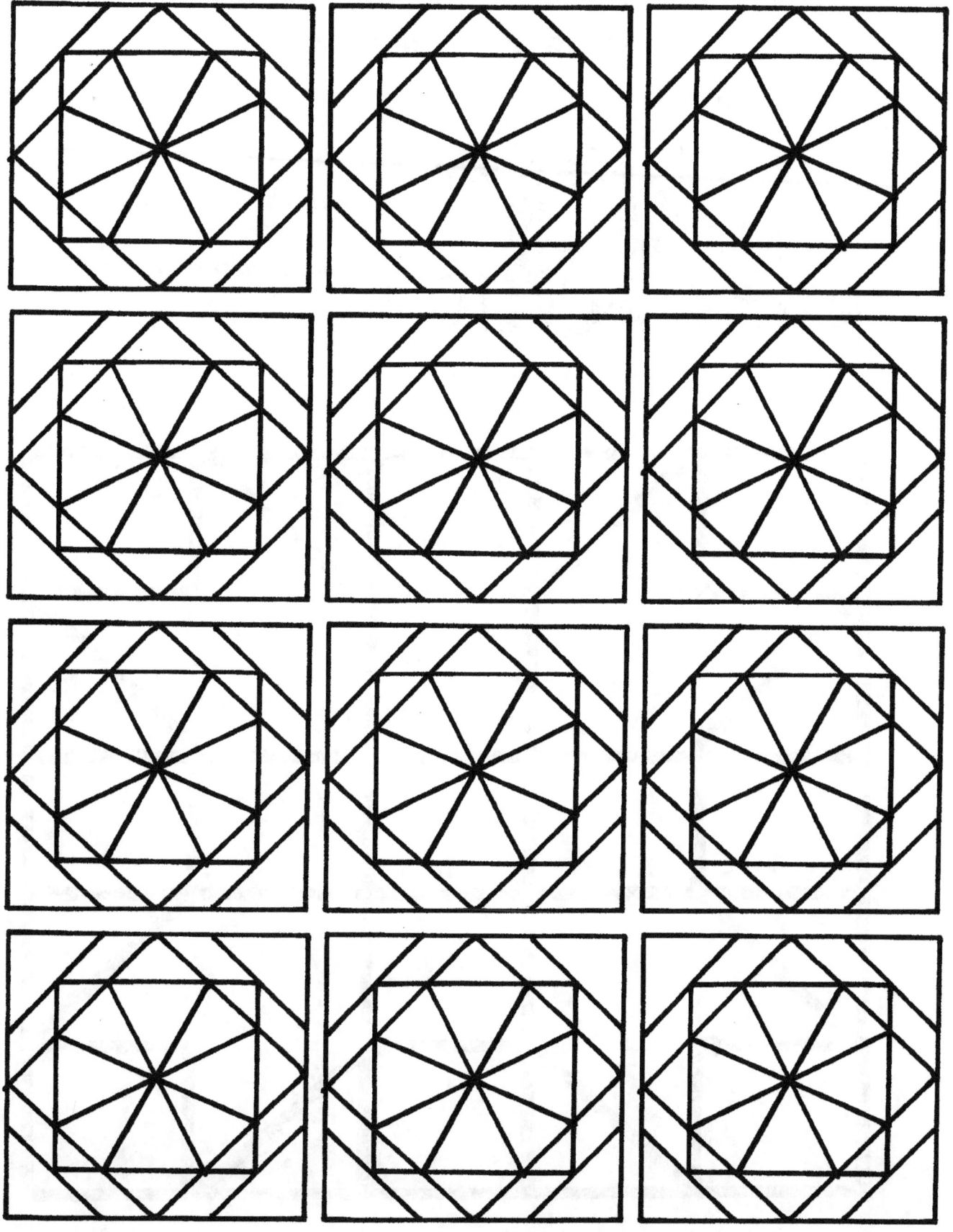

Barn Quilt Father's Choice
Delaware County Iowa

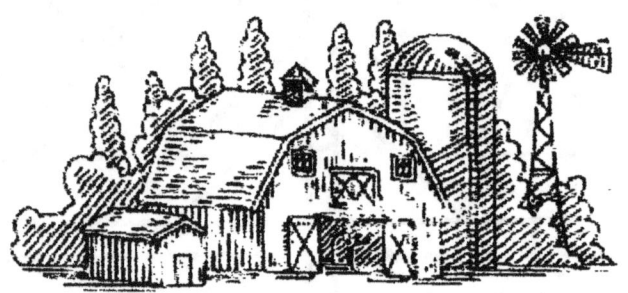

Barn Quilt Location
190th Ave
Manchester, Iowa

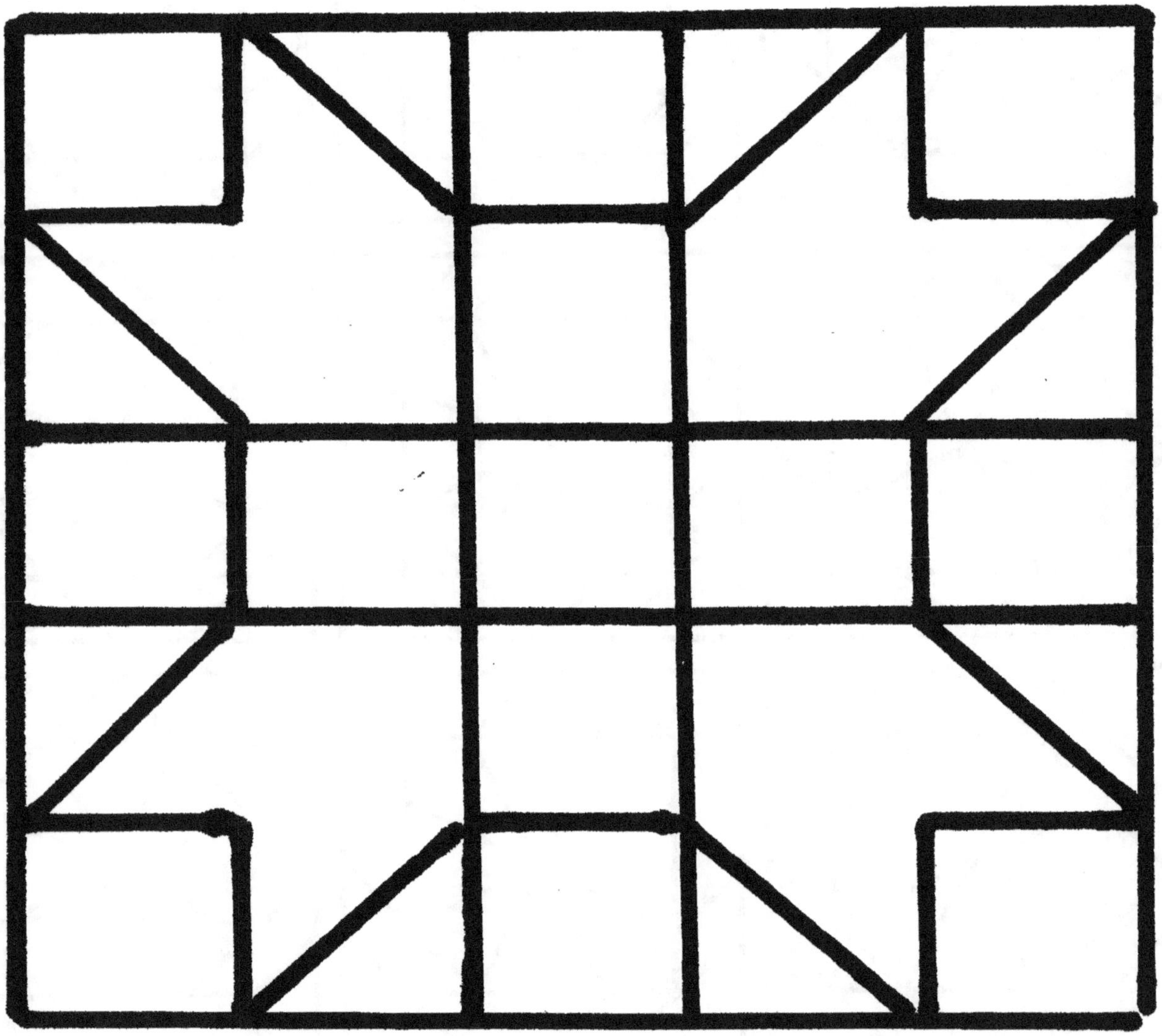

Barn Quilt Father's Choice

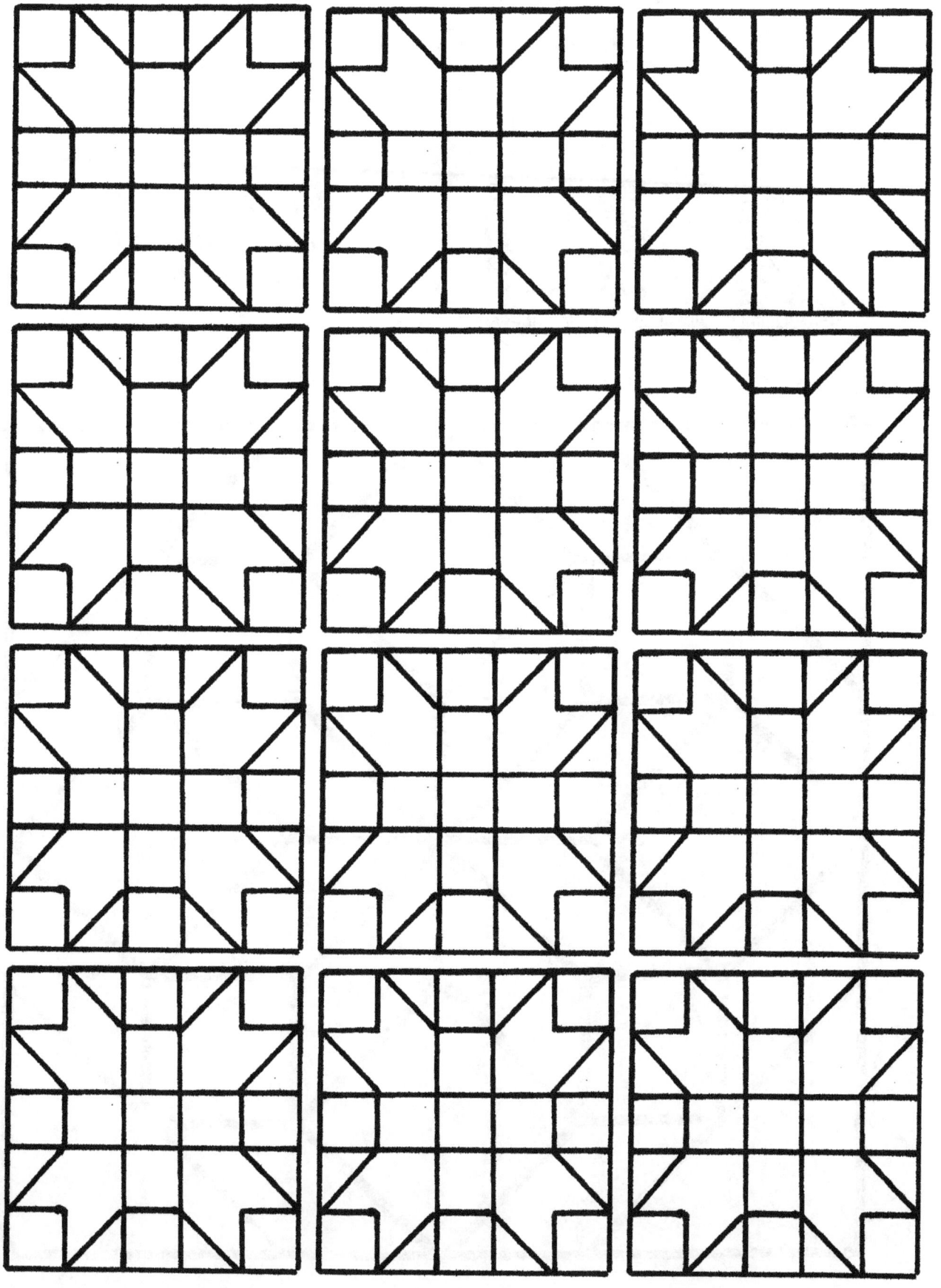

Barn Quilt Cross & Crown
Delaware County Iowa

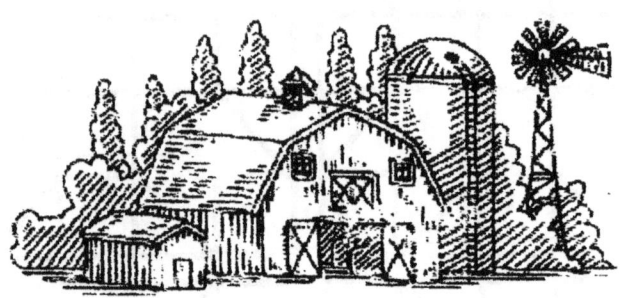

Barn Quilt Location
Linn-Delaware Rd
Coggon, Iowa

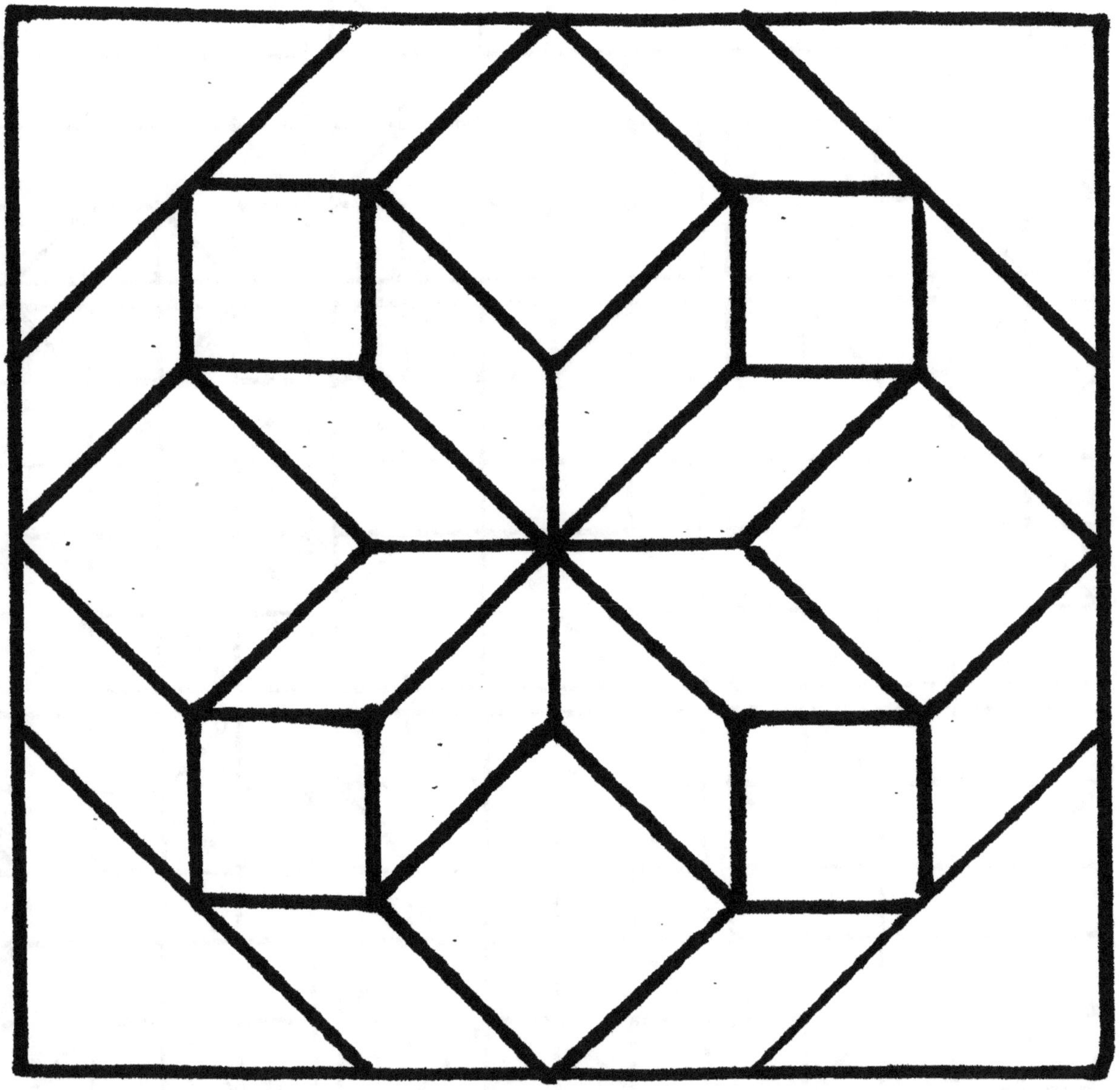

Barn Quilt Cross & Crown

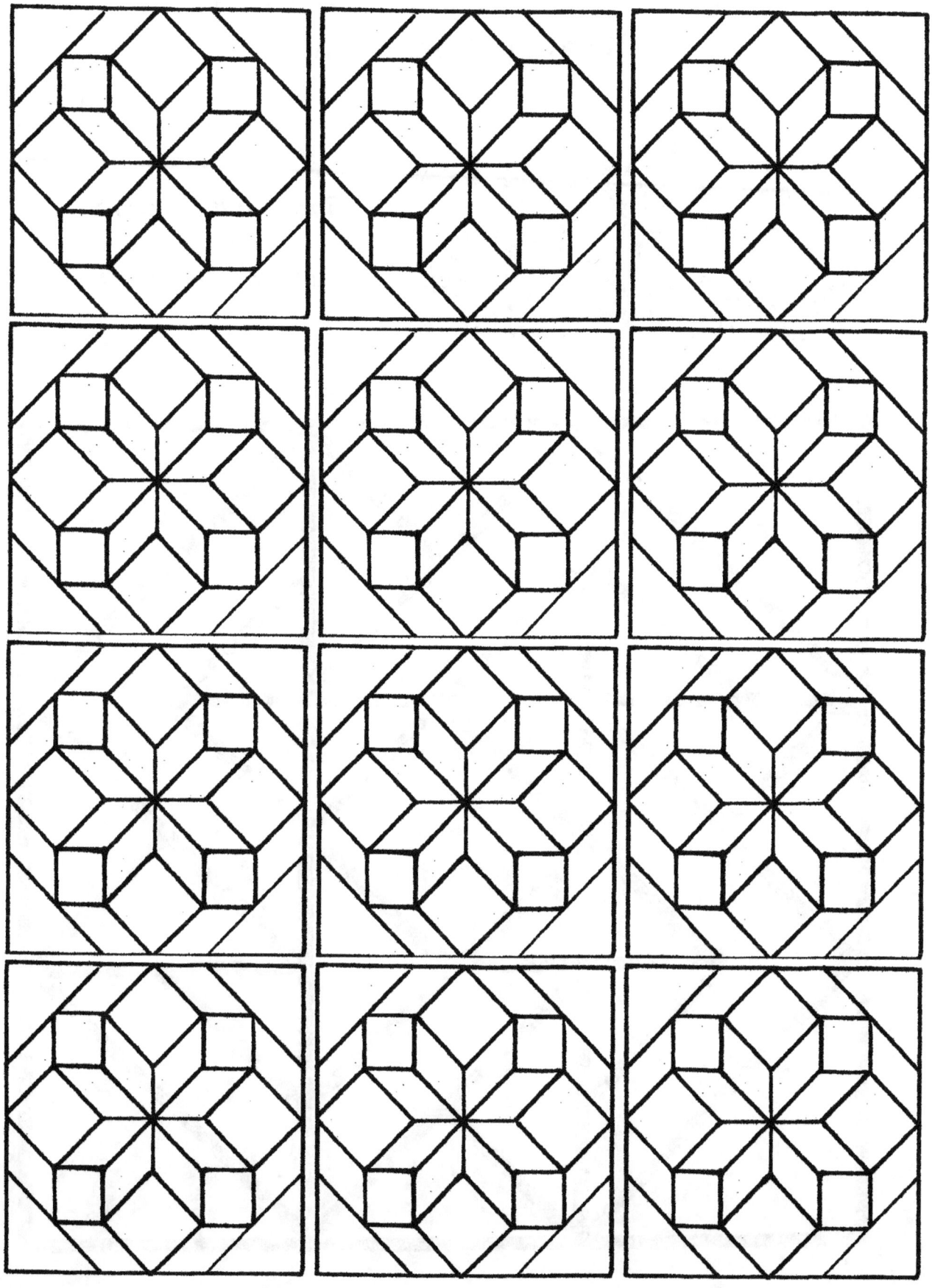

Barn Quilt An Iowa Sun
Delaware County Iowa

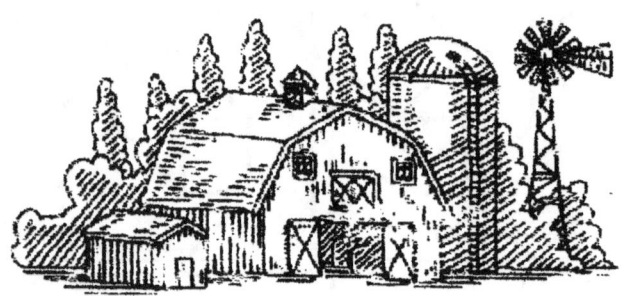

Barn Quilt Location
Hwy 13
Manchester, Iowa

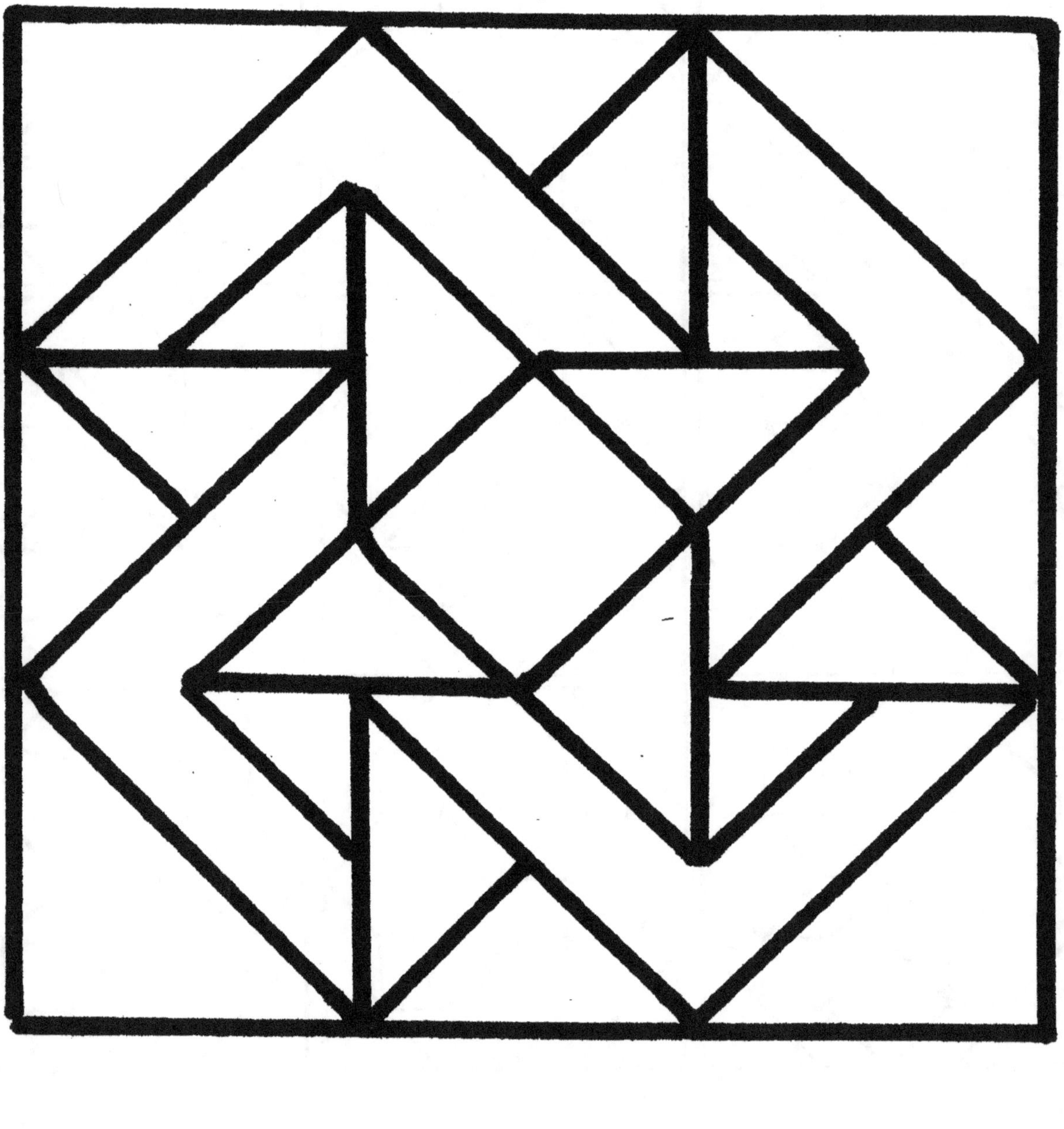

Barn Quilt An Iowa Sun

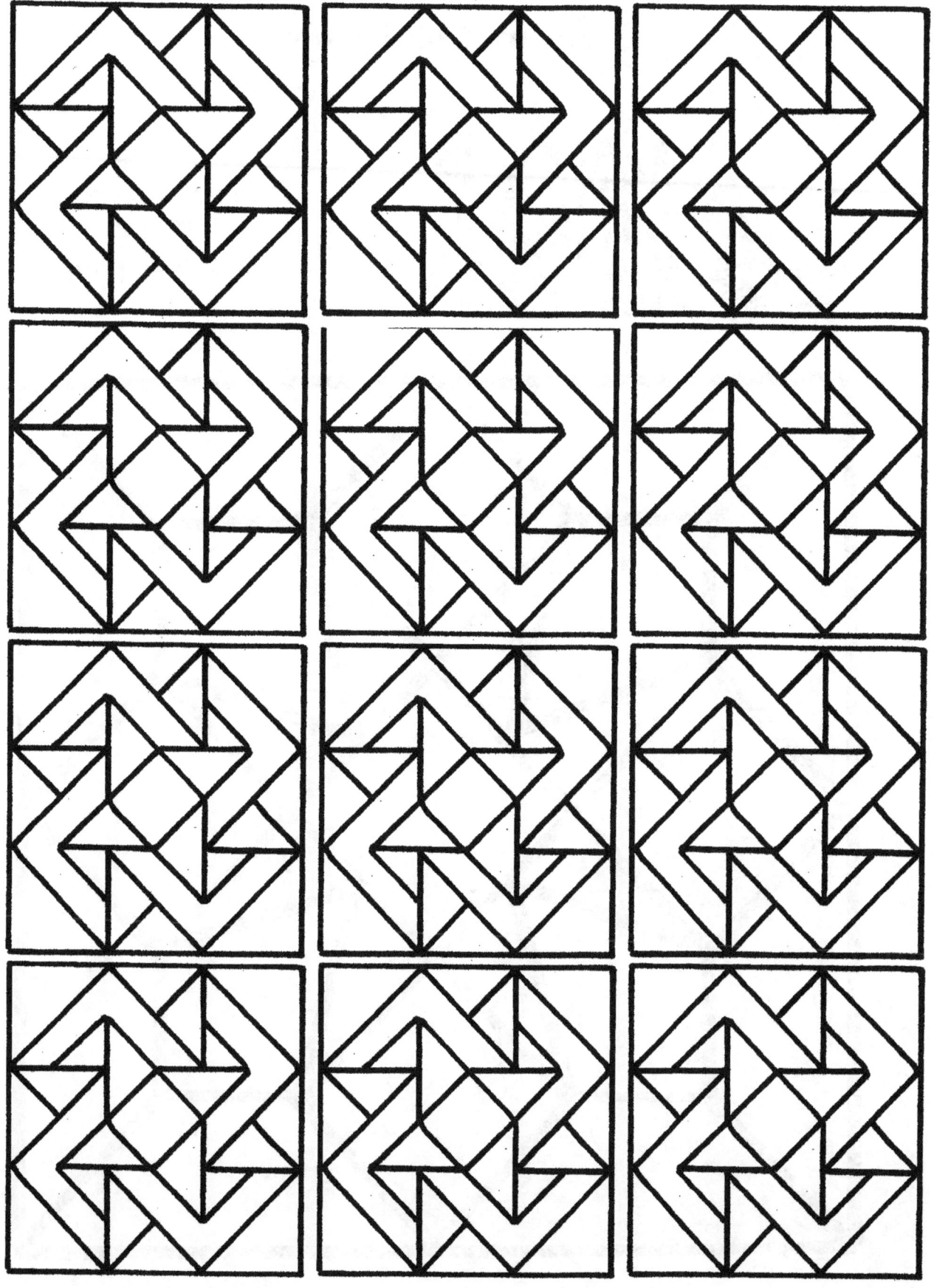

Barn Quilt Grandmother's Choice
Delaware County Iowa

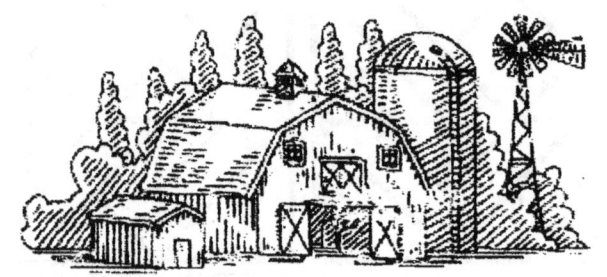

Barn Quilt Location
150th Ave
Manchester, Iowa

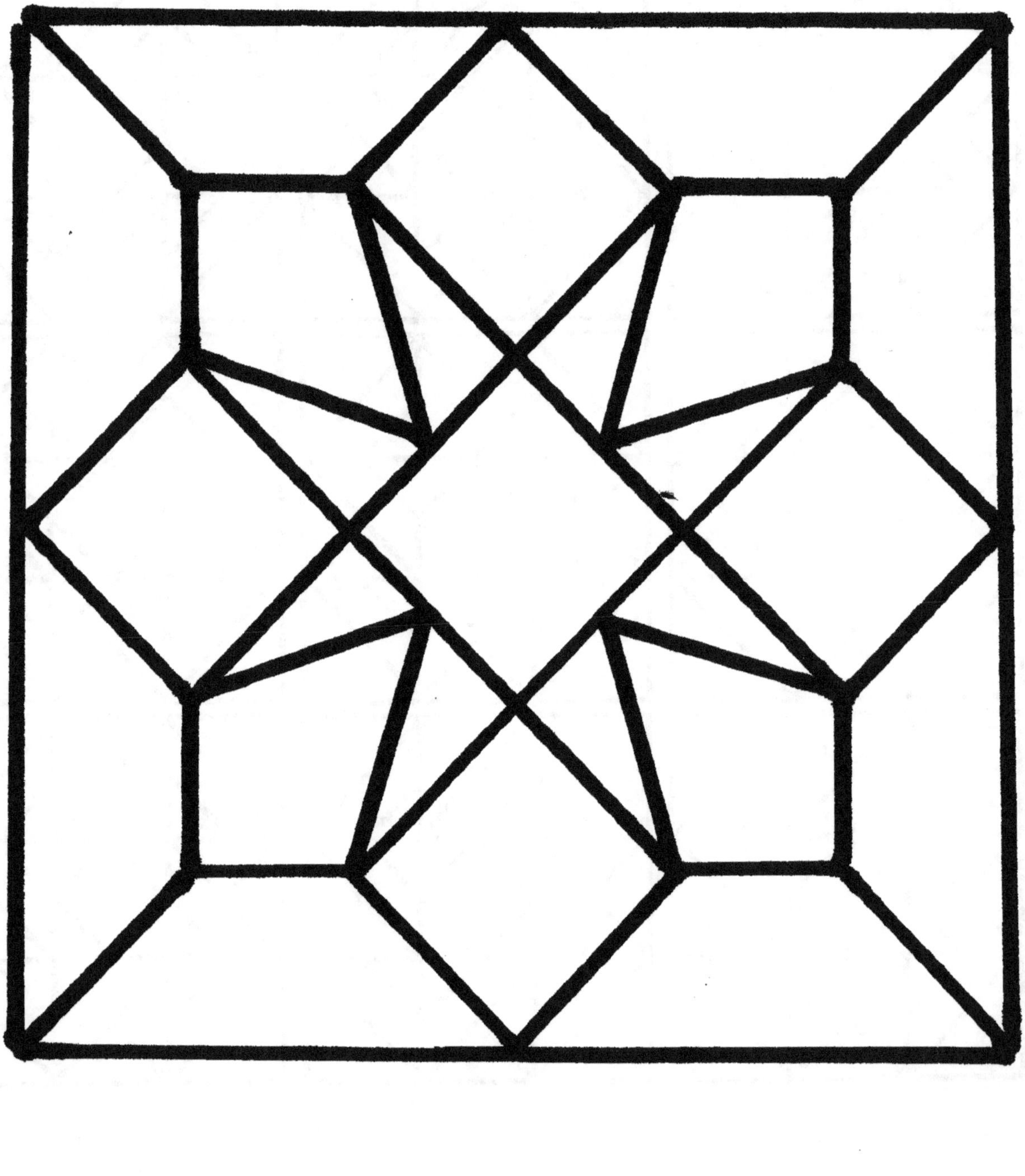

Barn Quilt Grandmother's Choice

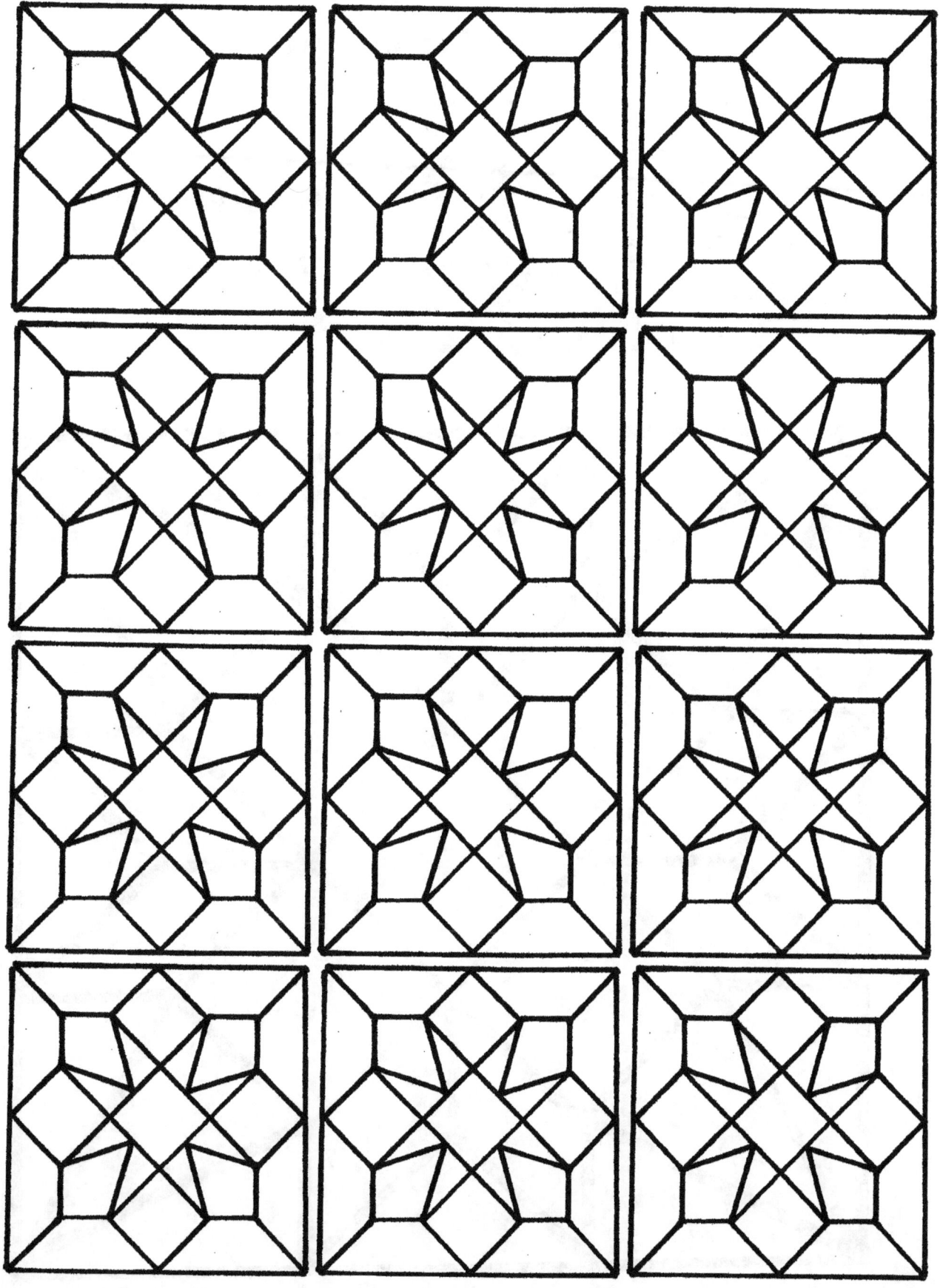

Barn Quilt Prairie Queen
Delaware County Iowa

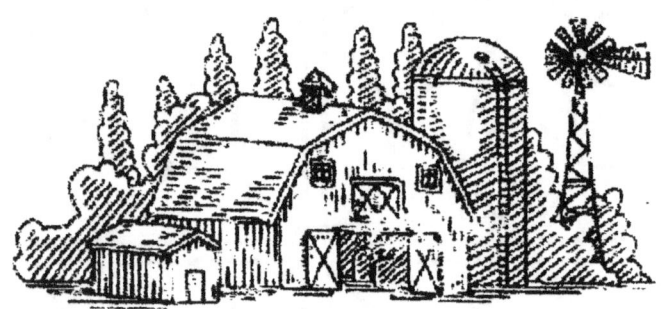

Barn Quilt Location
Thunder Rd
Hopkinton, Iowa

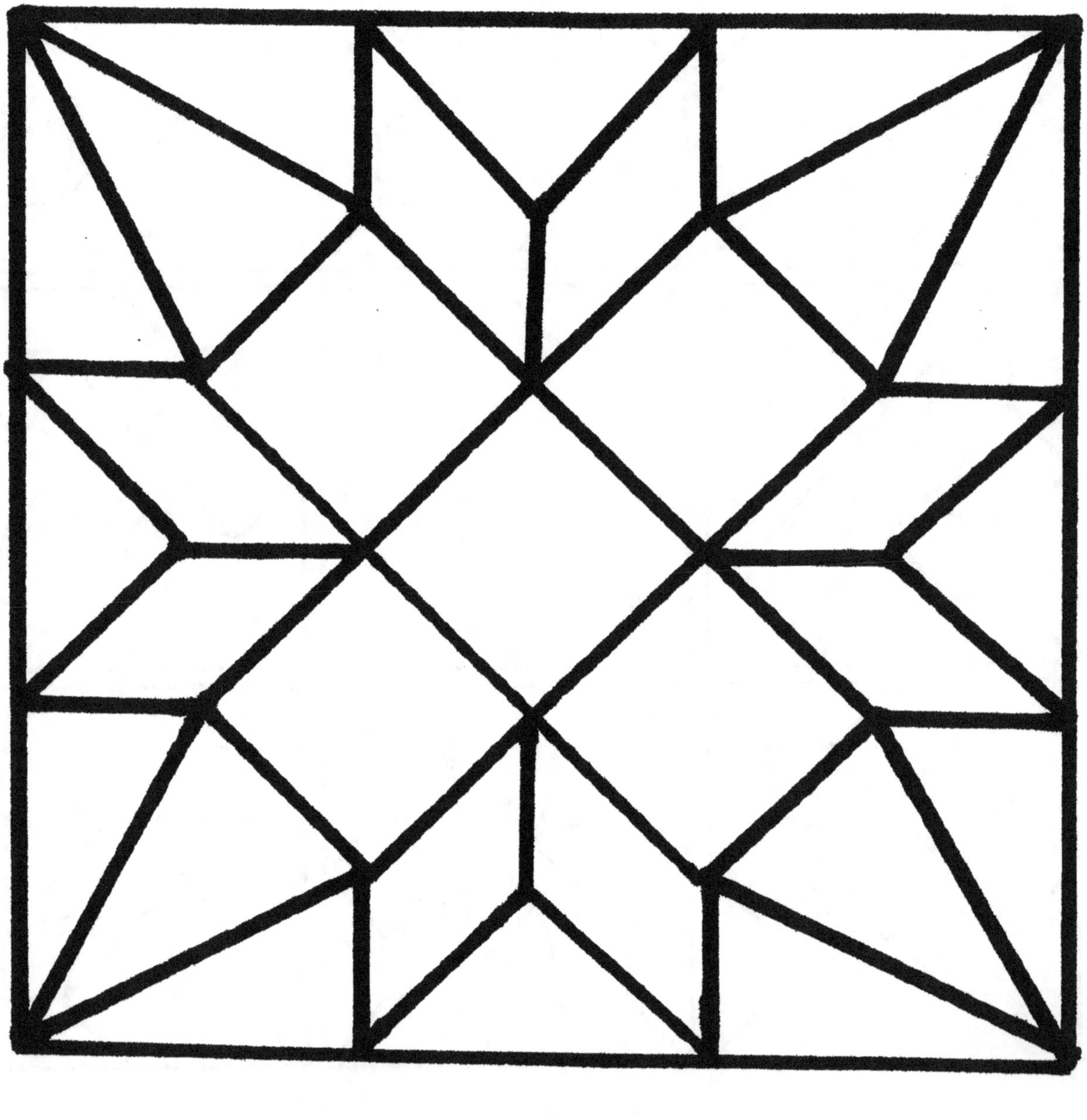

Barn Quilt Prairie Queen

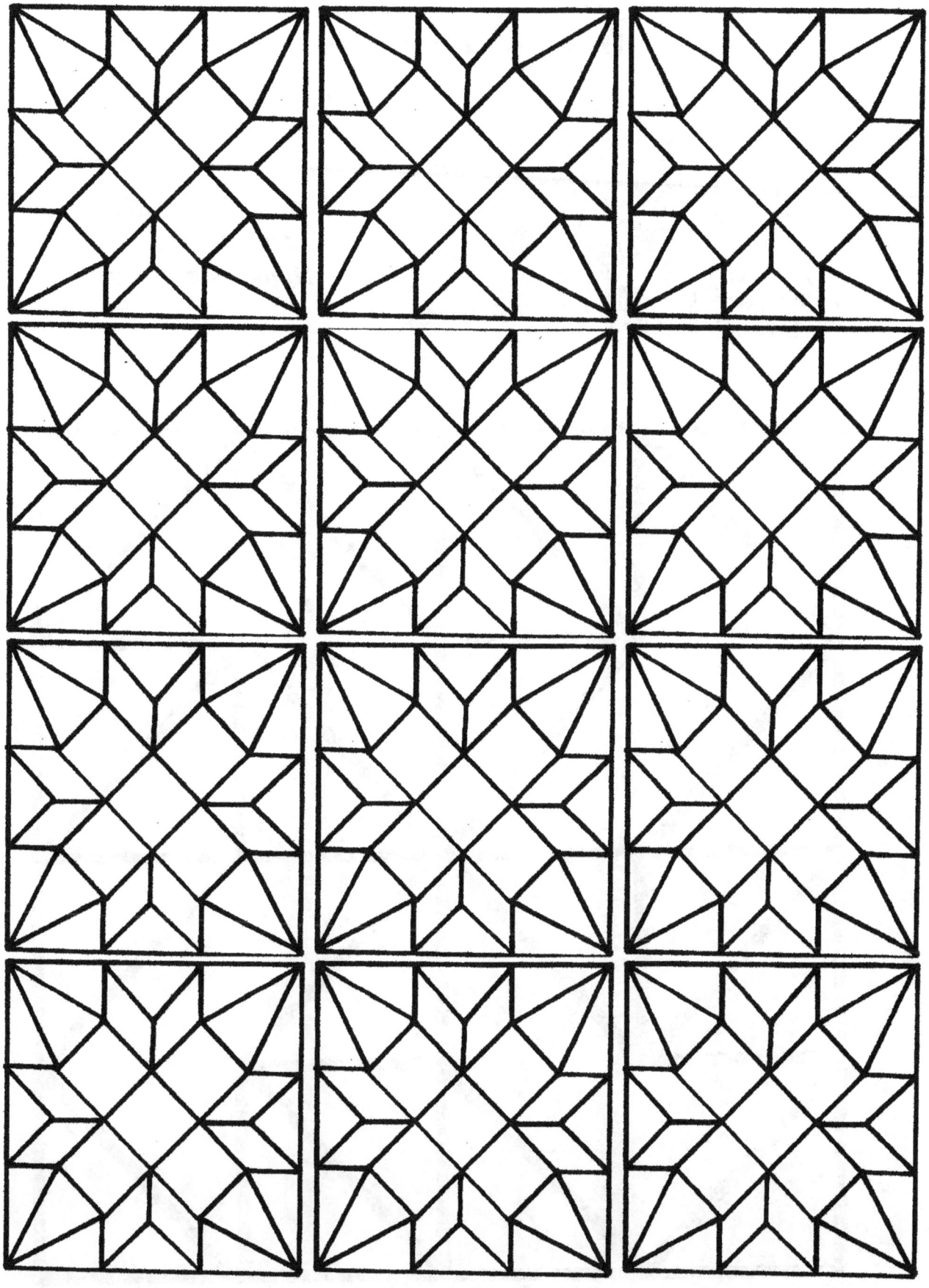

Barn Quilt Yankee Puzzle
Delaware County Iowa

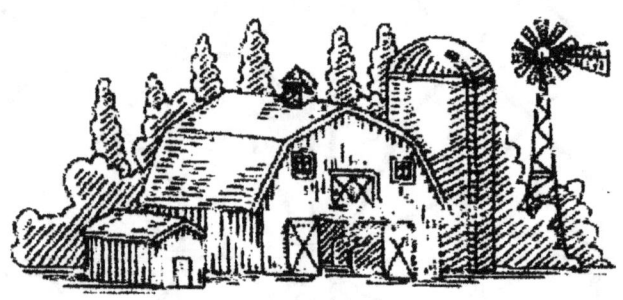

Barn Quilt Location
Quarter Rd
Hopkinton, Iowa

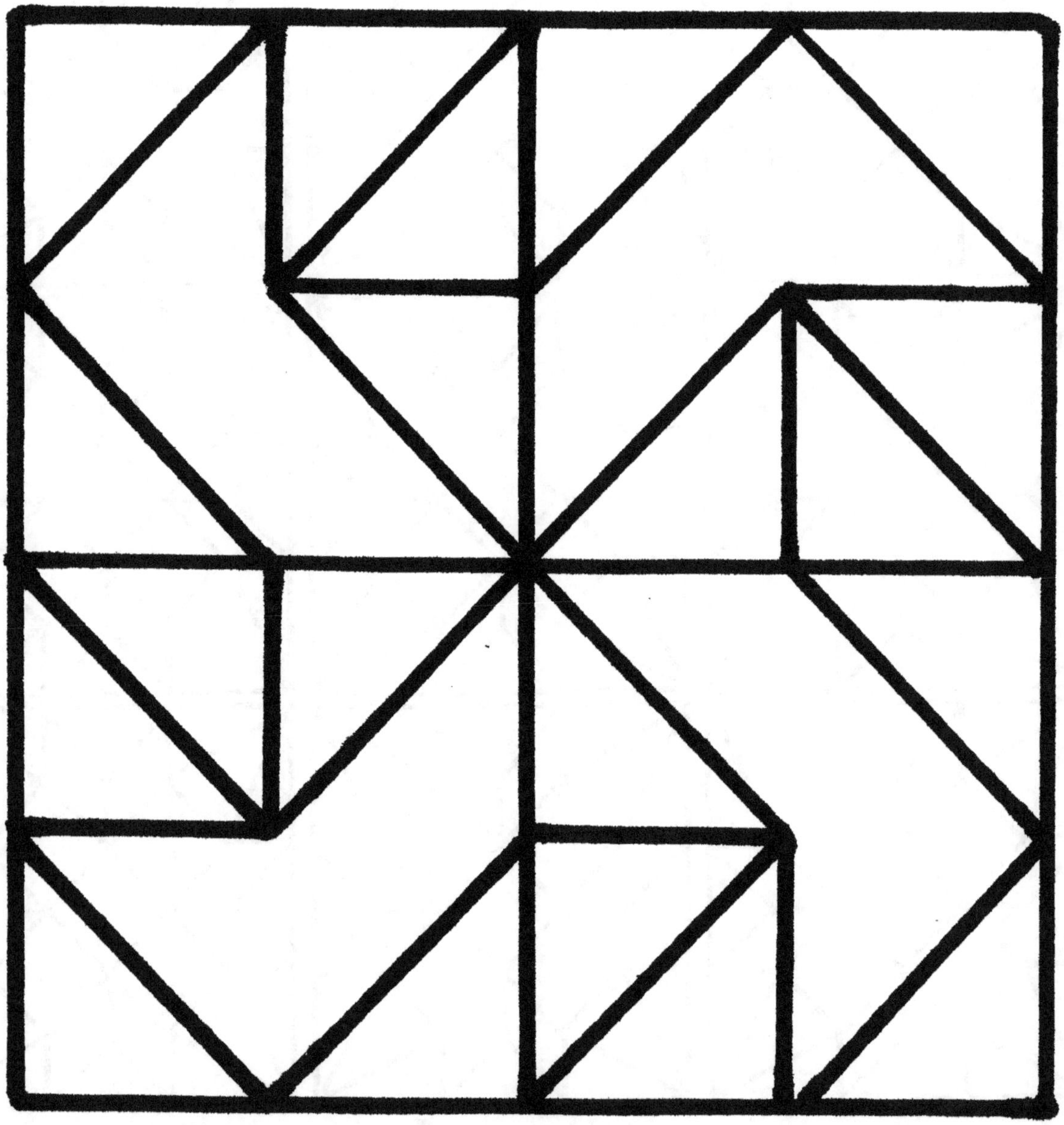

Barn Quilt Yankee Puzzle

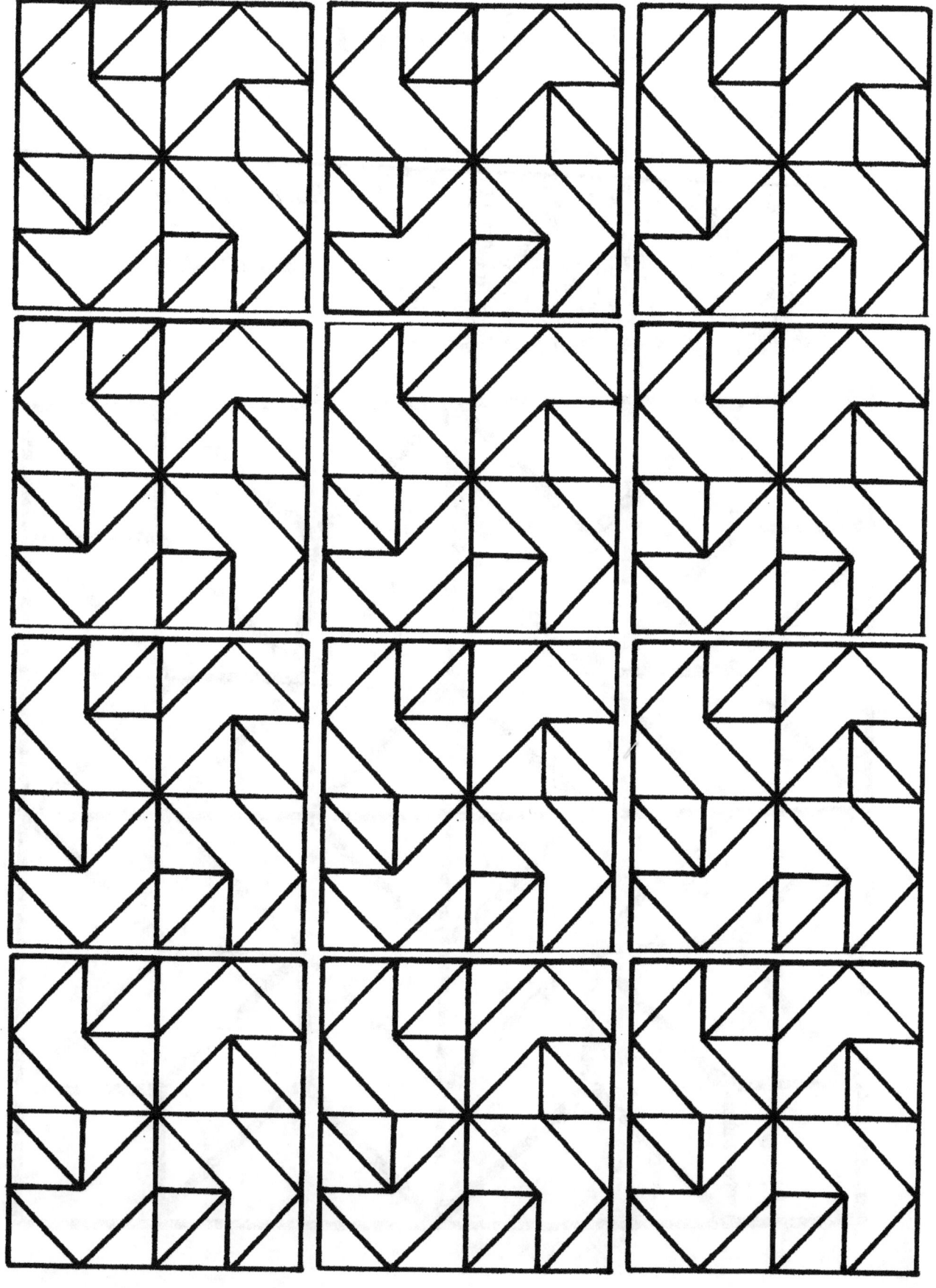

Barn Quilt Kansas
Delaware County Iowa

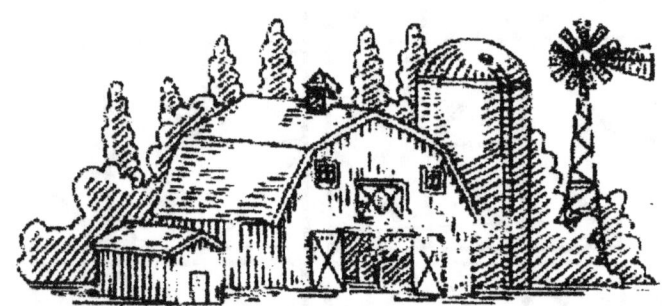

Barn Quilt Location
195ᵗʰ St
Manchester, Iowa

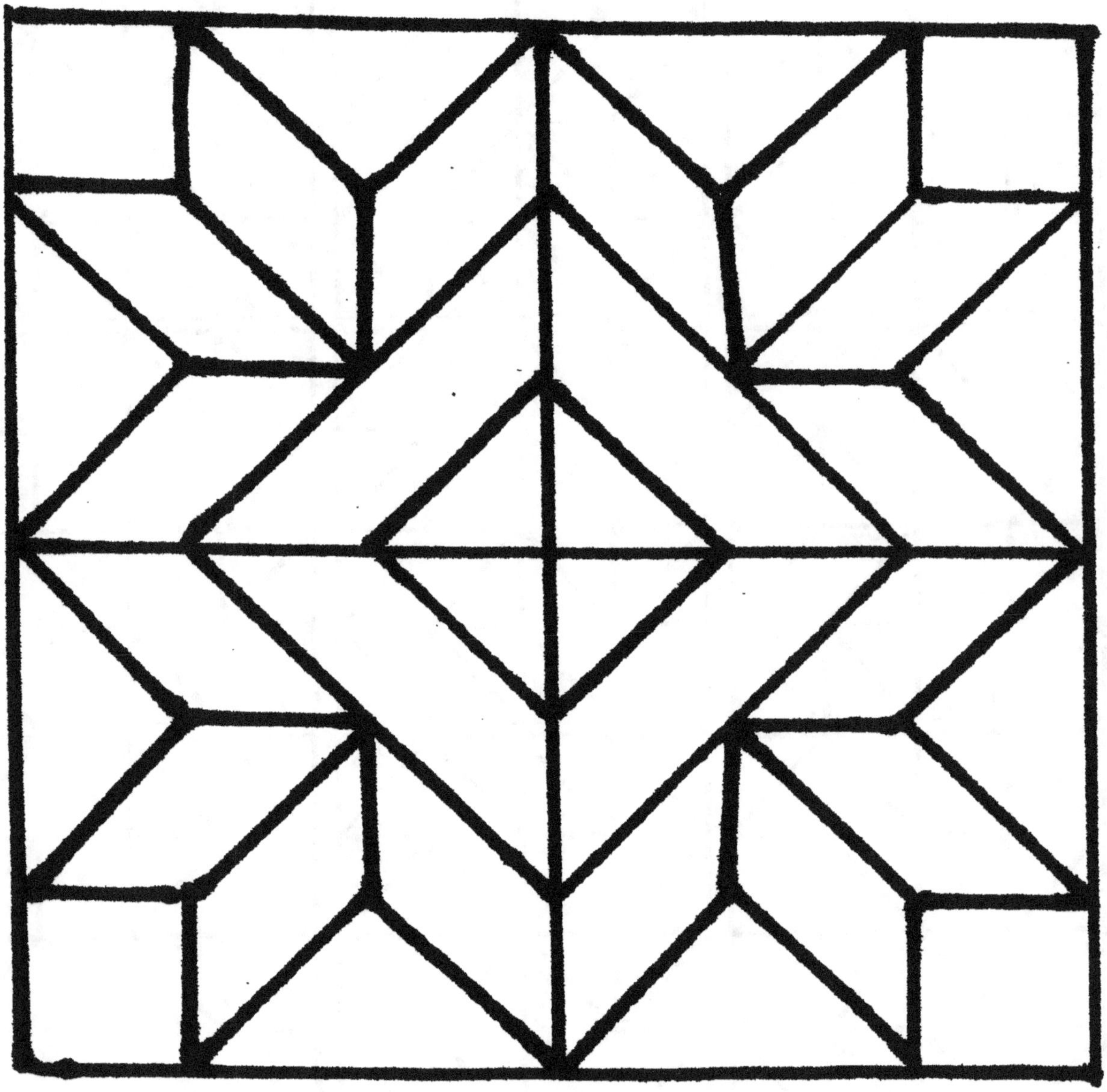

Barn Quilt Kansas

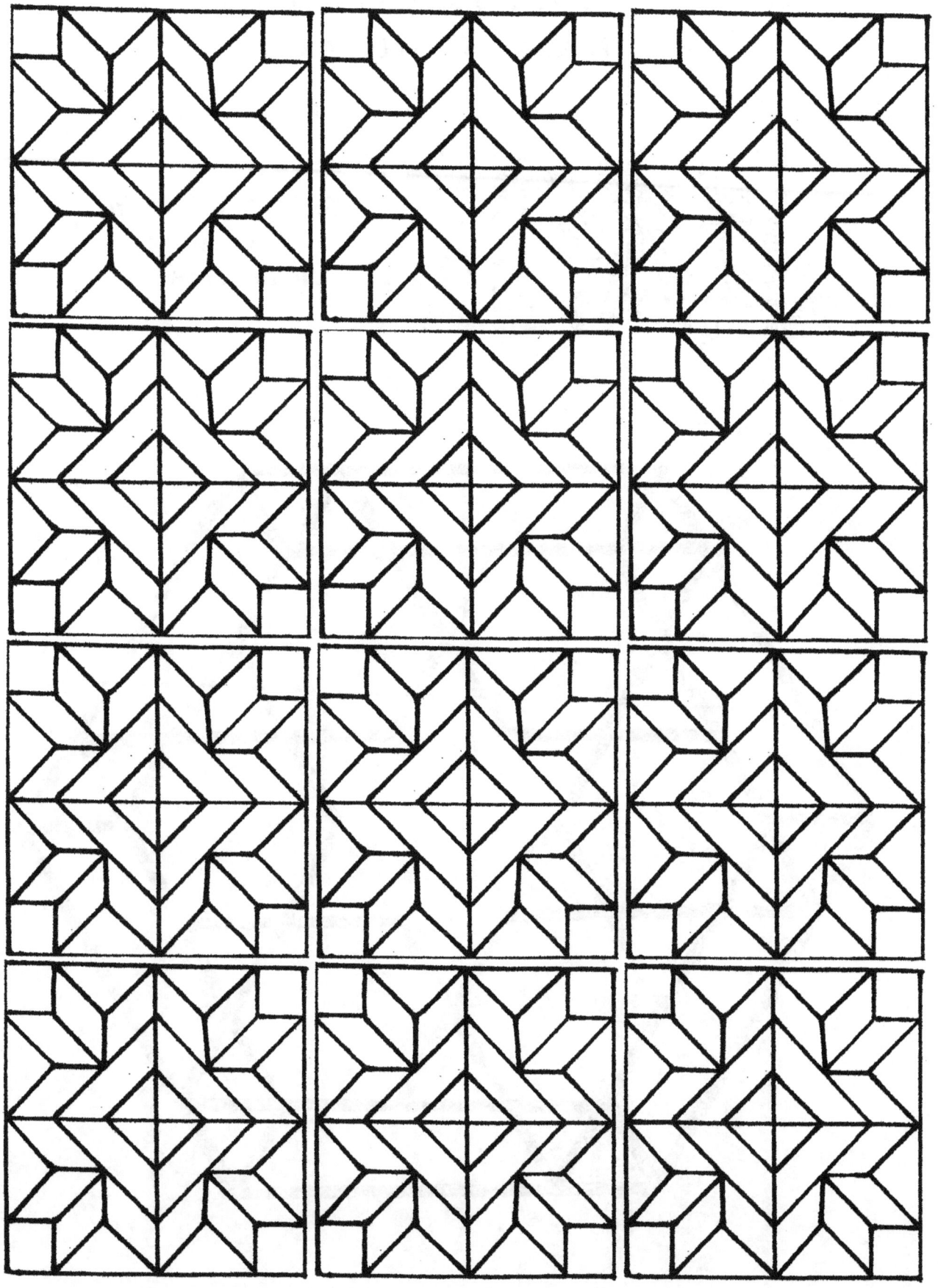

Barn Quilt Kaleidoscope
Delaware County Iowa

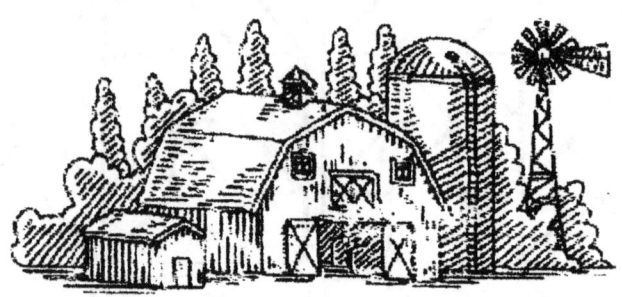

Barn Quilt Location
132nd St
Dundee, Iowa

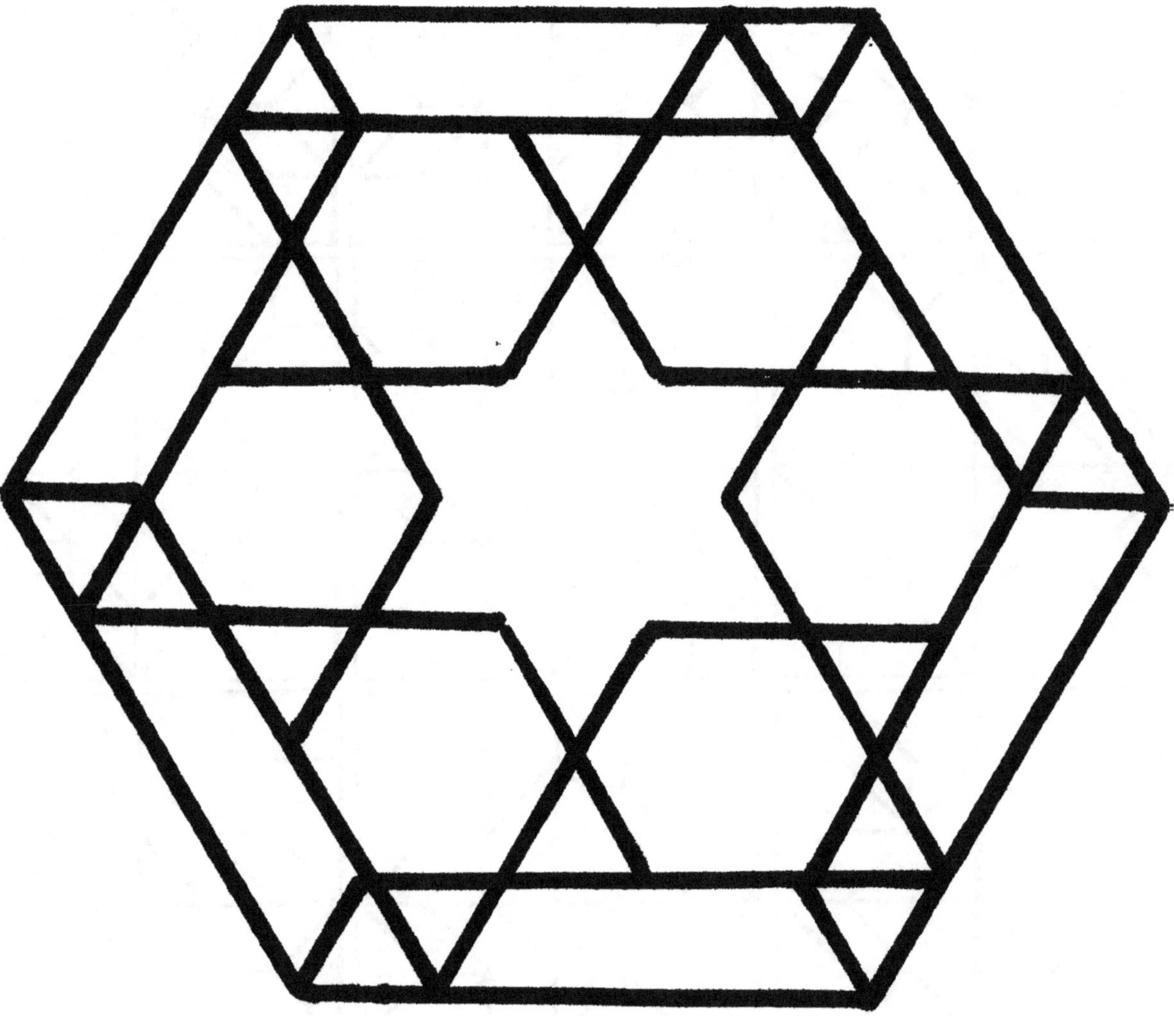

Barn Quilt Kaleidoscope

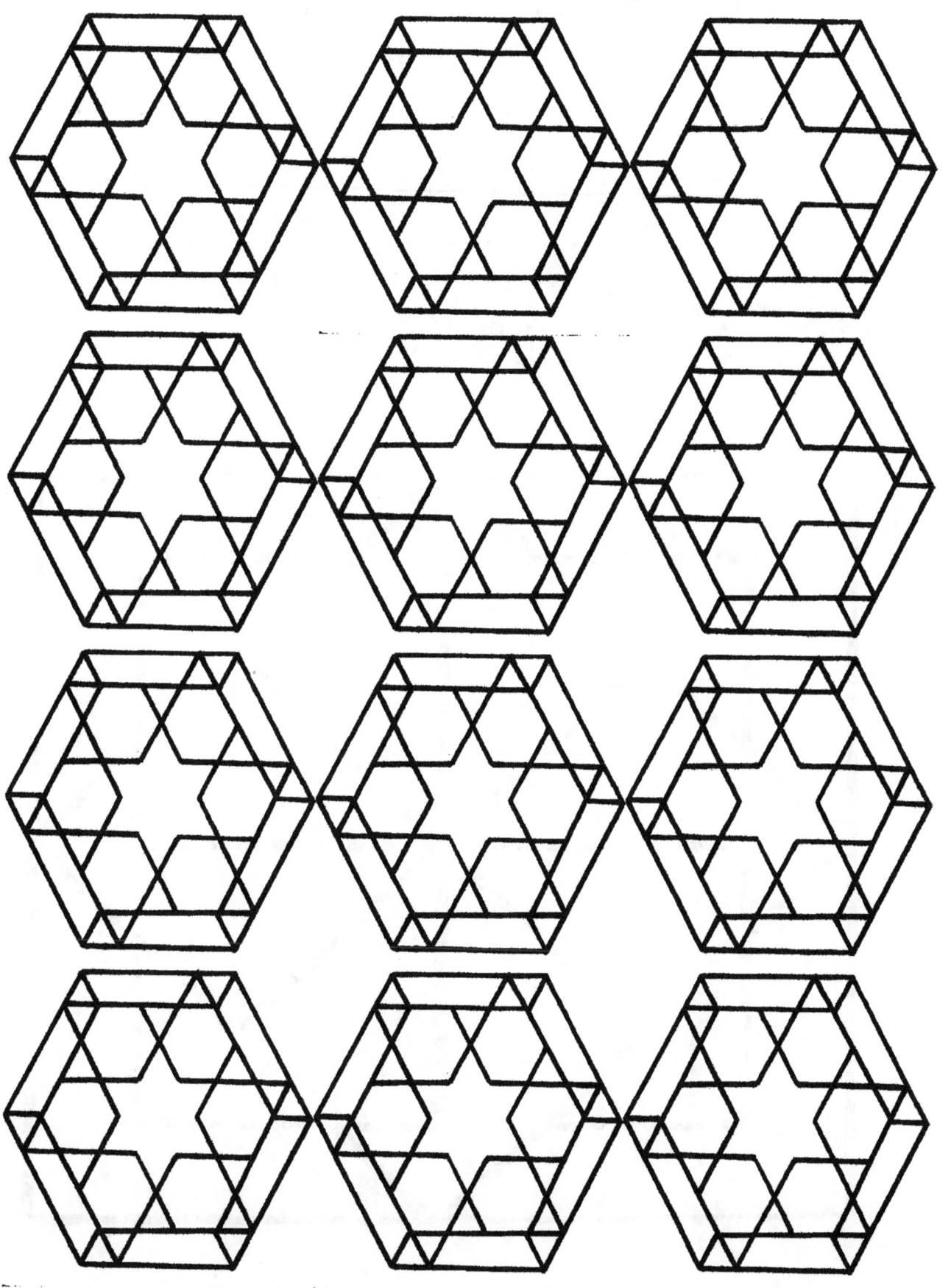

Barn Quilt Twisting Star
Delaware County Iowa

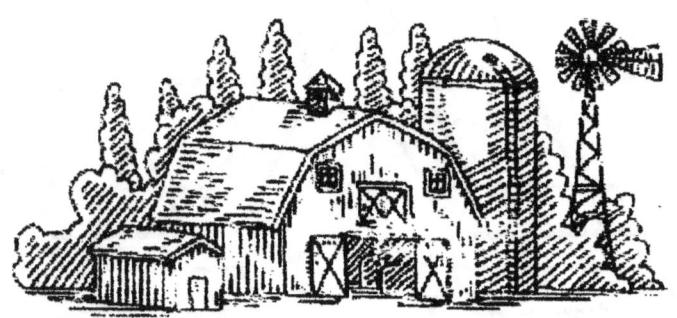

Barn Quilt Location
275th St
Delhi, Iowa

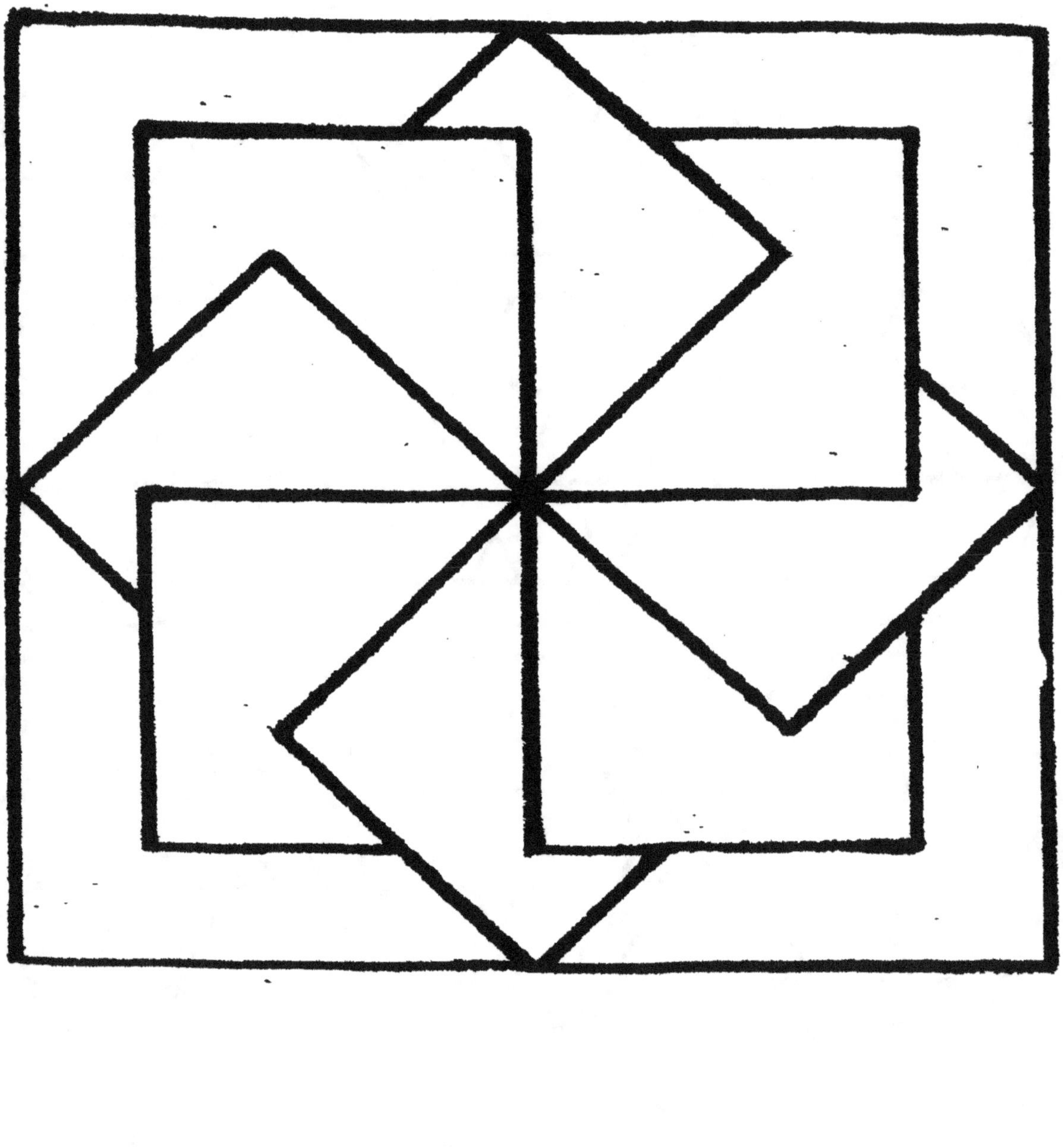

Barn Quilt Twisting Star

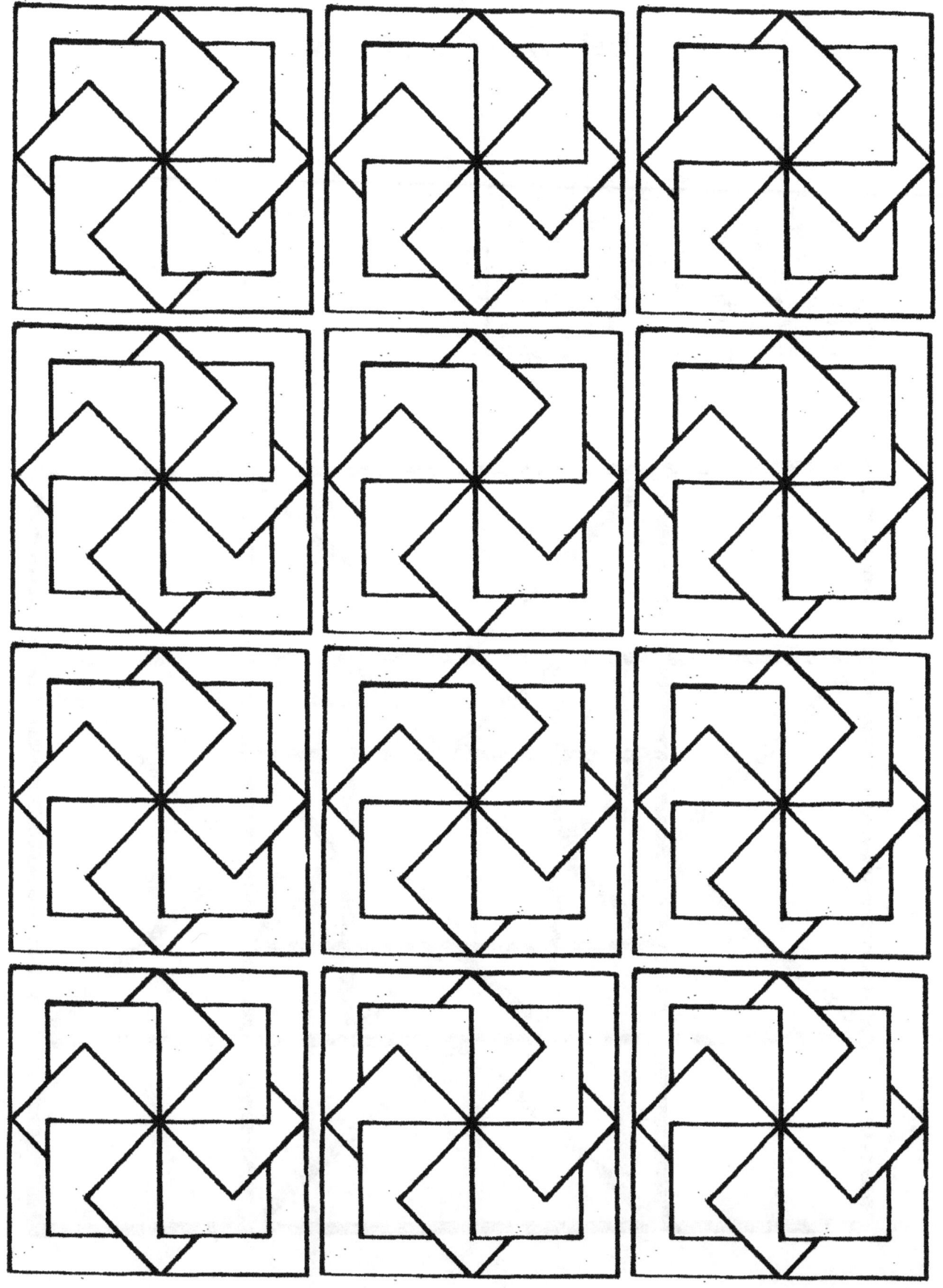

Barn Quilt Double Star
Delaware County Iowa

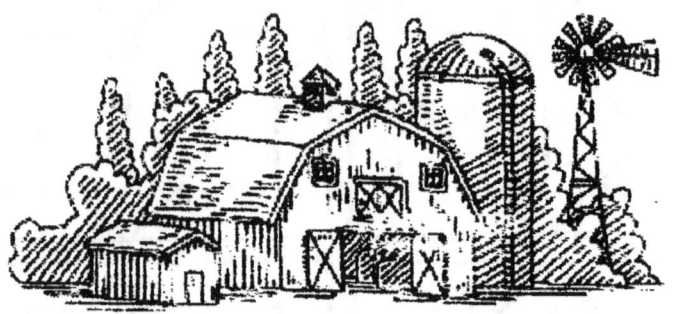

Barn Quilt Location
110th Ave
Masonville, Iowa

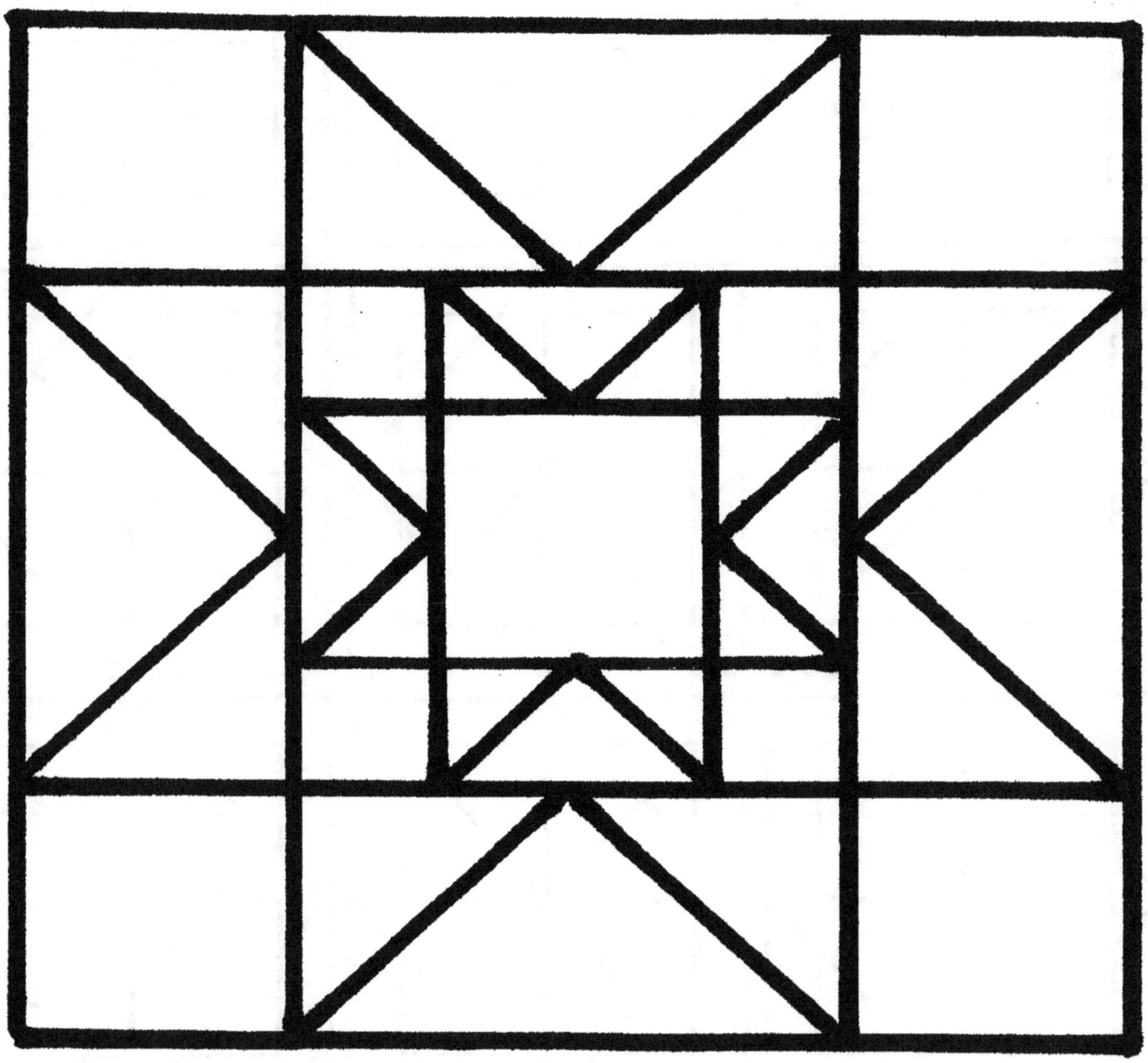

Barn Quilt Double Star

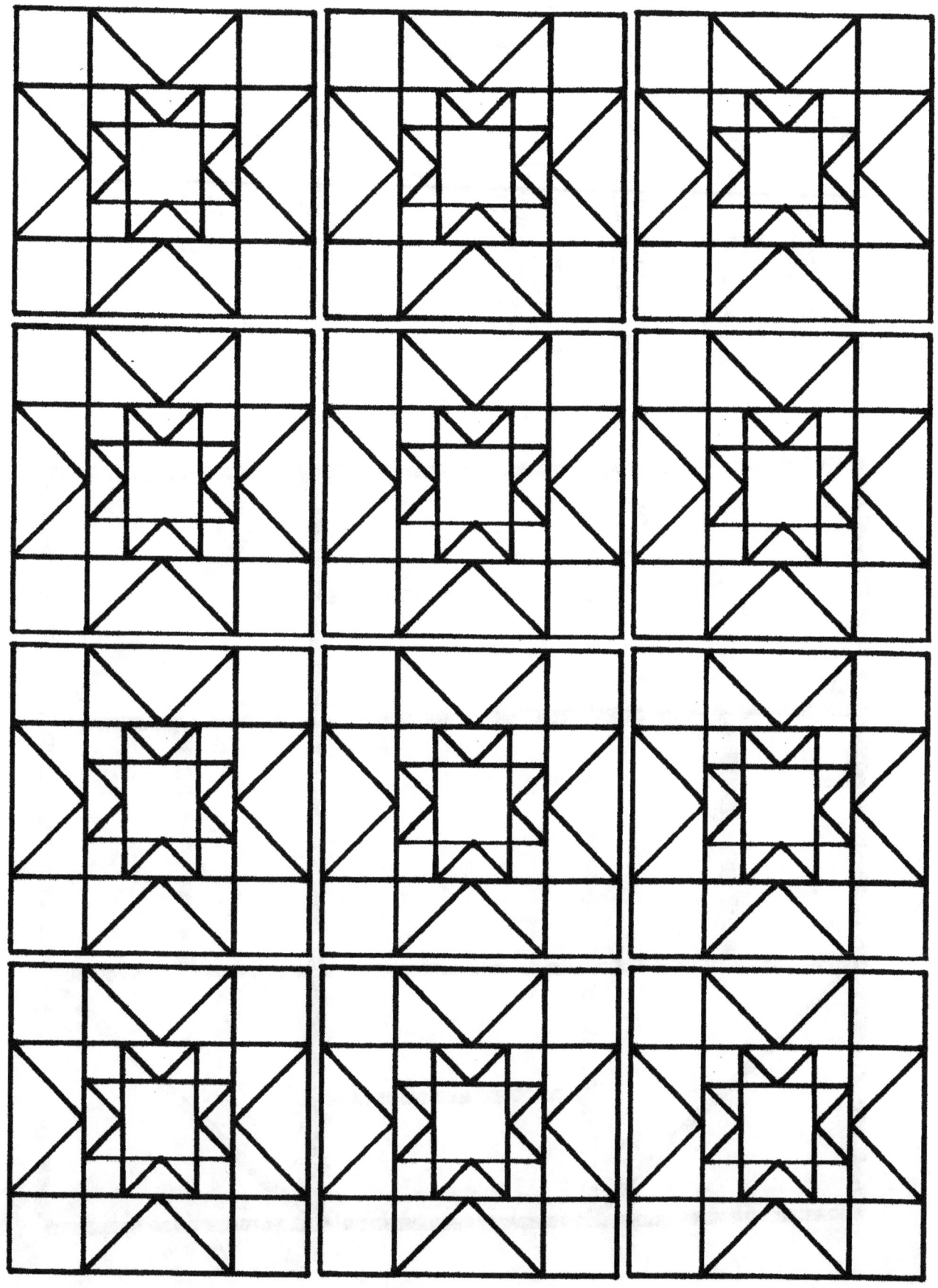

Barn Quilt Hole in the Barn Door
Delaware County Iowa

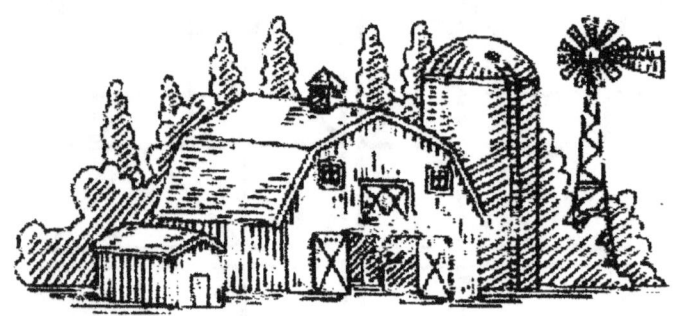

Barn Quilt Location
137ᵗʰ St
Dundee, Iowa

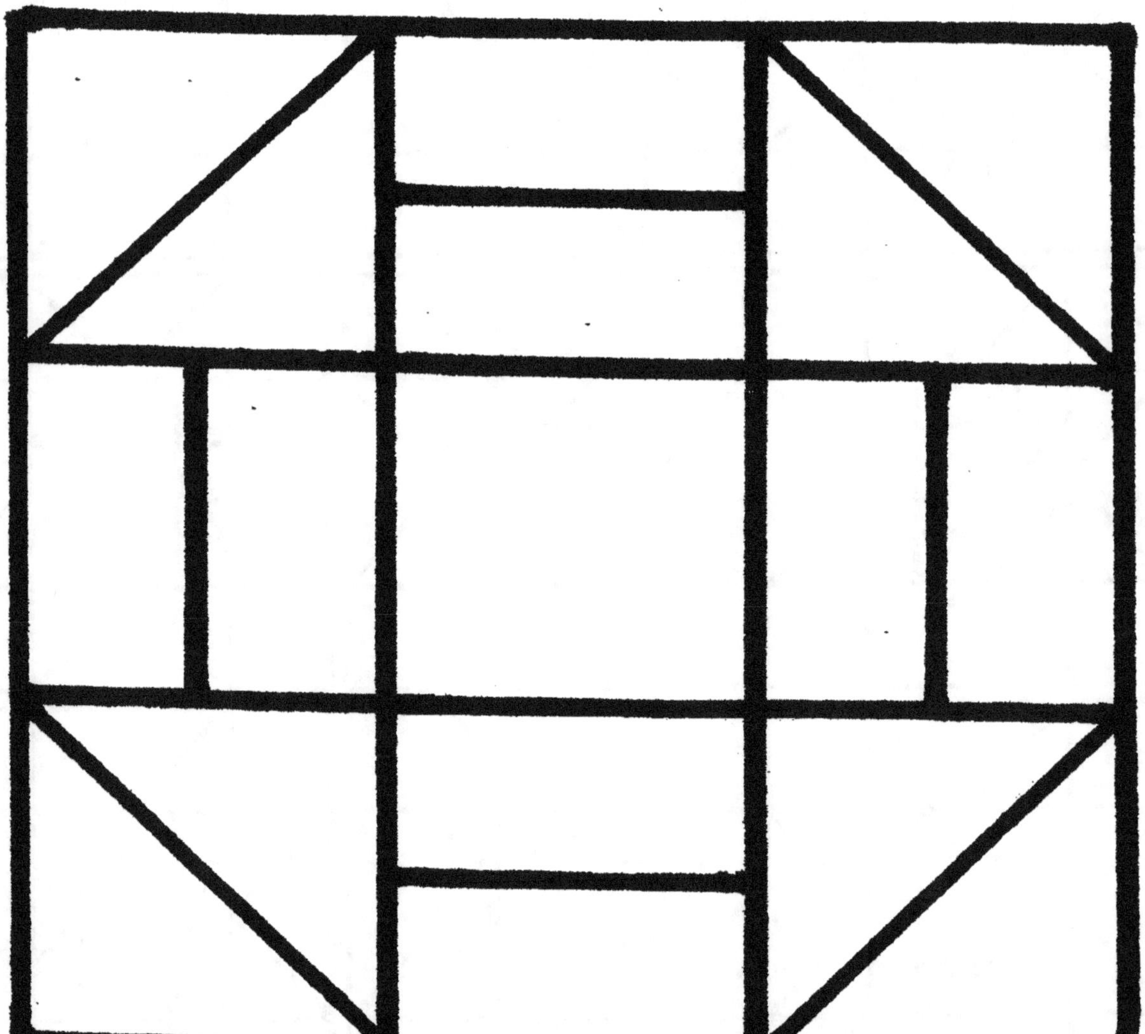

Barn Quilt Hole in the Barn Door

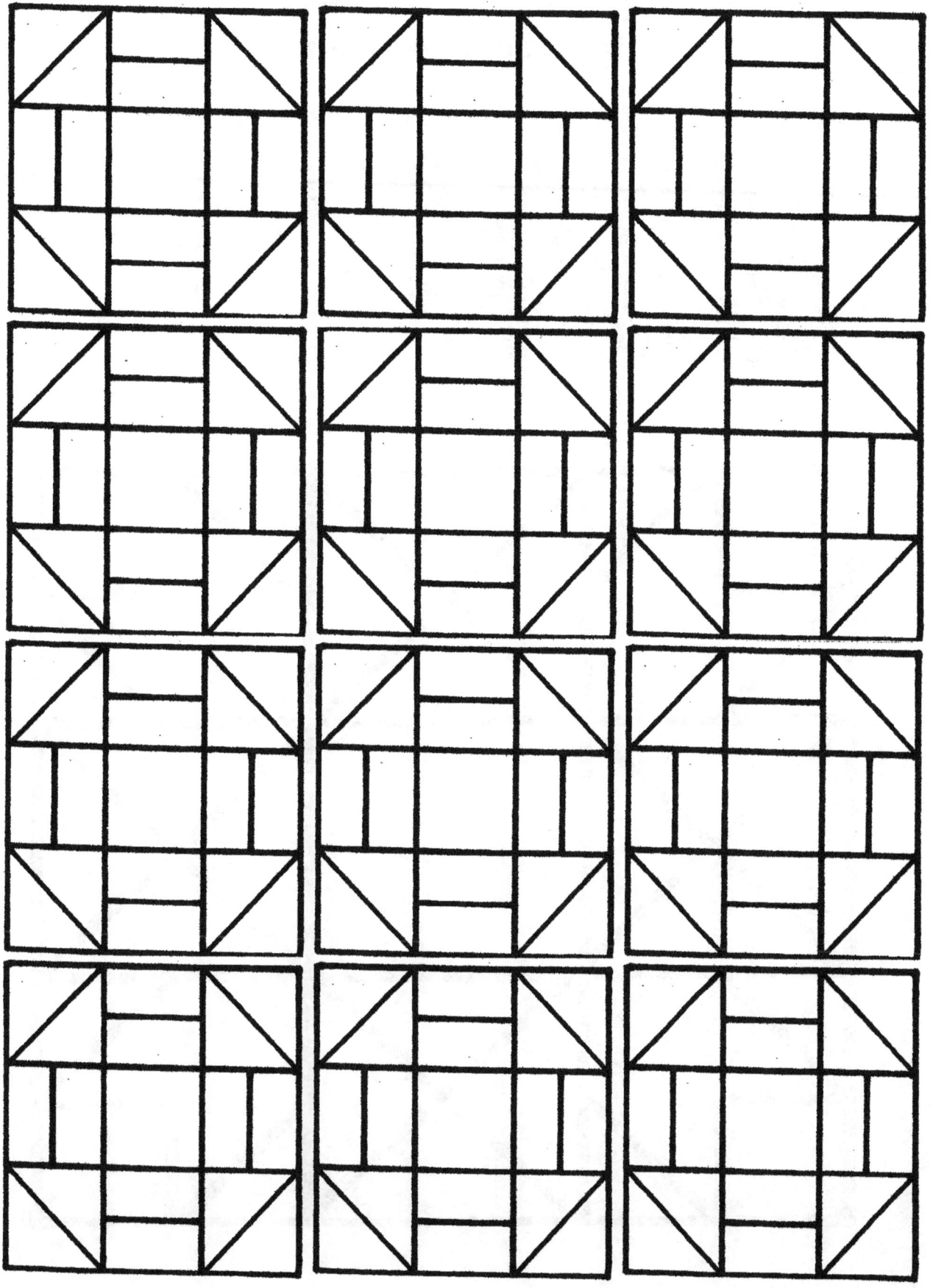

Barn Quilt Mountain Star
Delaware County Iowa

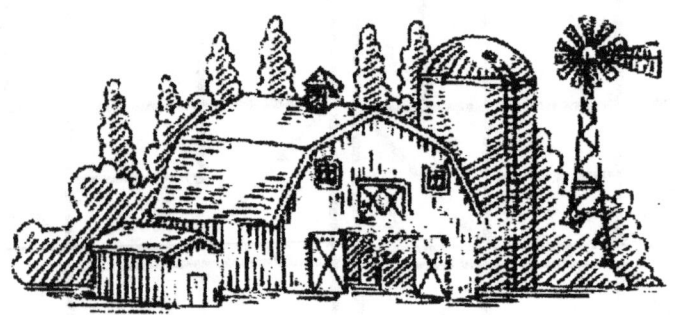

Barn Quilt Location
Franklin St
Delhi, Iowa

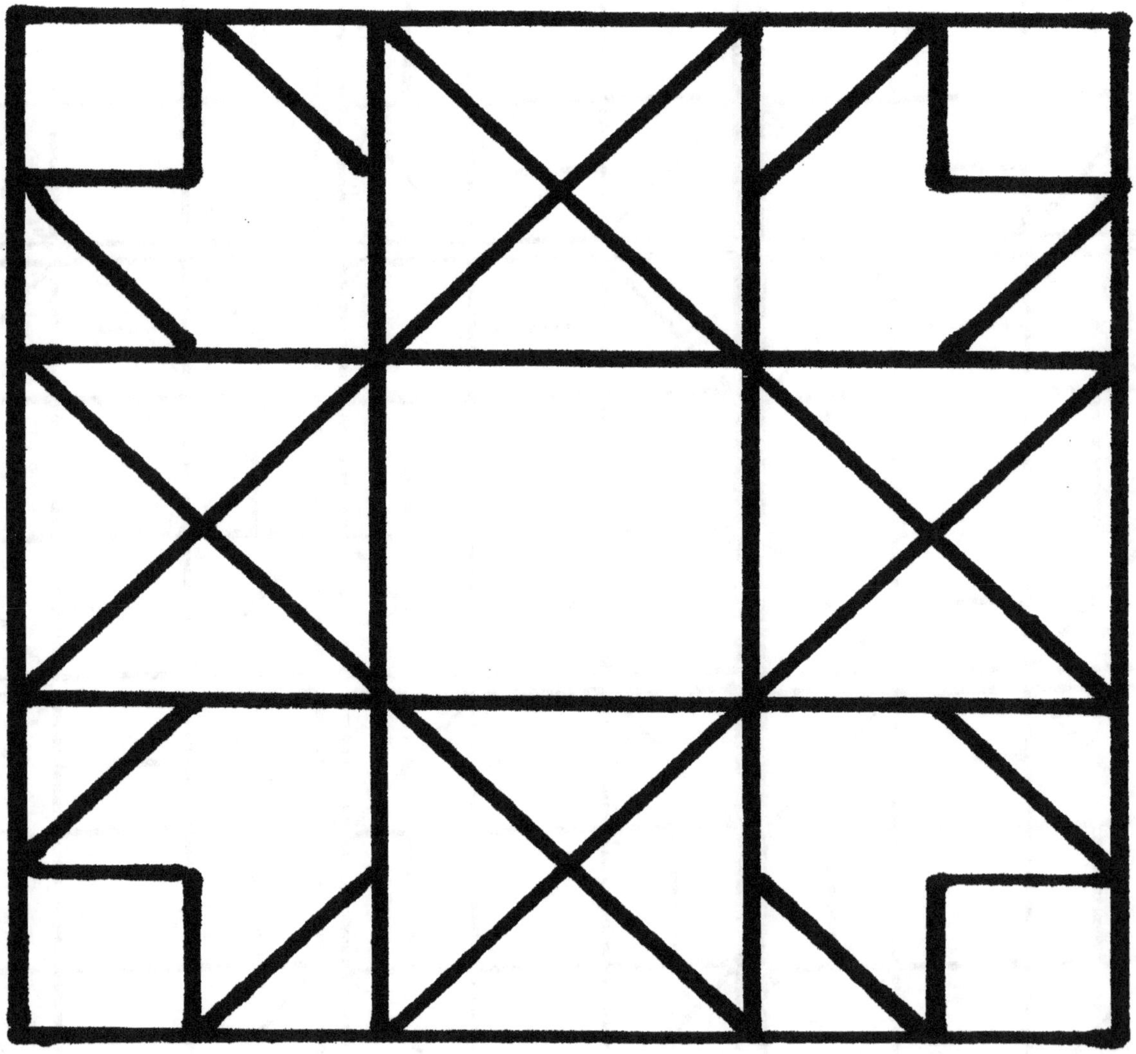

Barn Quilt Mountain Star

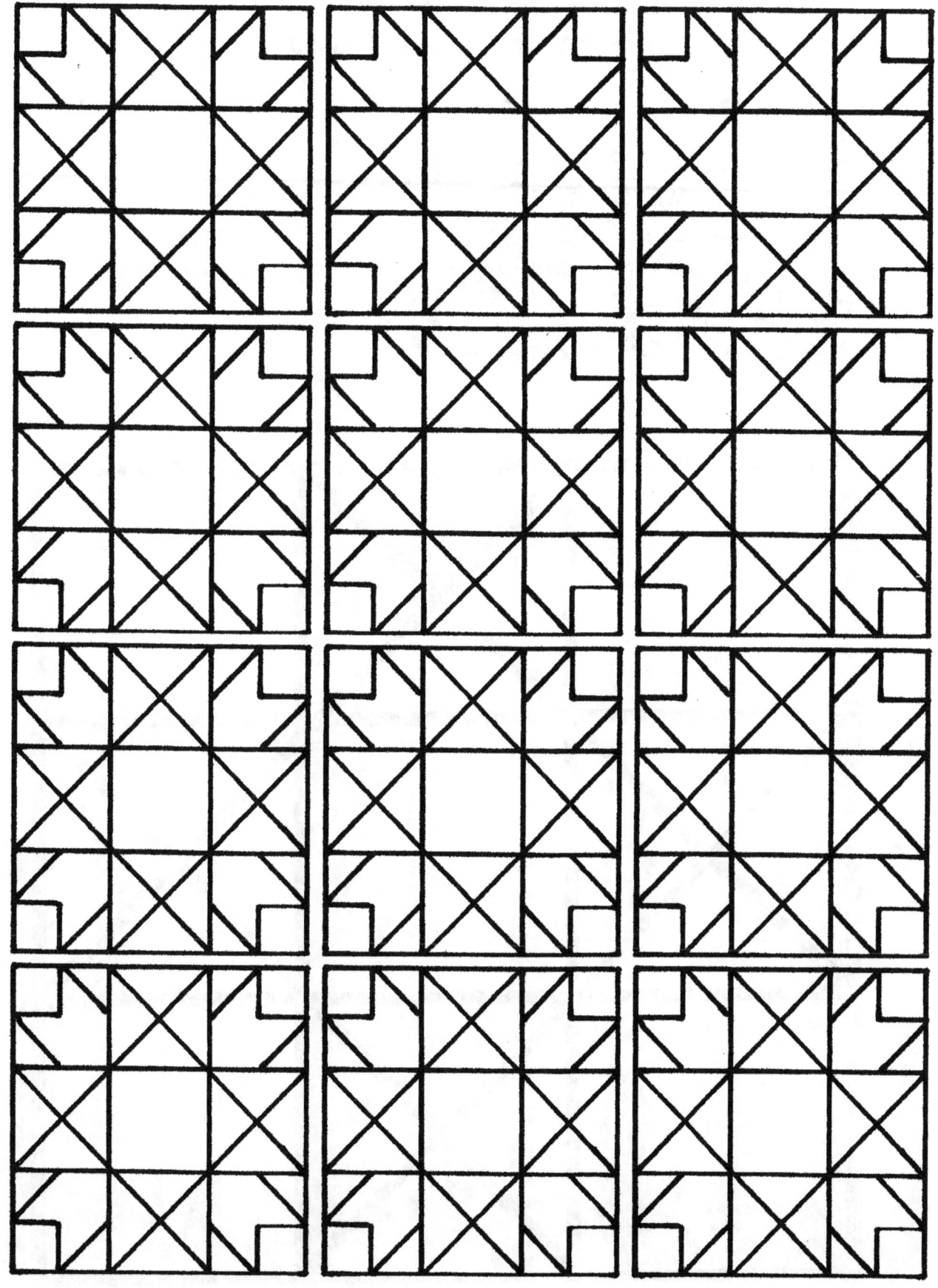

Barn Quilt Ohio Star
Delaware County Iowa

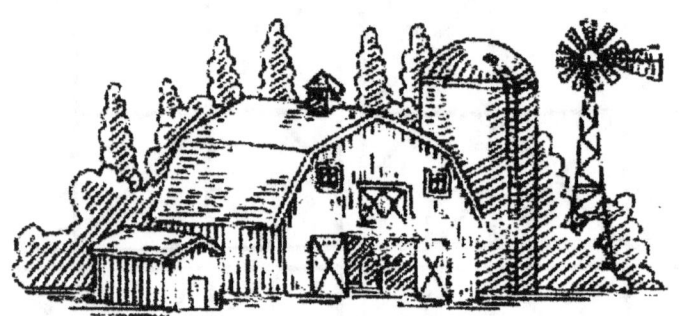

Barn Quilt Location
150ᵗʰ Ave
Manchester, Iowa

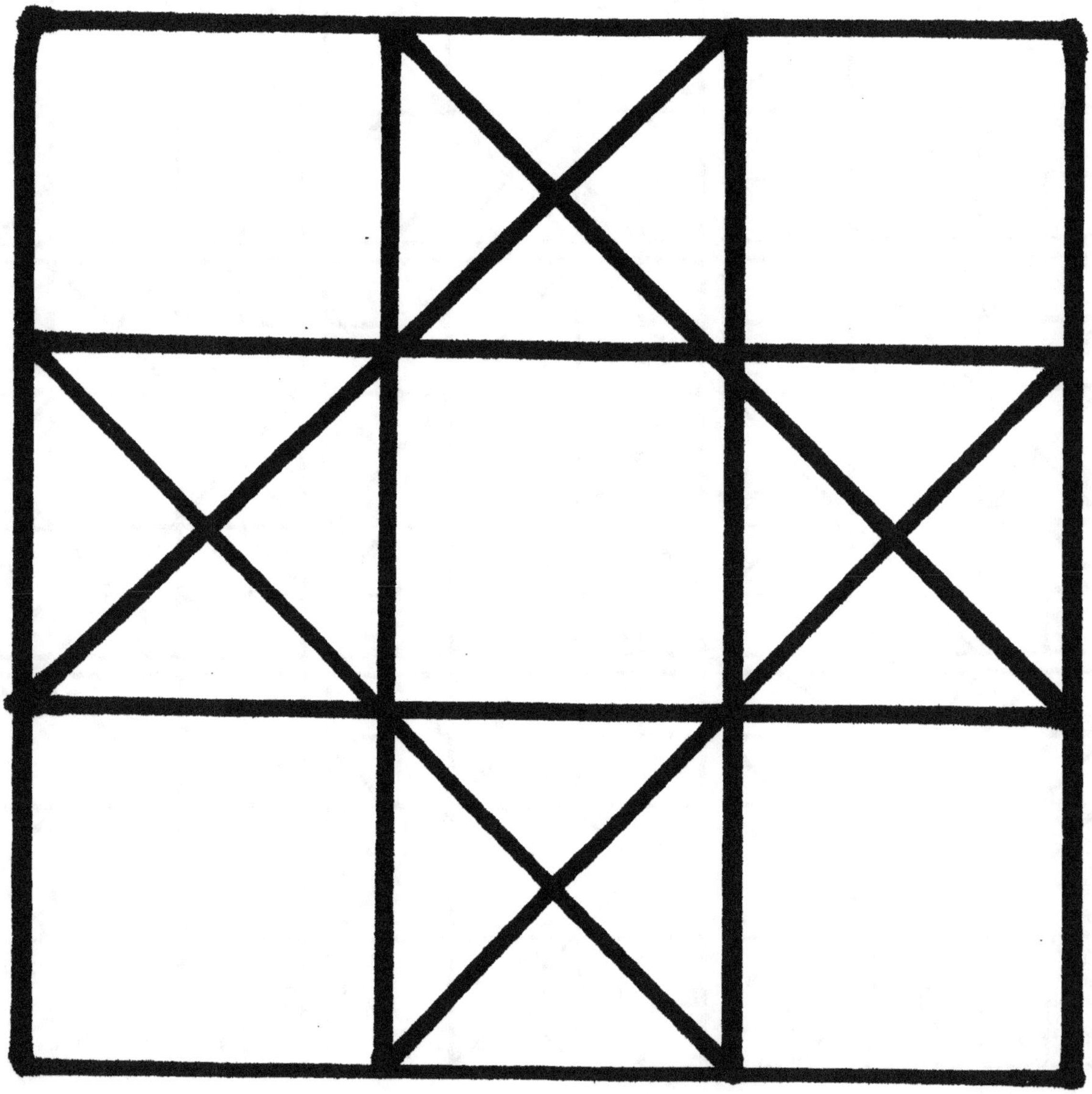

Barn Quilt Ohio Star

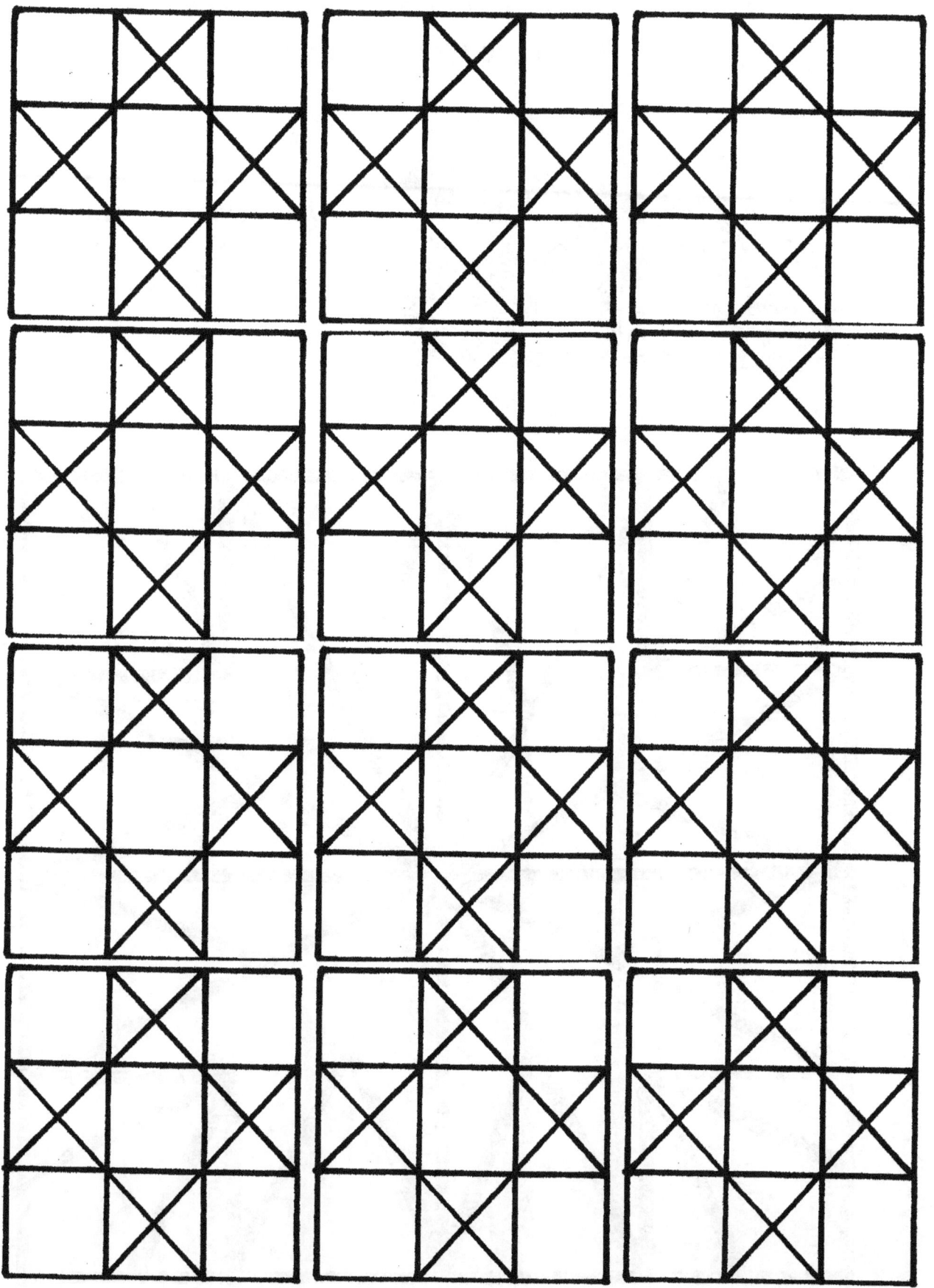

Barn Quilt North Star
Delaware County Iowa

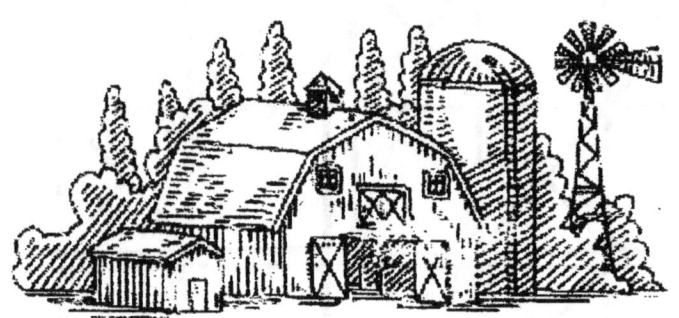

Barn Quilt Location
275ᵗʰ St
Delhi, Iowa

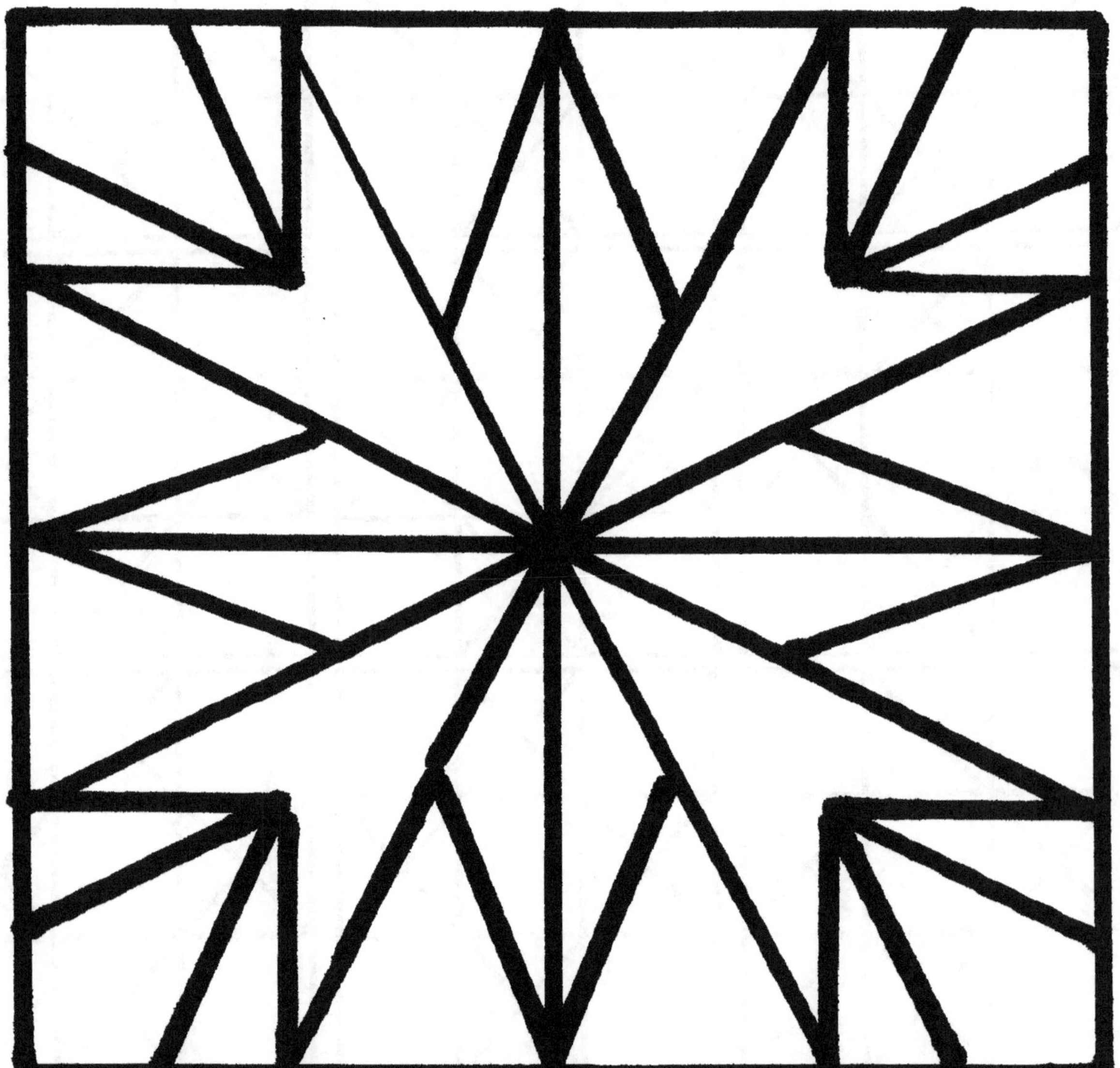

Barn Quilt North Star

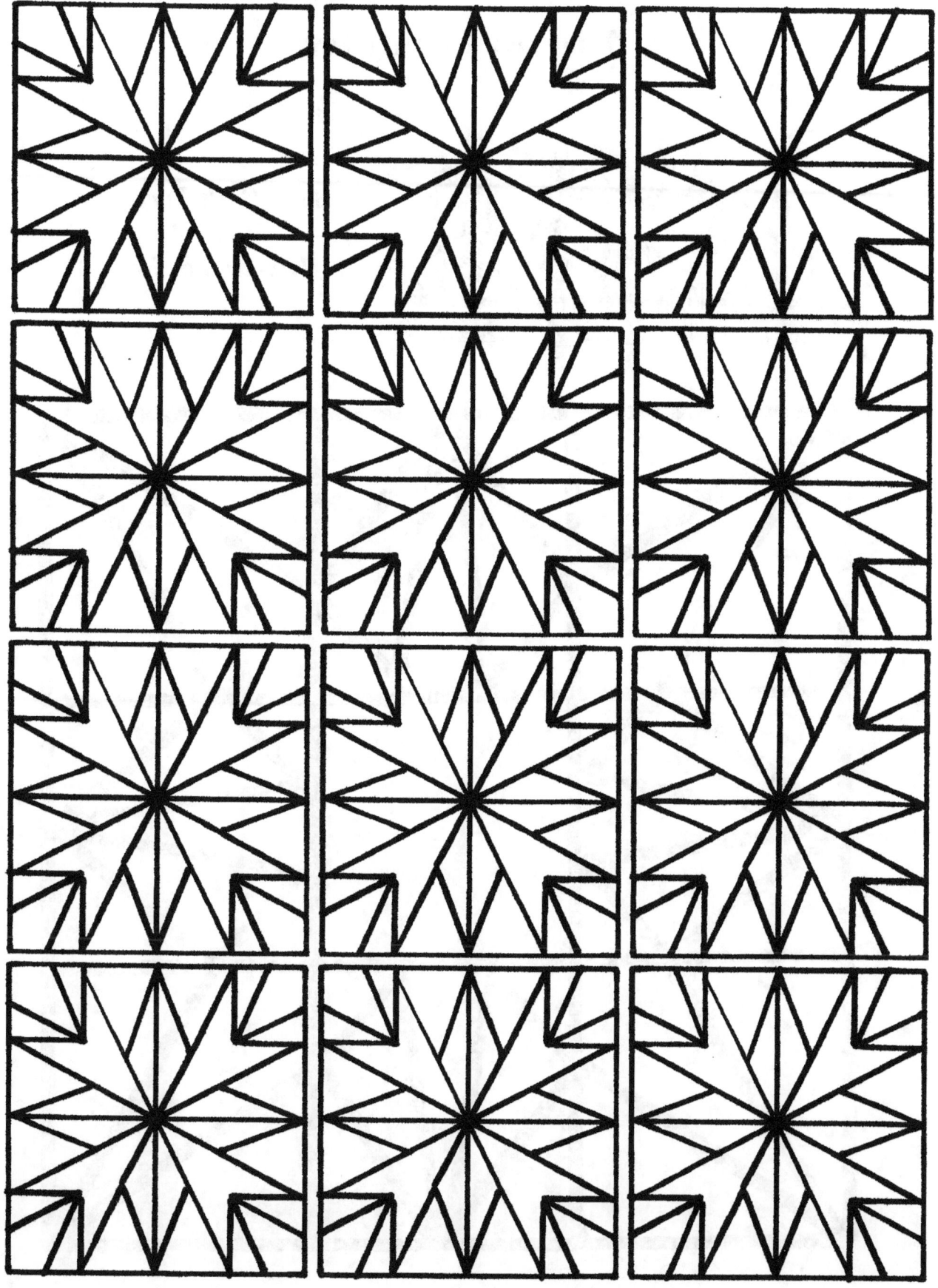

Barn Quilt Wisconsin Star
Delaware County Iowa

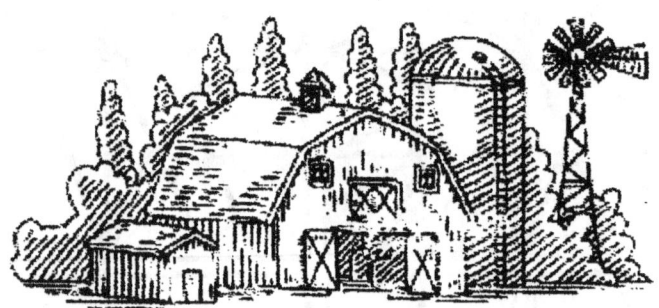

Barn Quilt Location
Hwy 38
Hopkinton, Iowa

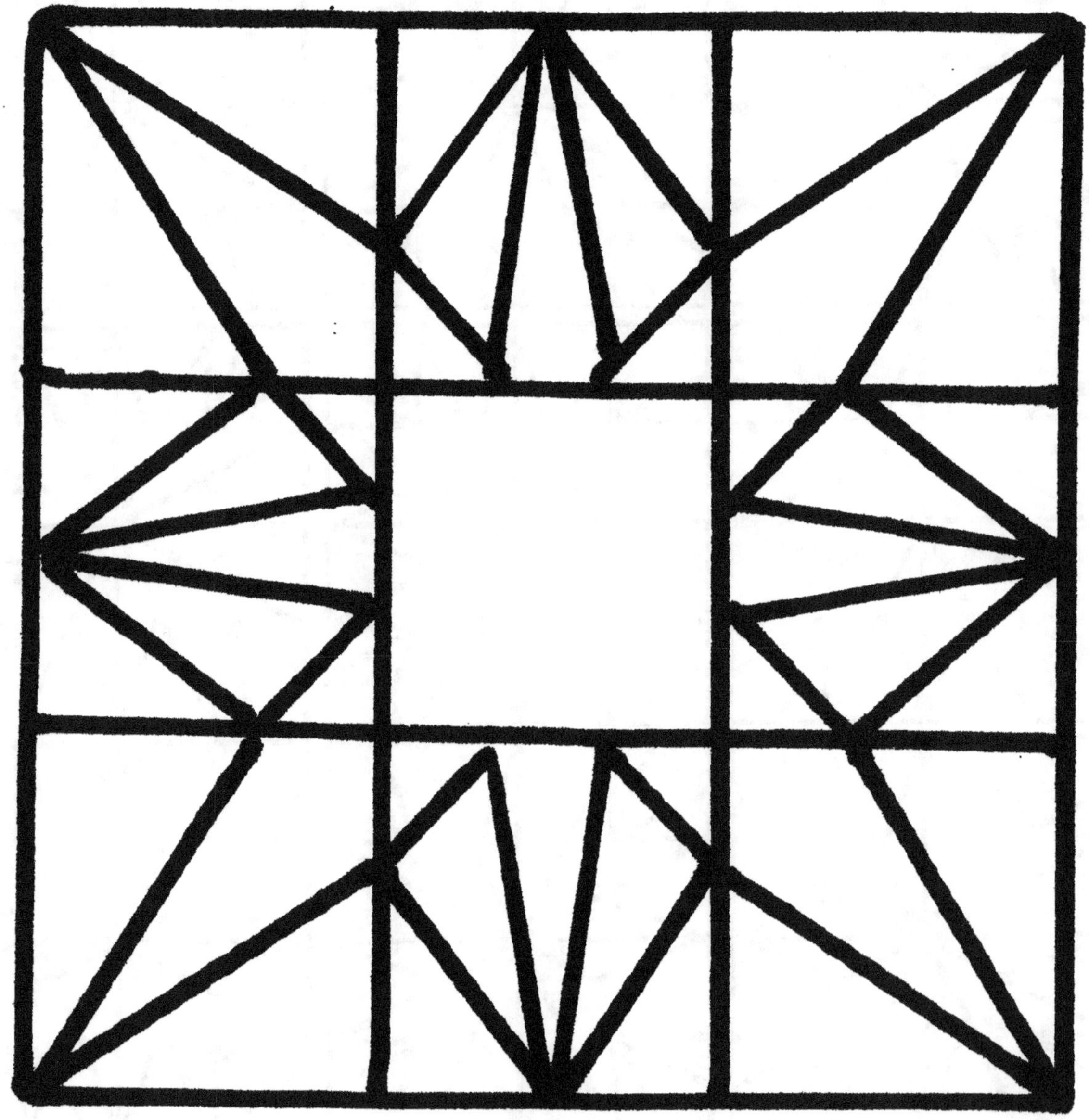

Barn Quilt Wisconsin Star

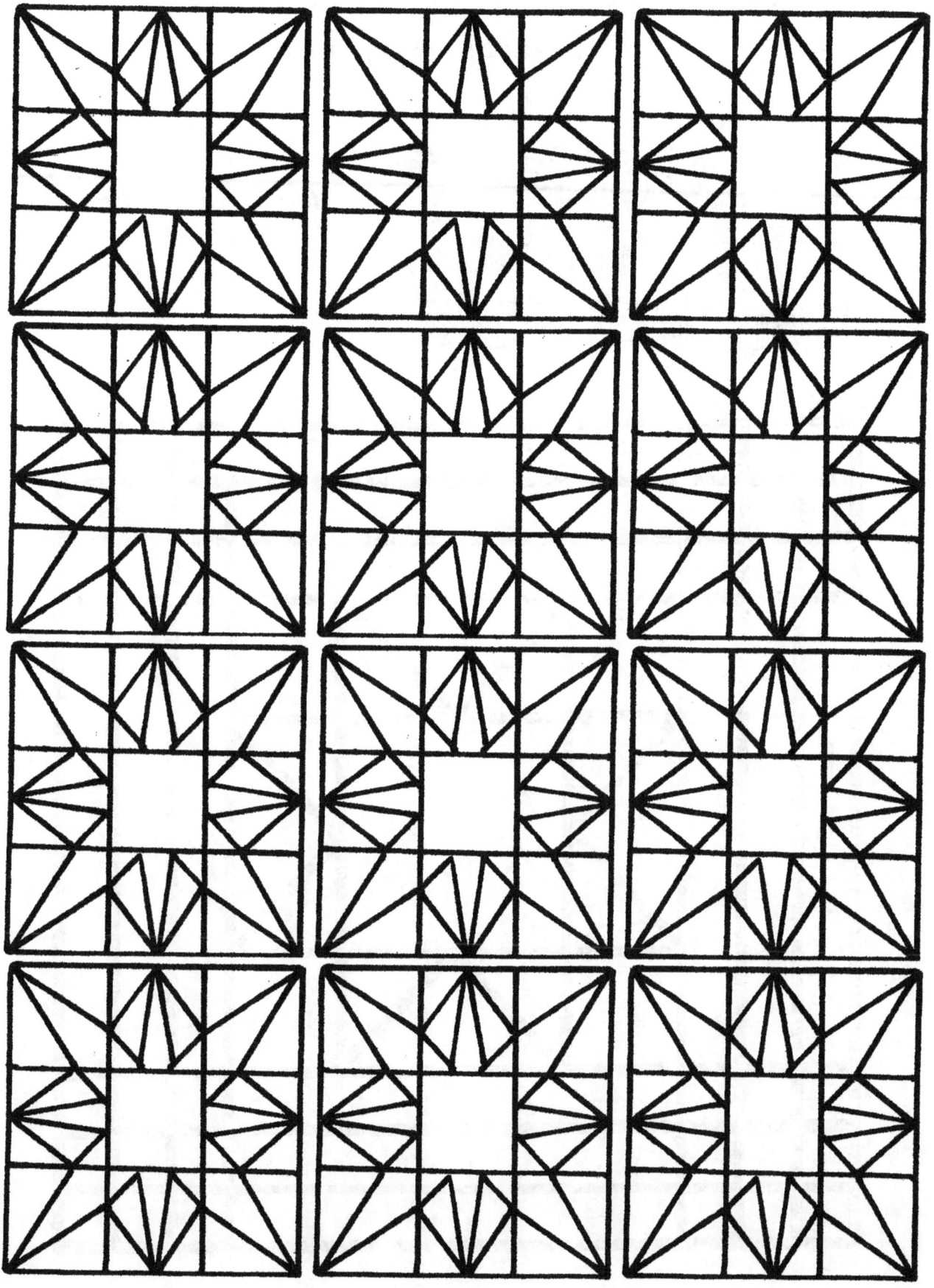

Barn Quilt Mother's Fancy
Delaware County Iowa

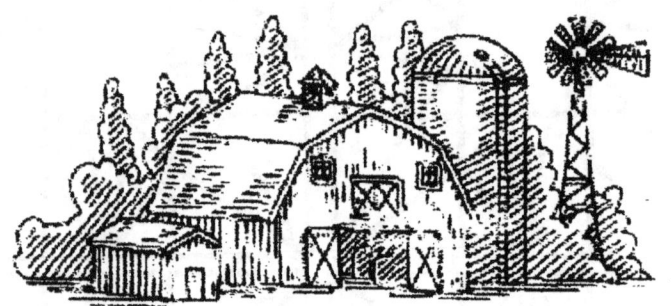

Barn Quilt Location
310ᵗʰ Ave
Hopkinton, Iowa

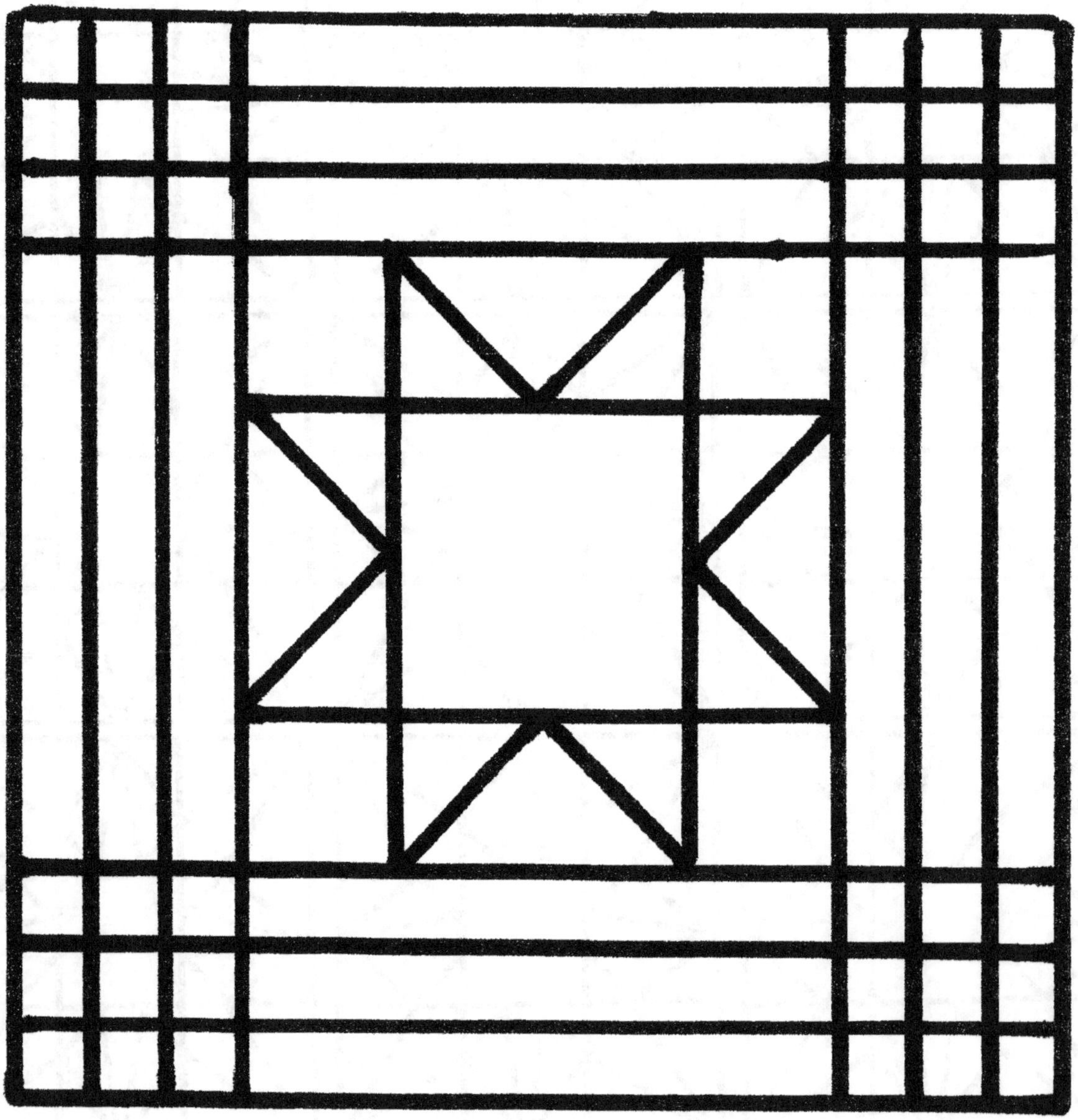

Barn Quilt Mother's Fancy

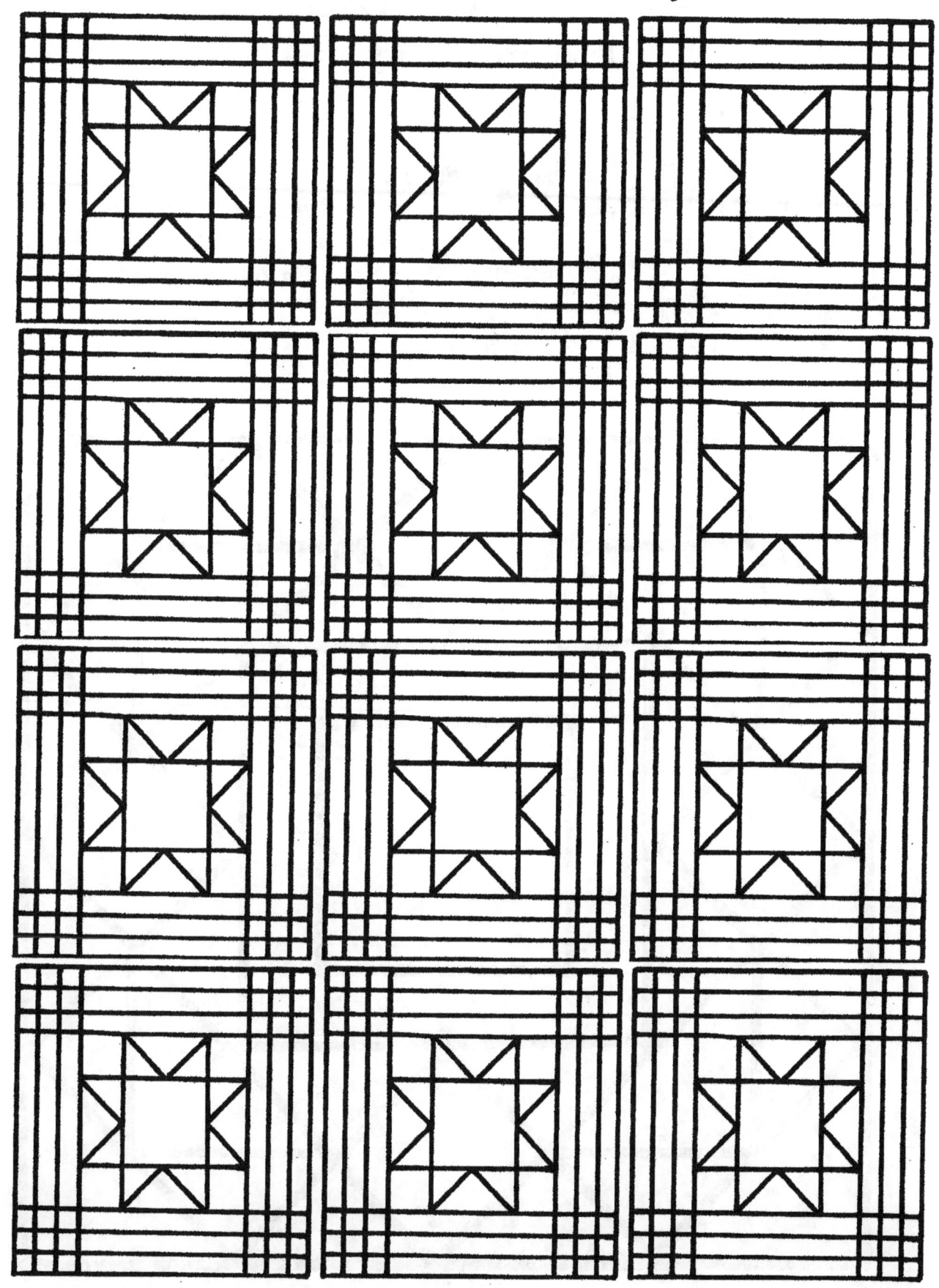

Barn Quilt Colonial Garden
Delaware County Iowa

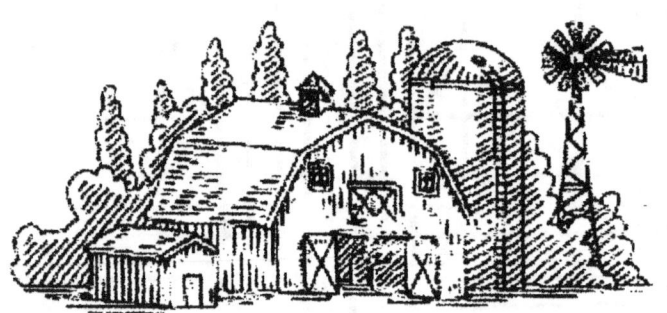

Barn Quilt Location
218th St
Earlville, Iowa

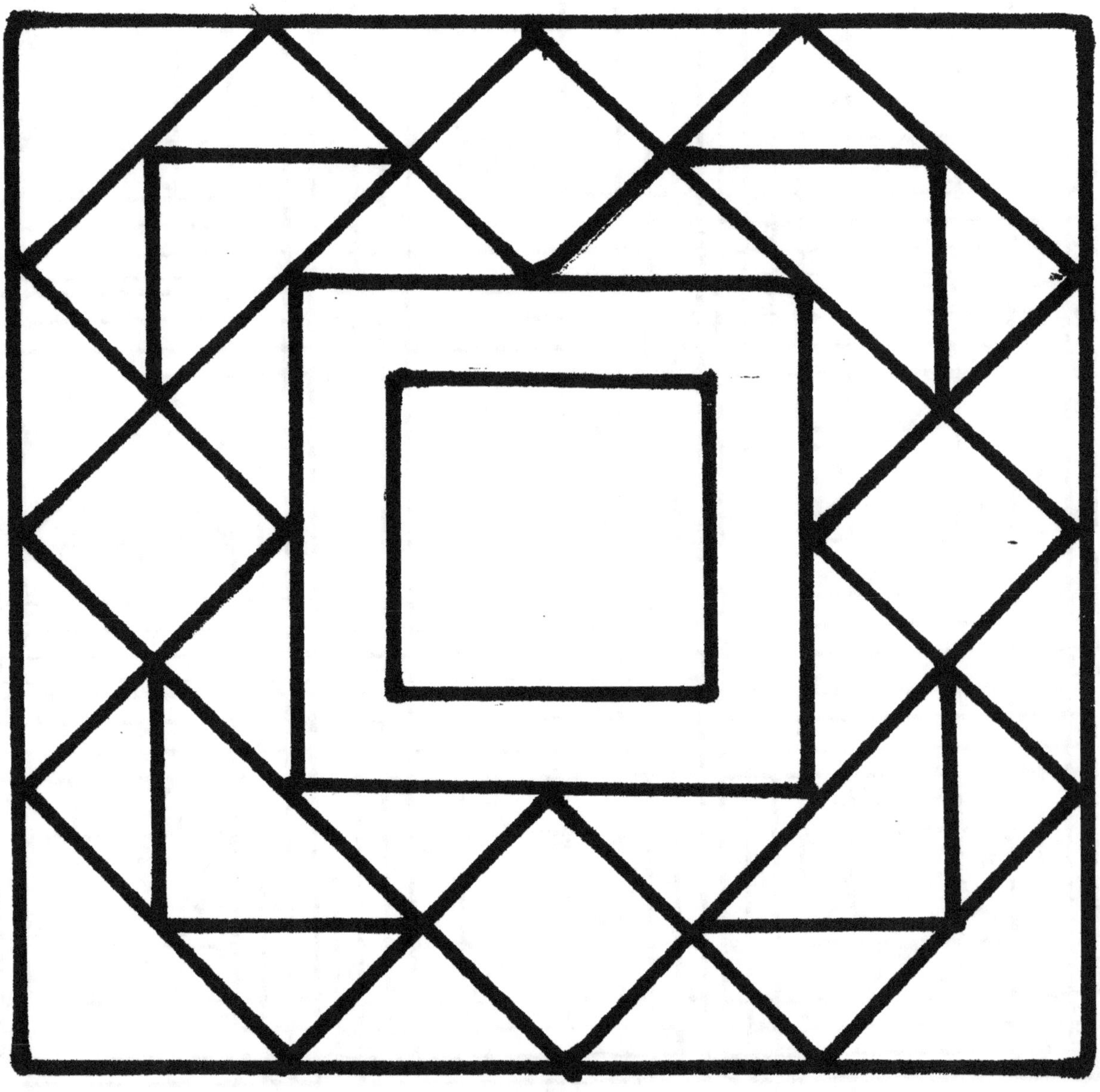

Barn Quilt Colonial Garden

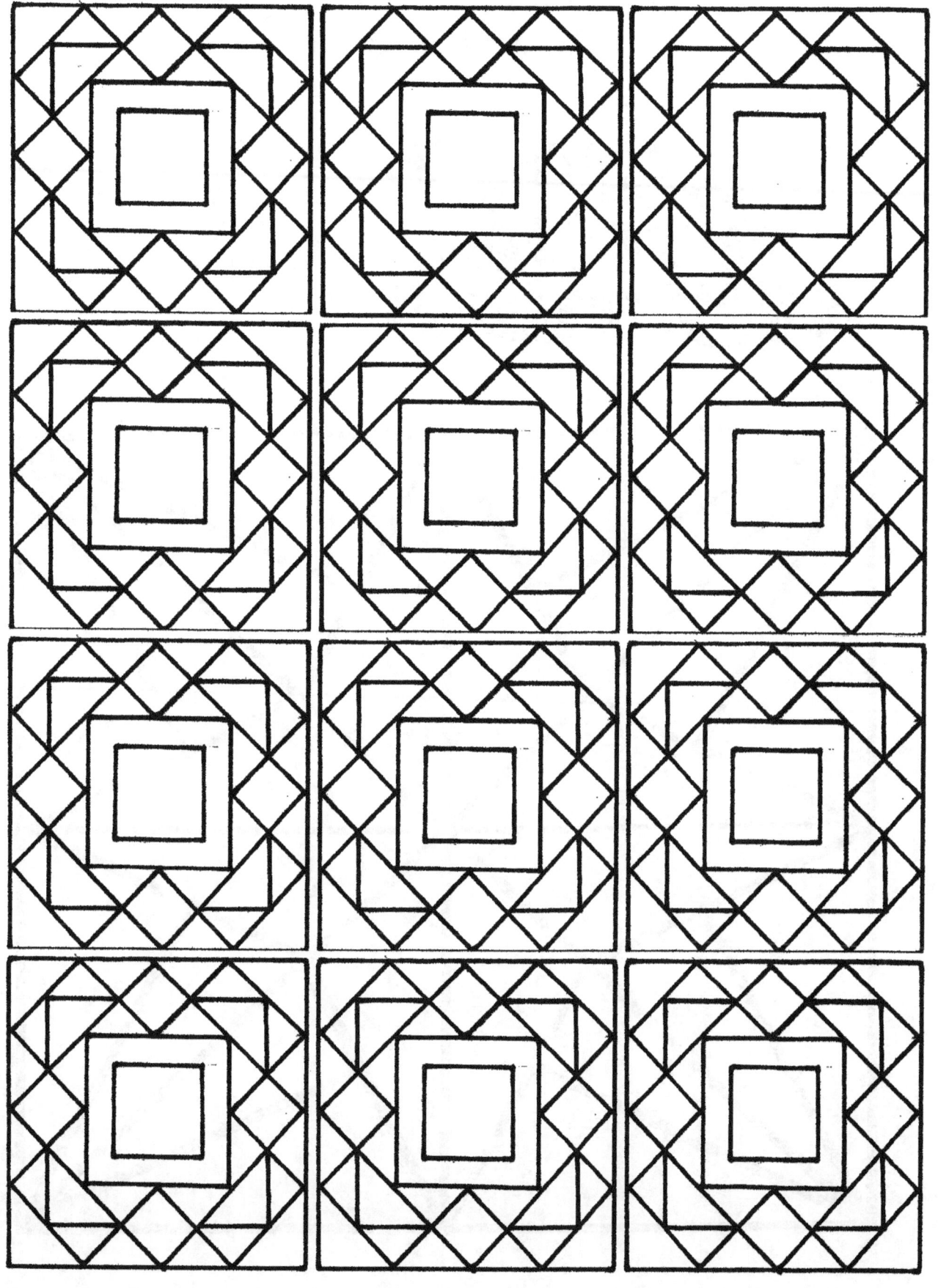

Barn Quilt Blazing Star
Delaware County Iowa

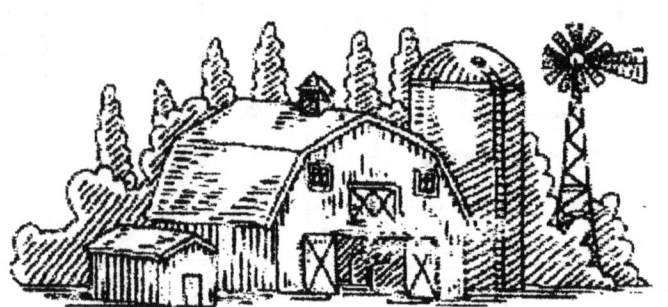

Barn Quilt Location
Jet Rd
Greeley, Iowa

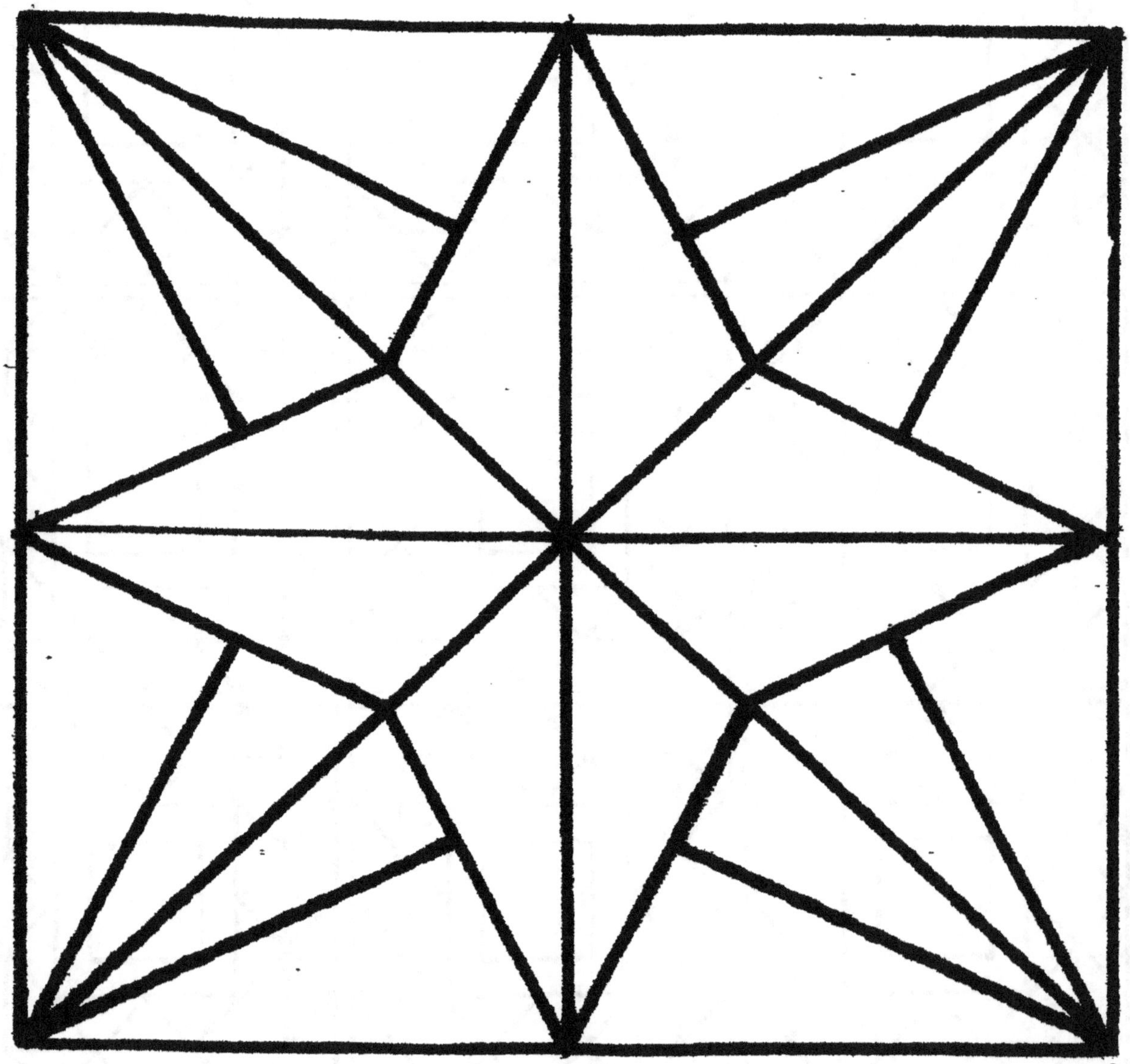

Barn Quilt Blazing Star

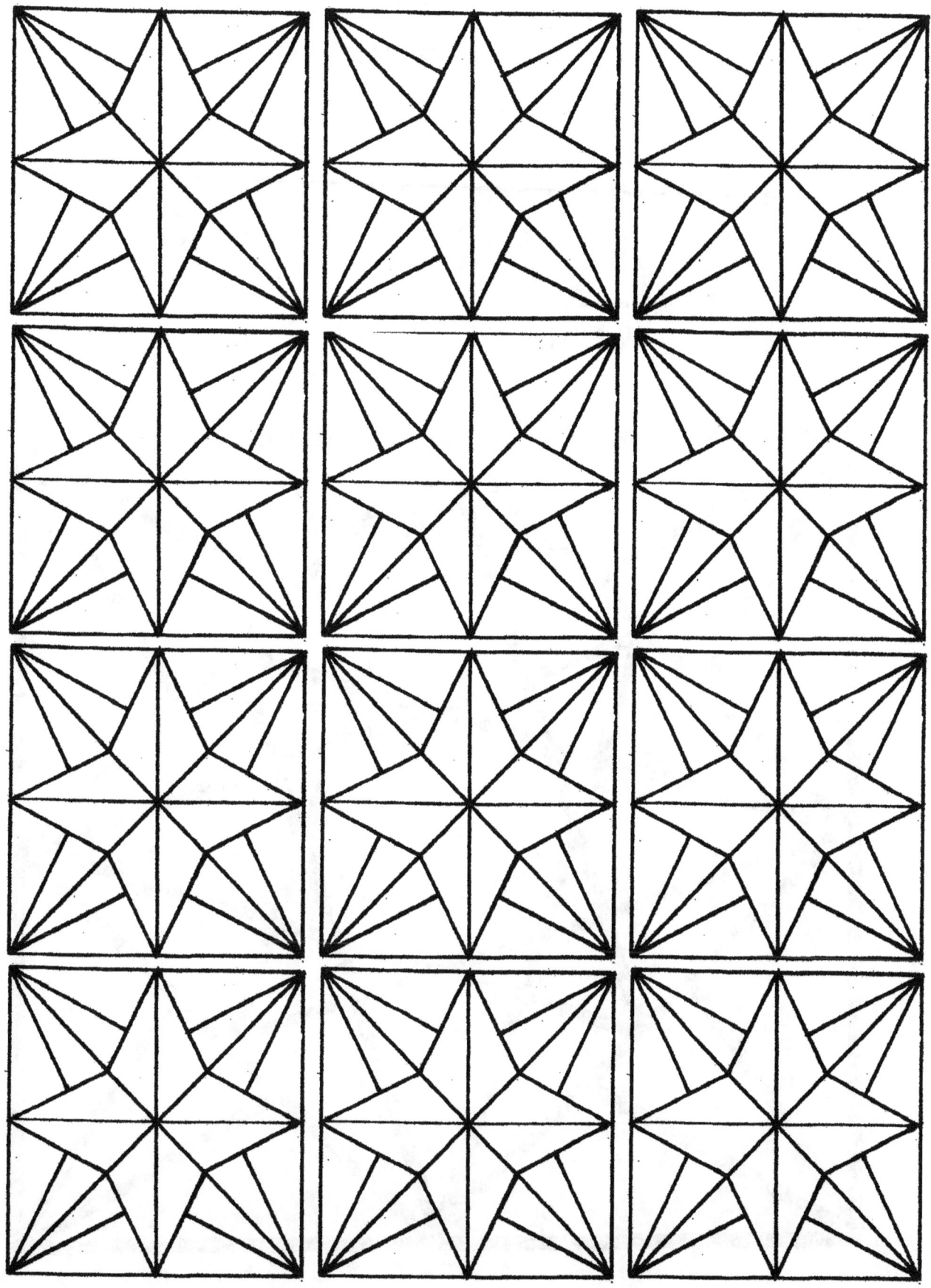

Barn Quilt Season's Joy
Delaware County Iowa

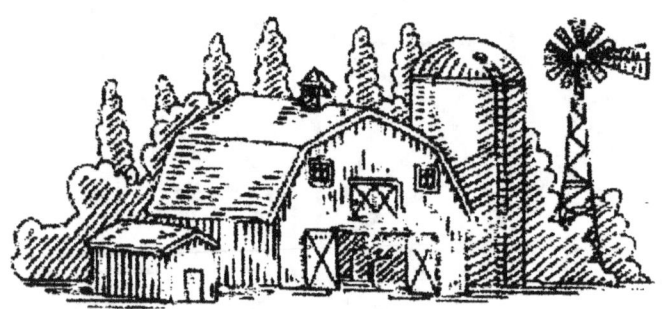

Barn Quilt Location
320th Ave
Worthington, Iowa

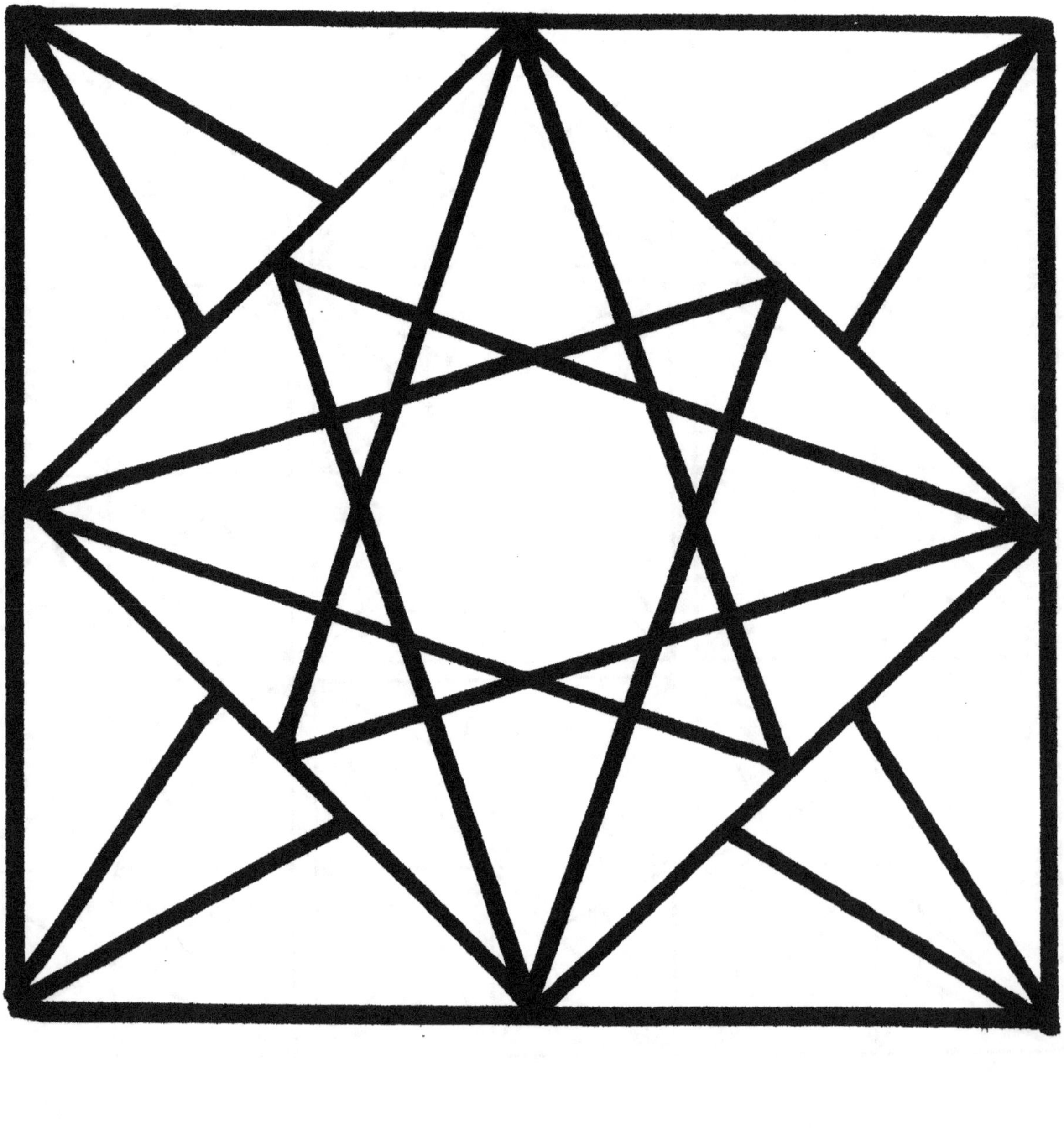

Barn Quilt Season's Joy

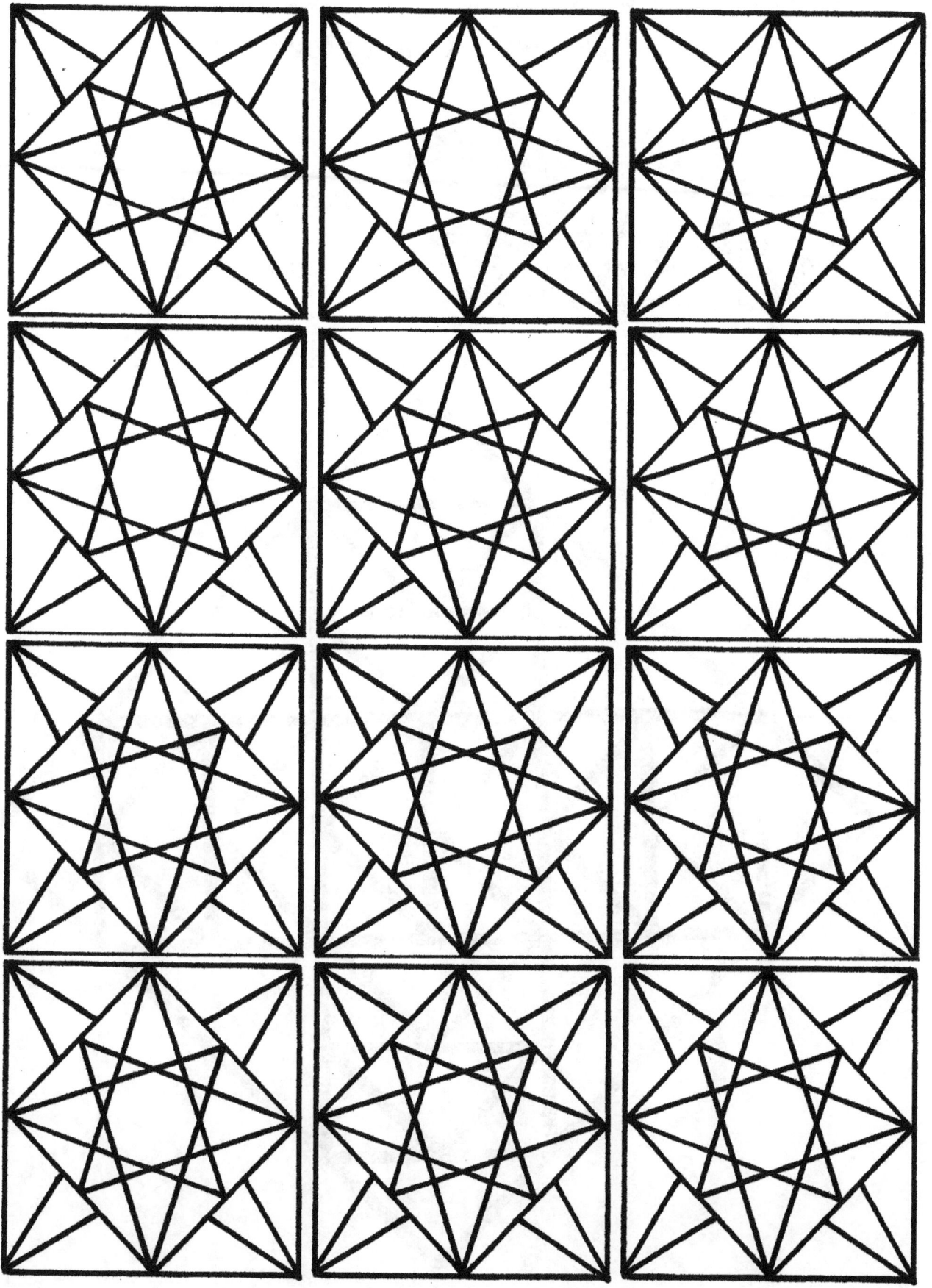

Barn Quilt Railroad Crossing
Delaware County Iowa

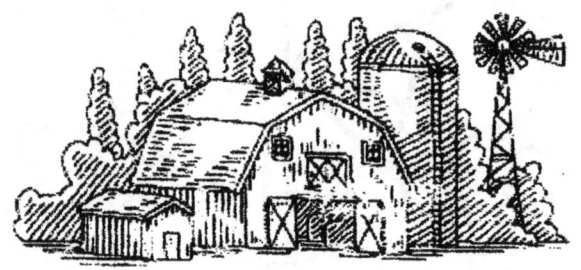

Barn Quilt Location
275th St
Delhi, Iowa

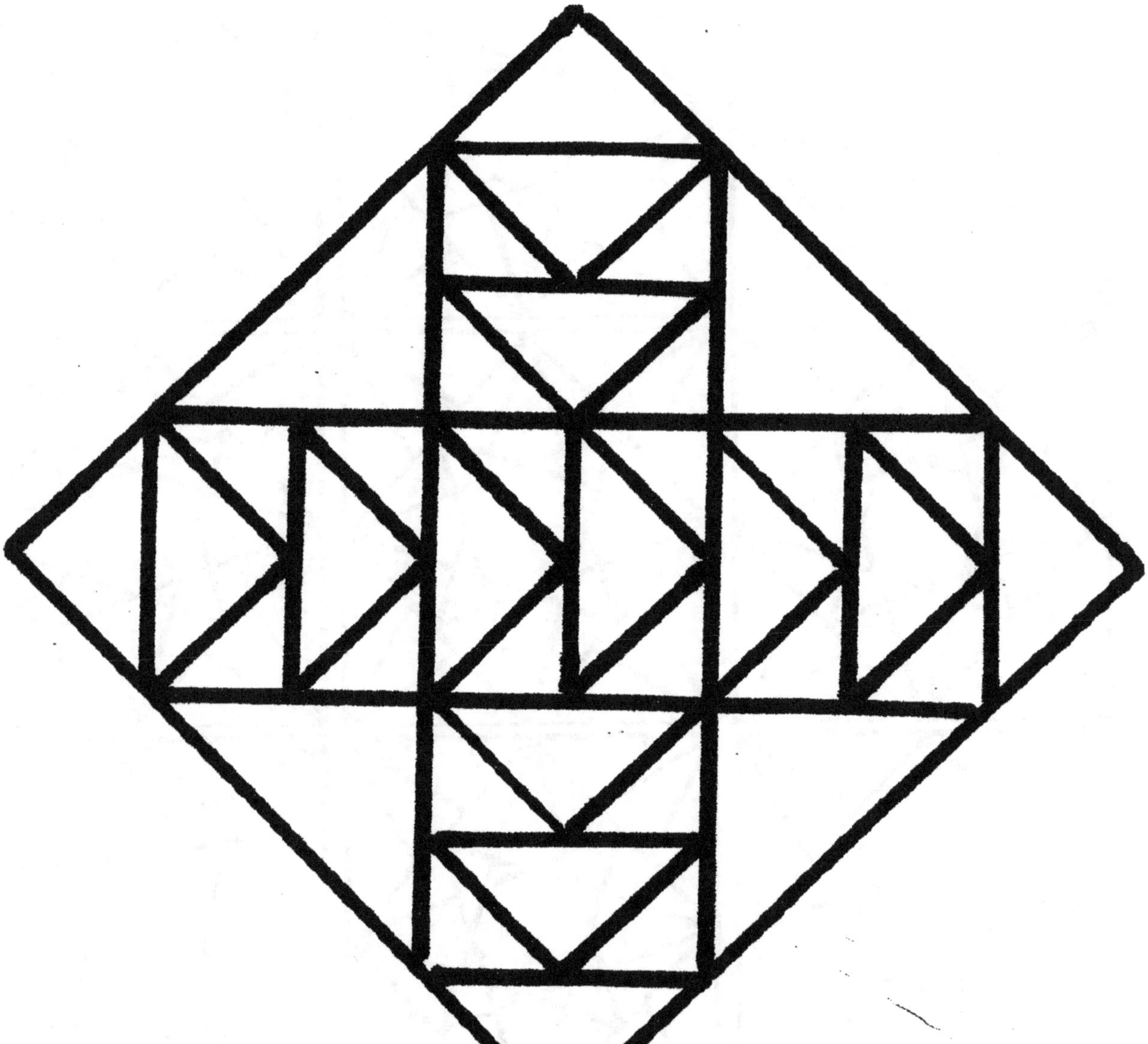

Barn Quilt Railroad Crossing

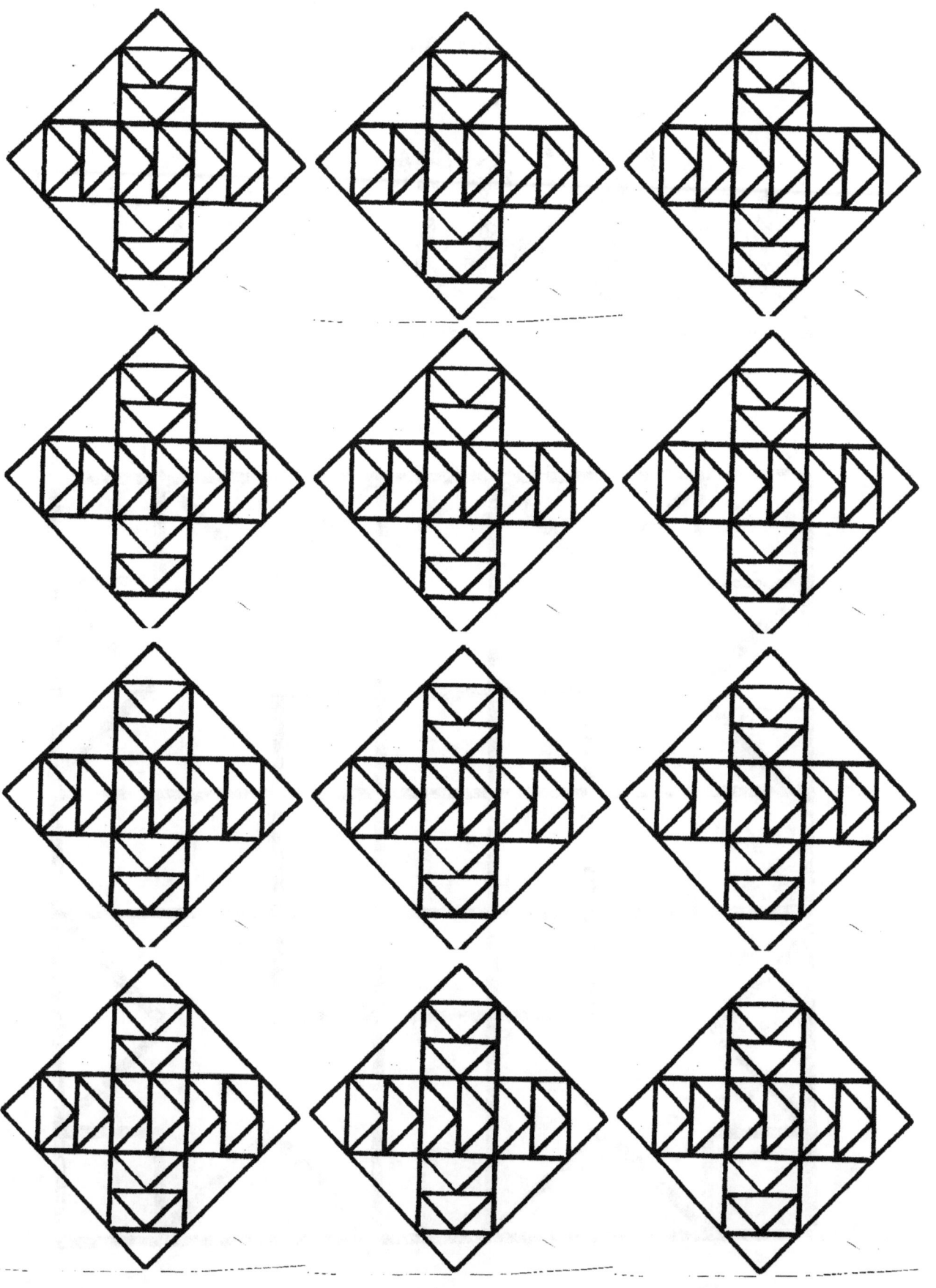

Barn Quilt Summer Blooms
Delaware County Iowa

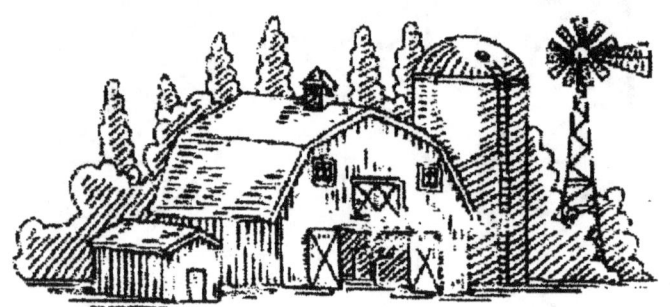

Barn Quilt Location
150th Ave
Ryan, Iowa

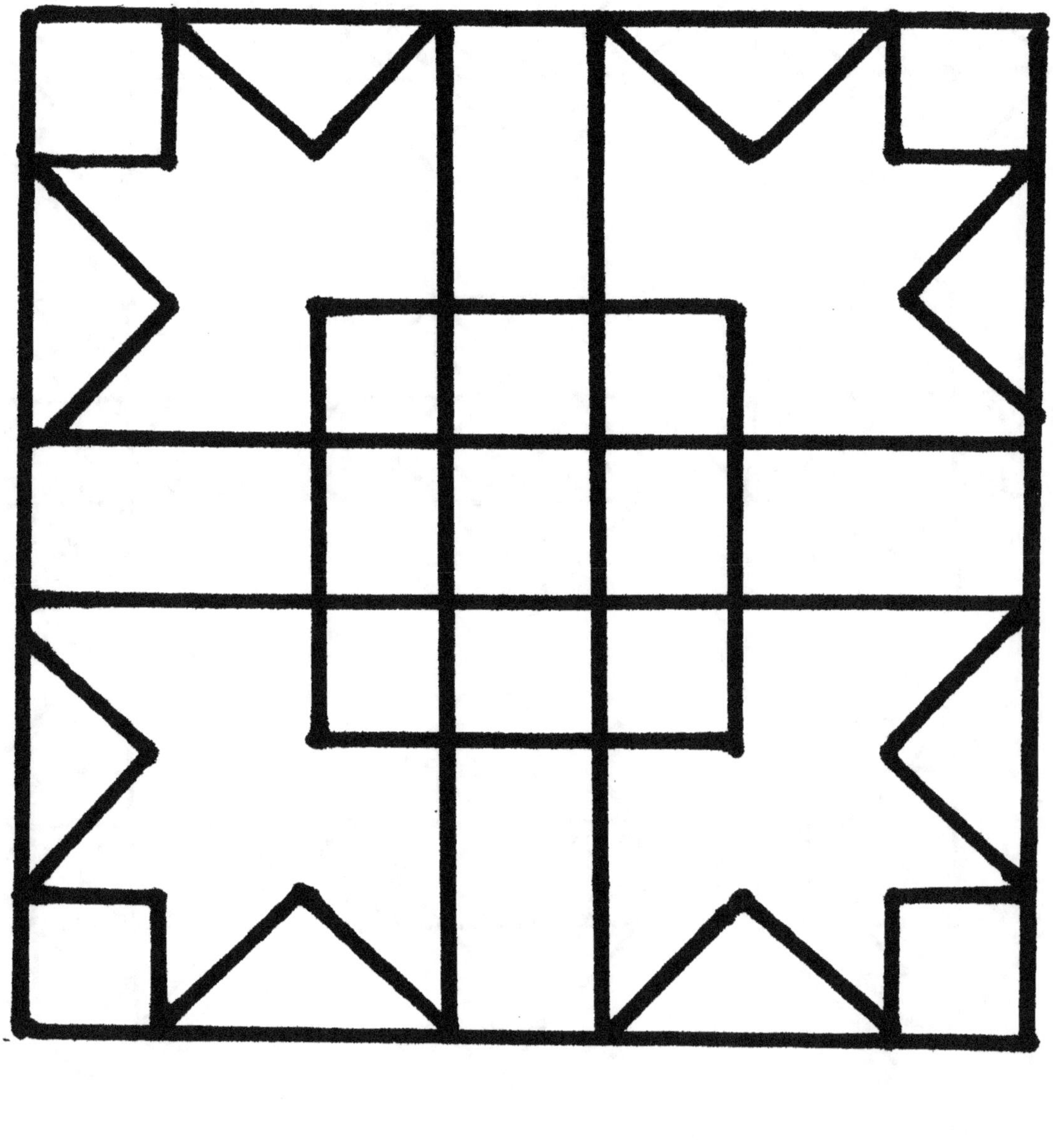

Barn Quilt Summer Blooms

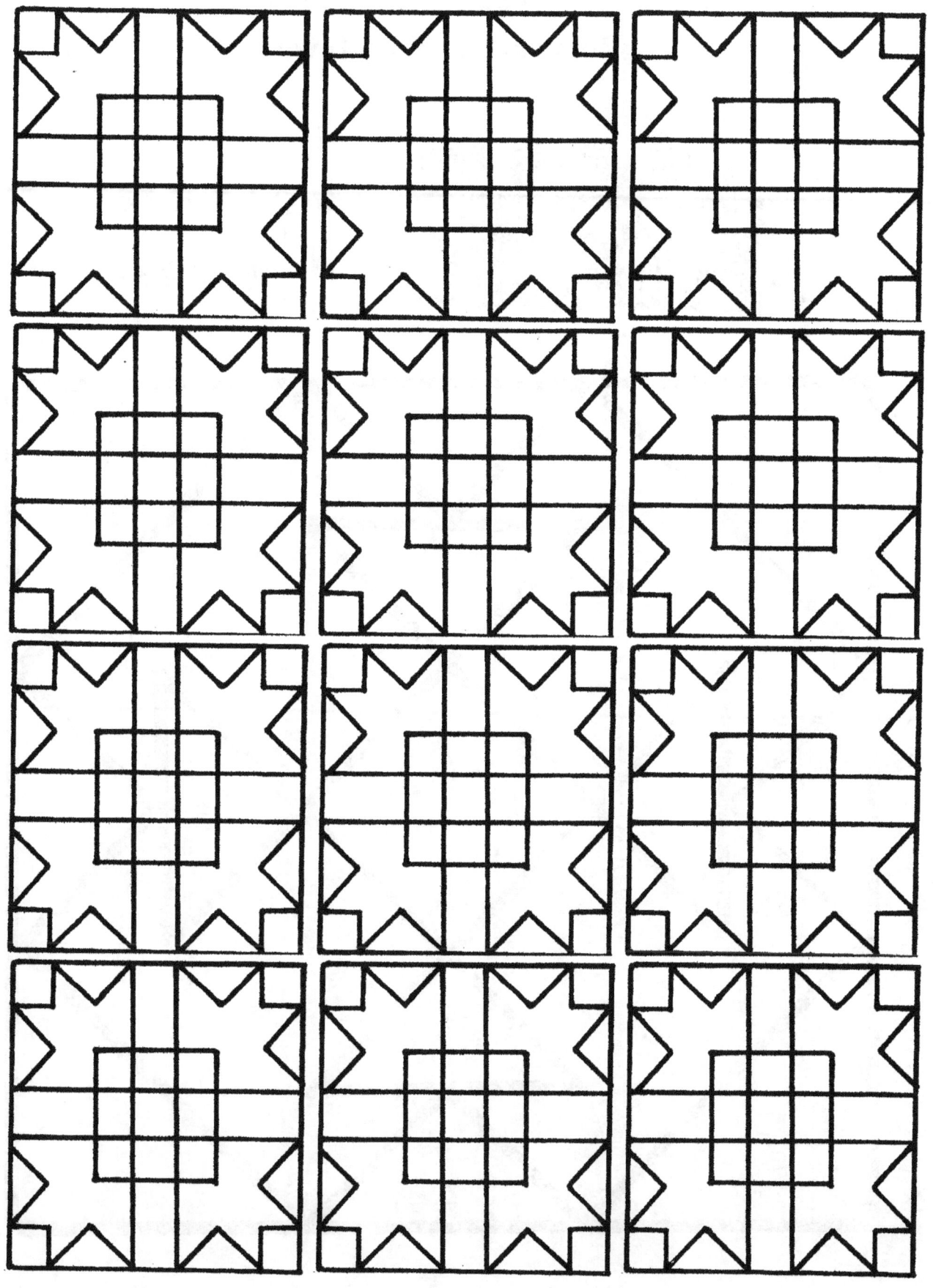

Barn Quilt Double T
Delaware County Iowa

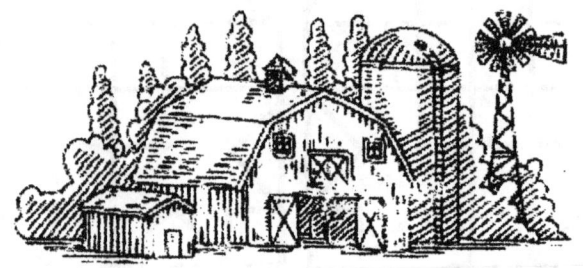

Barn Quilt Location
195th St
Manchester, Iowa

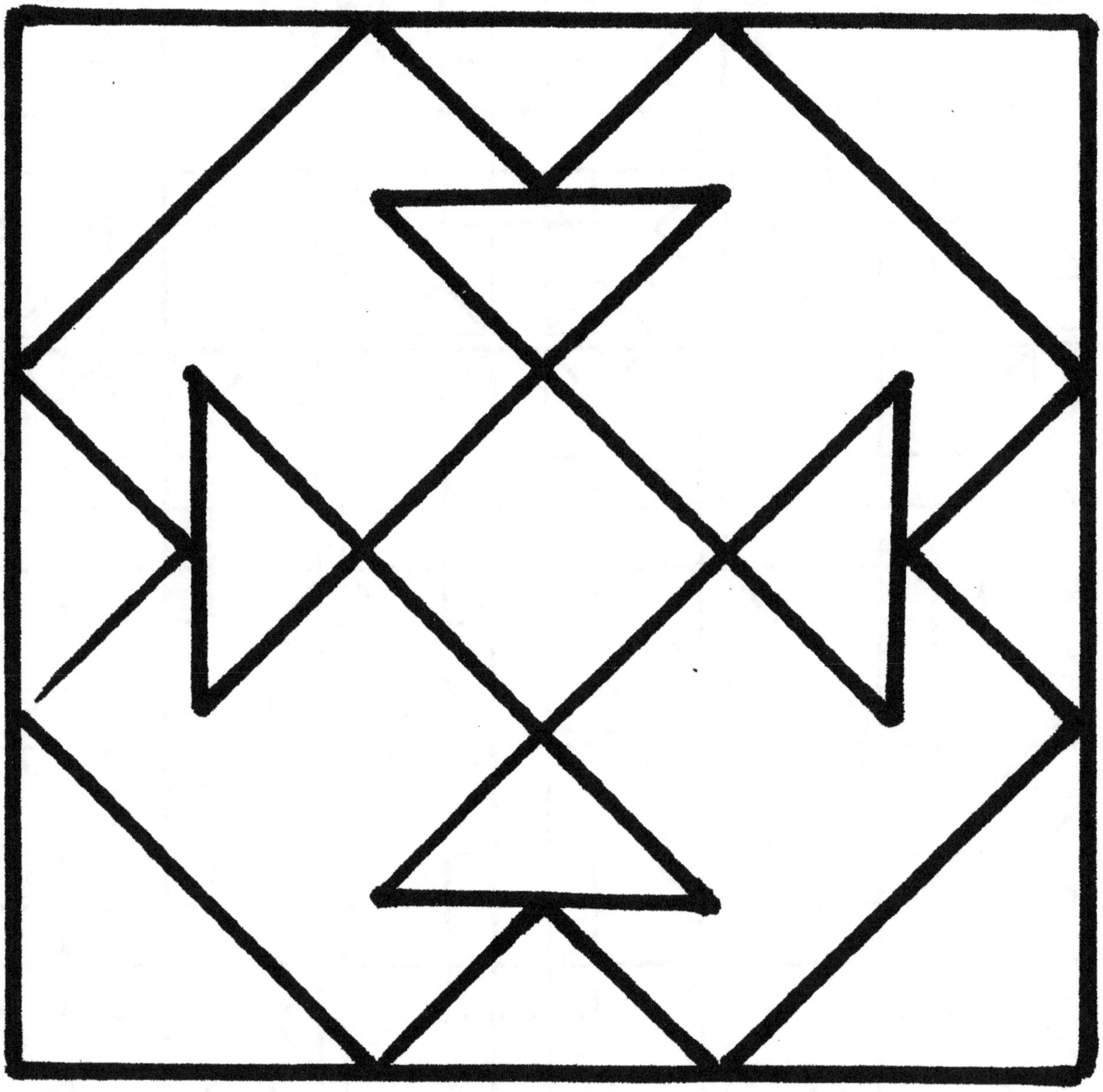

Barn Quilt Double T

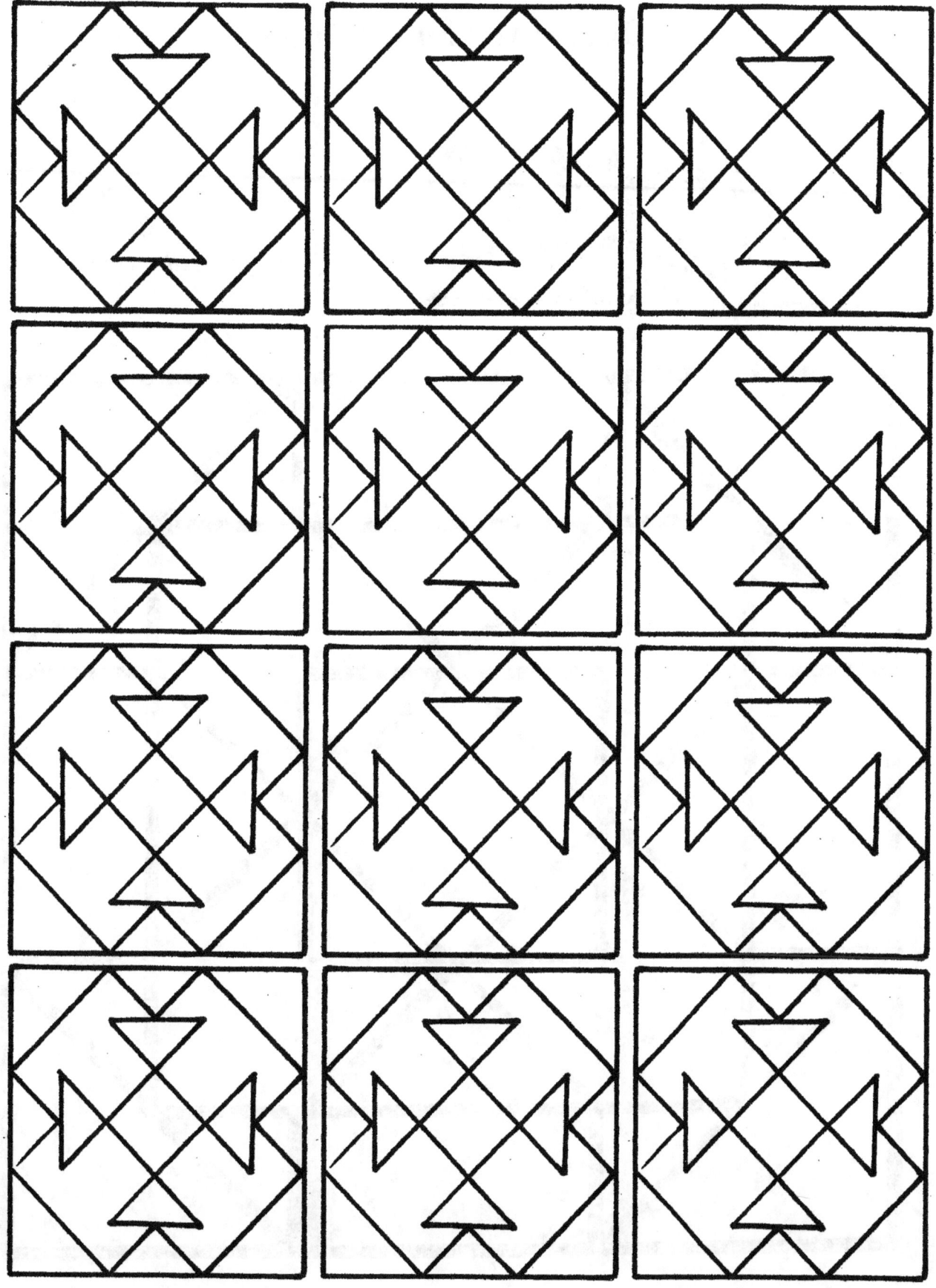

Barn Quilt Broken Band
Delaware County Iowa

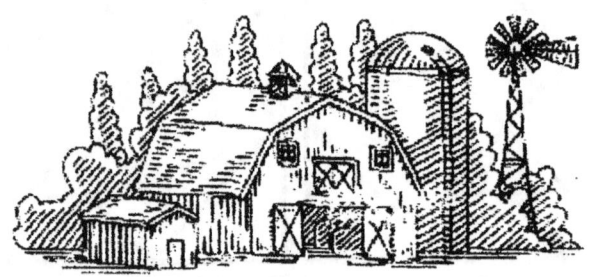

Barn Quilt Location
182nd St
Dryersville, Iowa

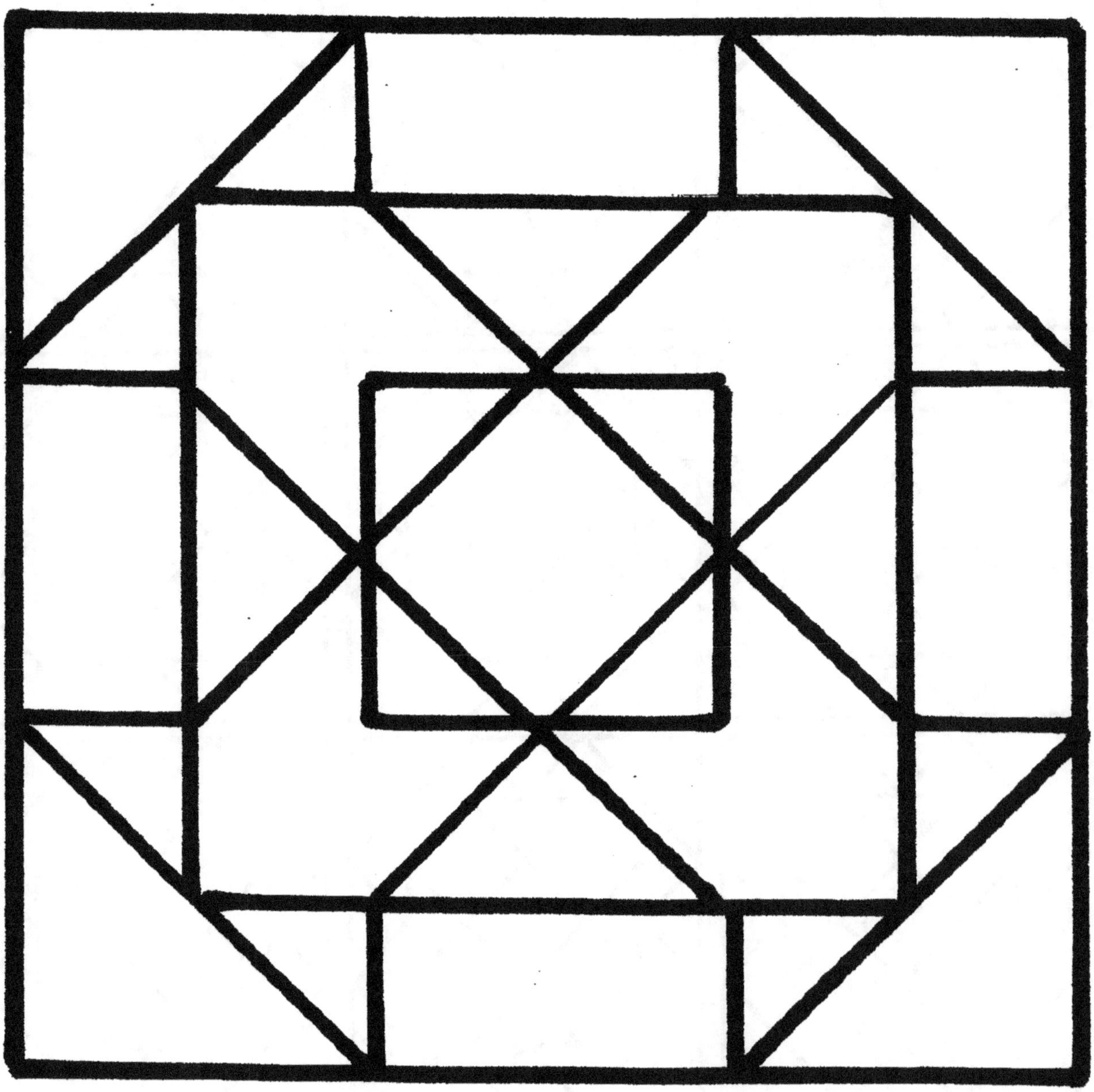

Barn Quilt Broken Band

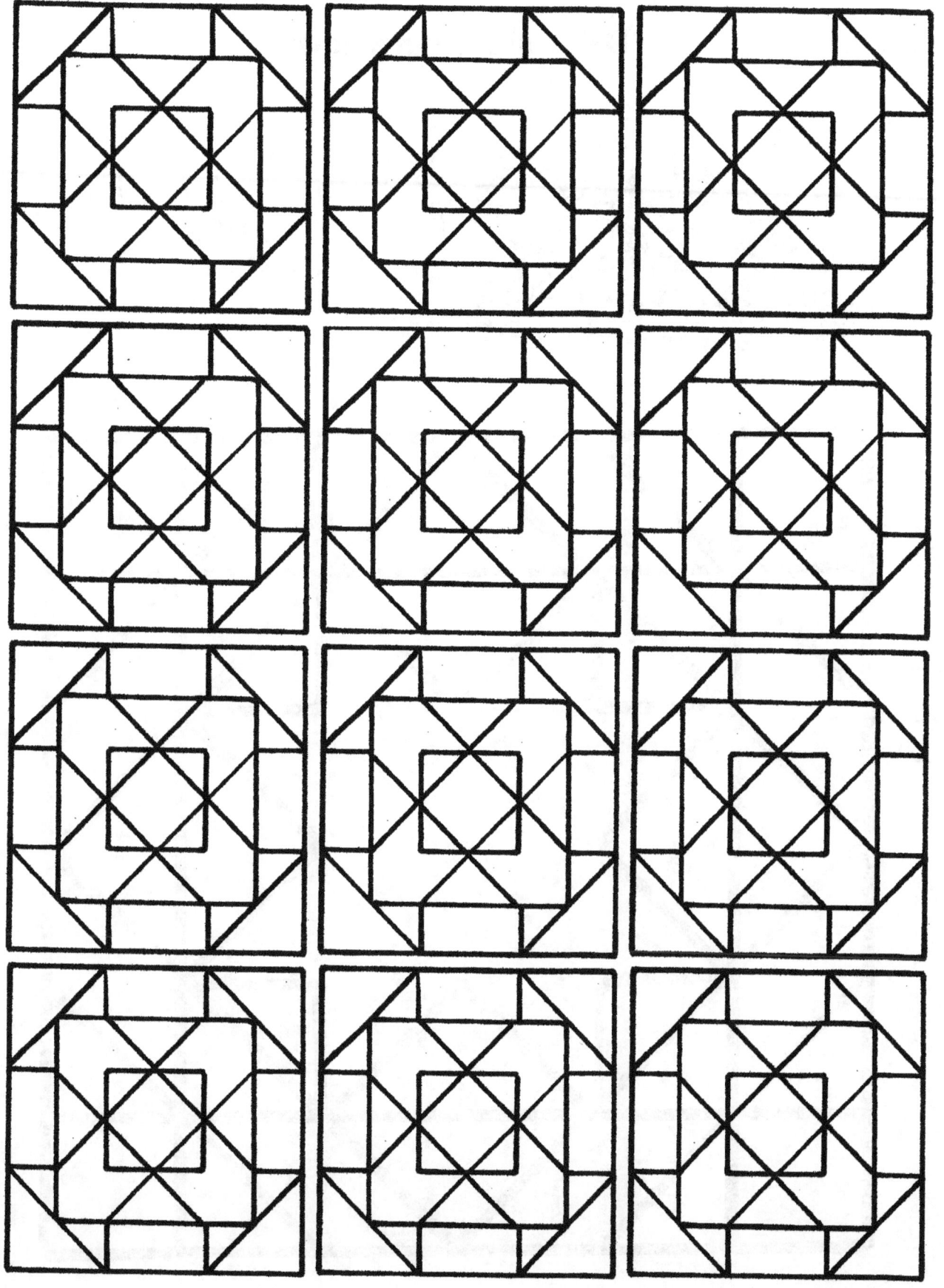

Barn Quilt Union Star
Delaware County Iowa

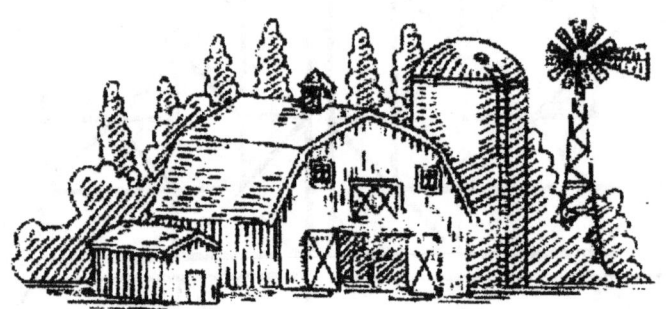

Barn Quilt Location
315th St
Hopkinton, Iowa

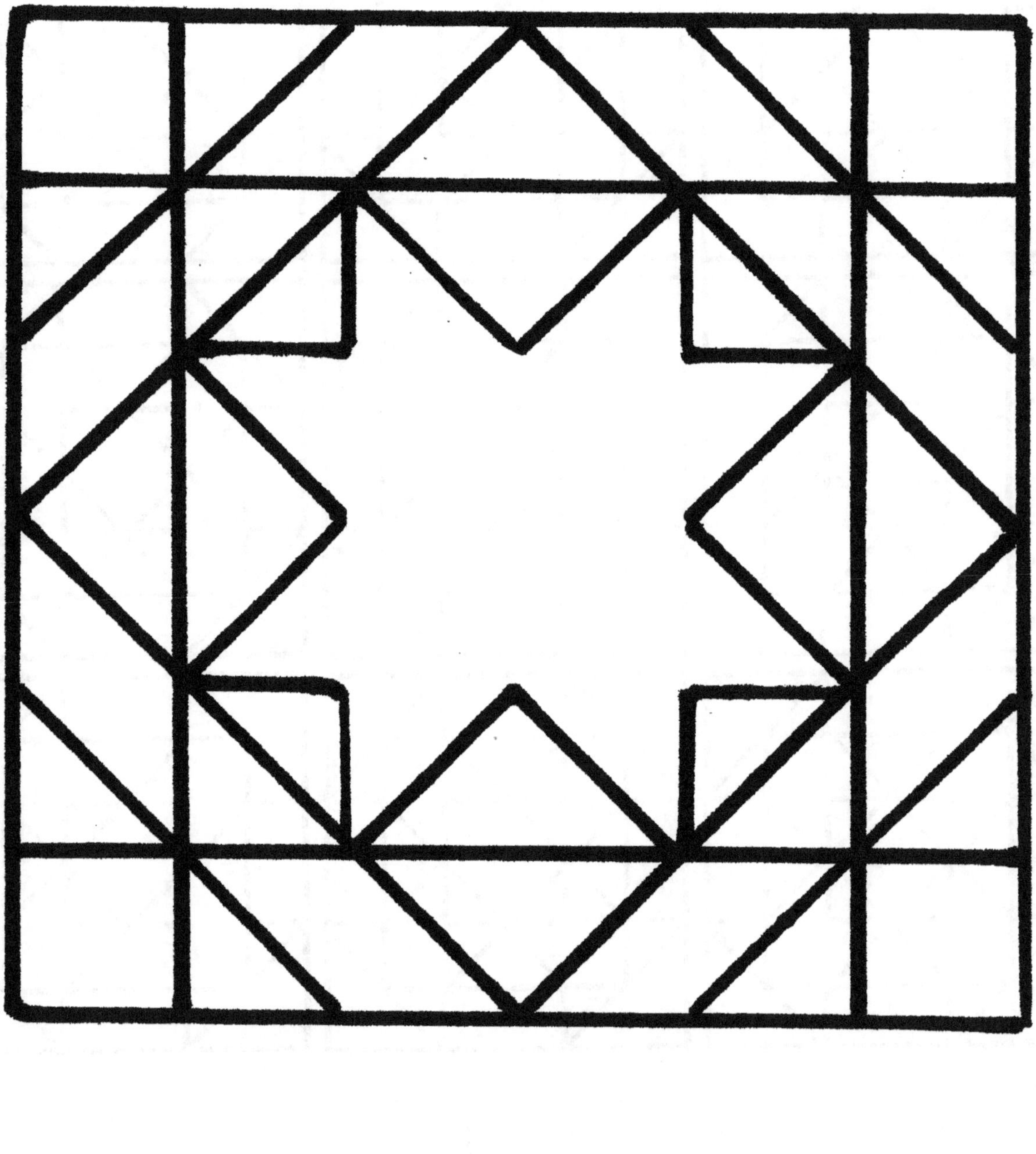

Barn Quilt Union Star

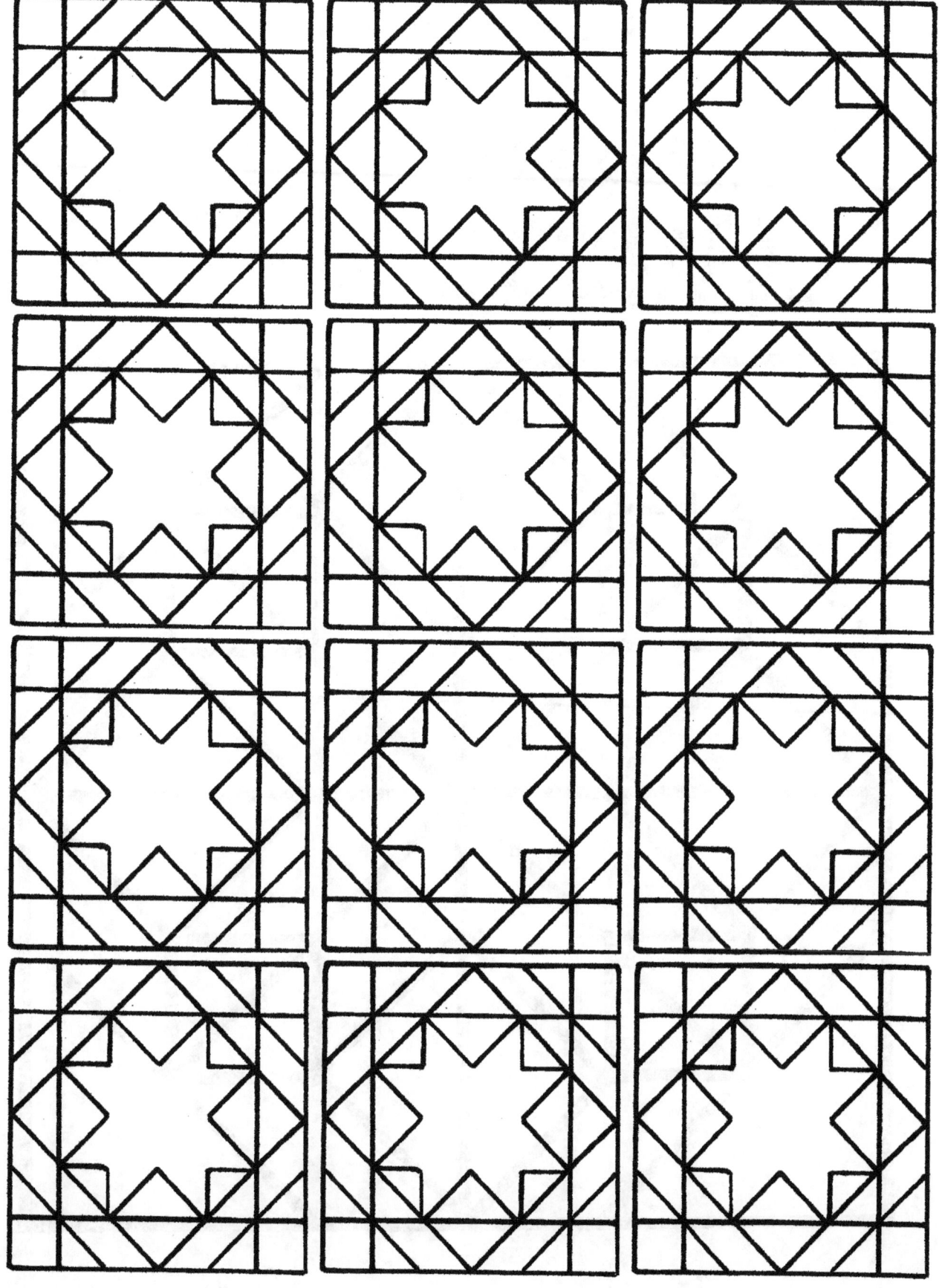

Barn Quilt Rolling Star
Delaware Count Iowa

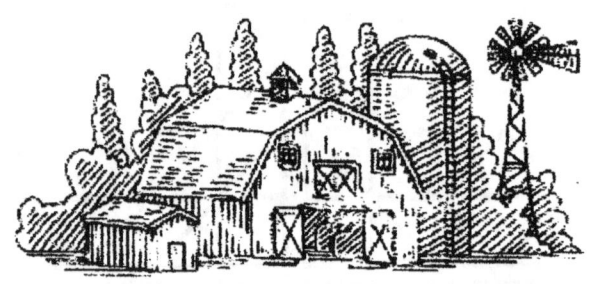

Barn Quilt Location
200th Ave
Hopkinton, Iowa

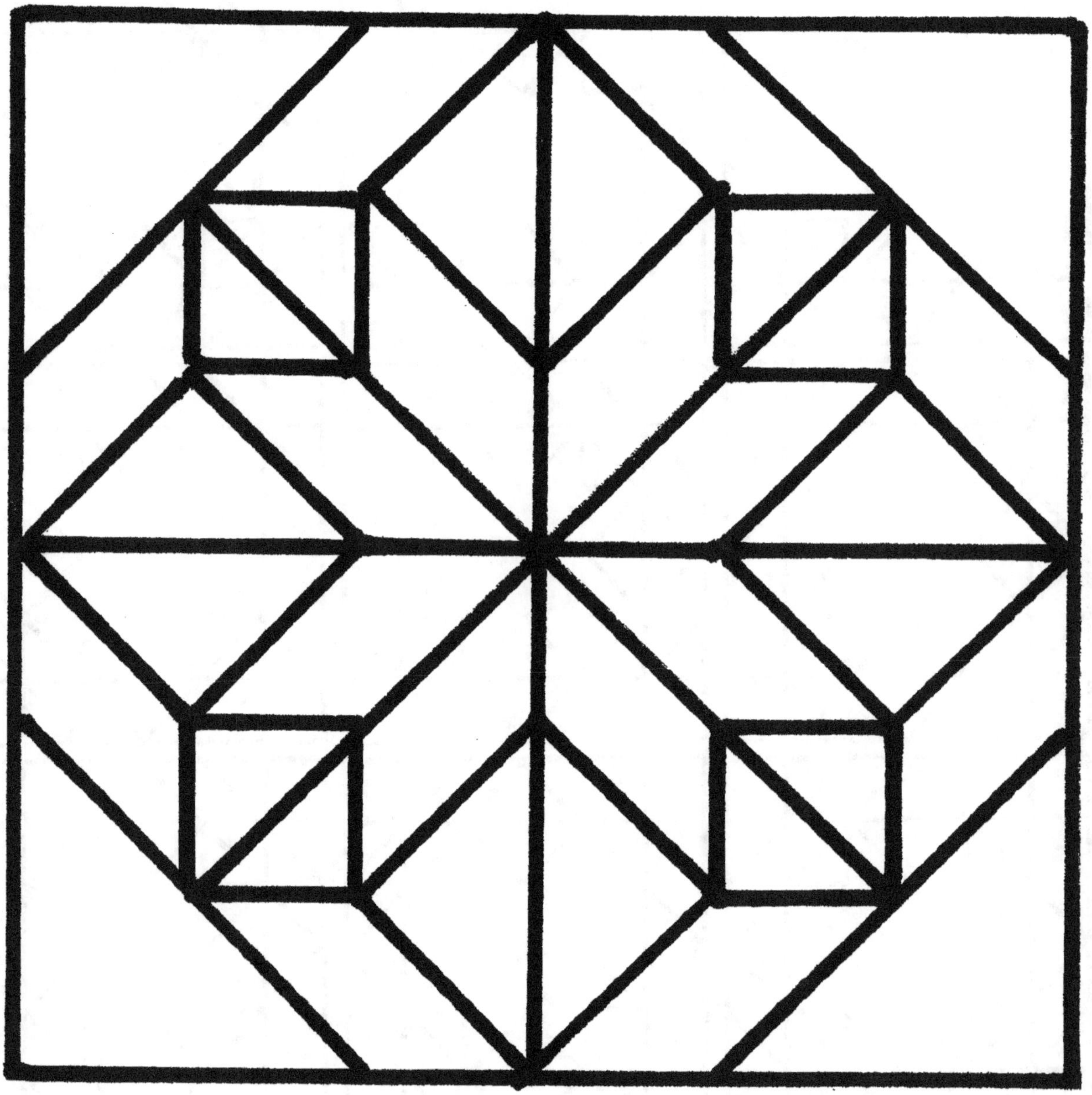

Barn Quilt Rolling Star

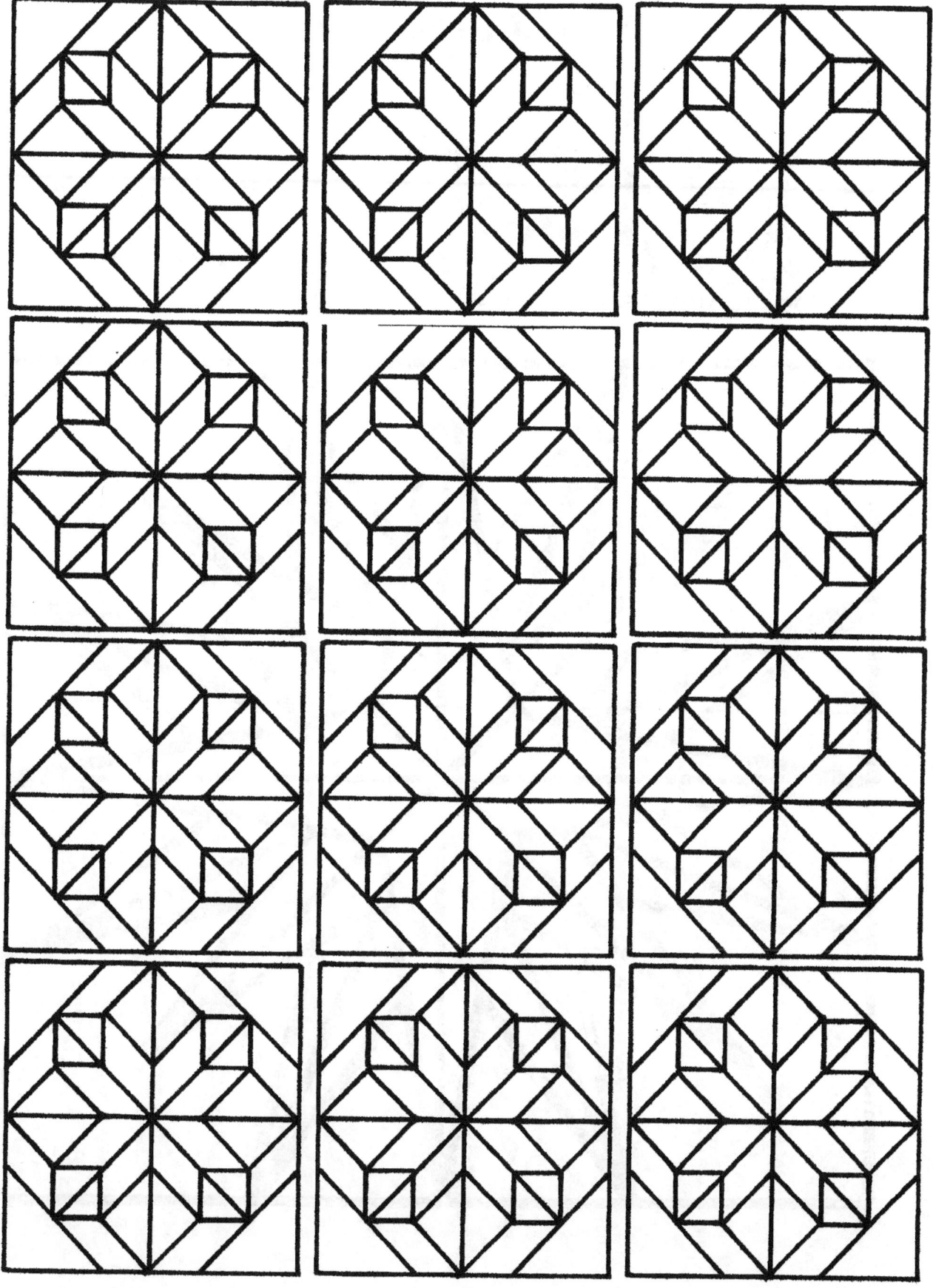

Barn Quilt Mariner's Star
Delaware County Iowa

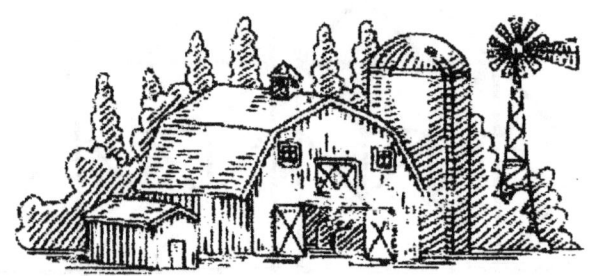

Barn Quilt Location
330ᵗʰ St
Coggon, Iowa

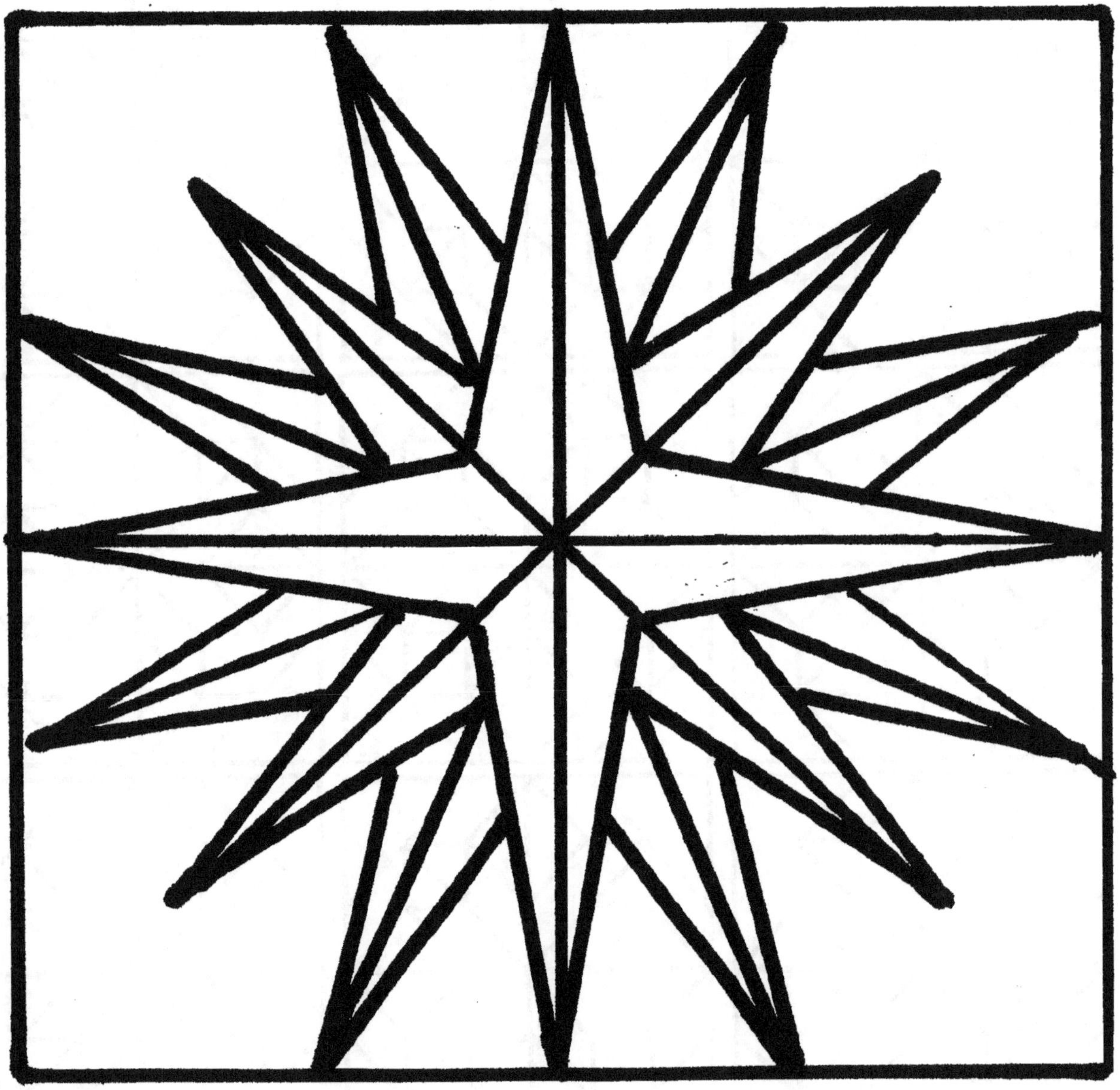

Barn Quilt Mariner's Star

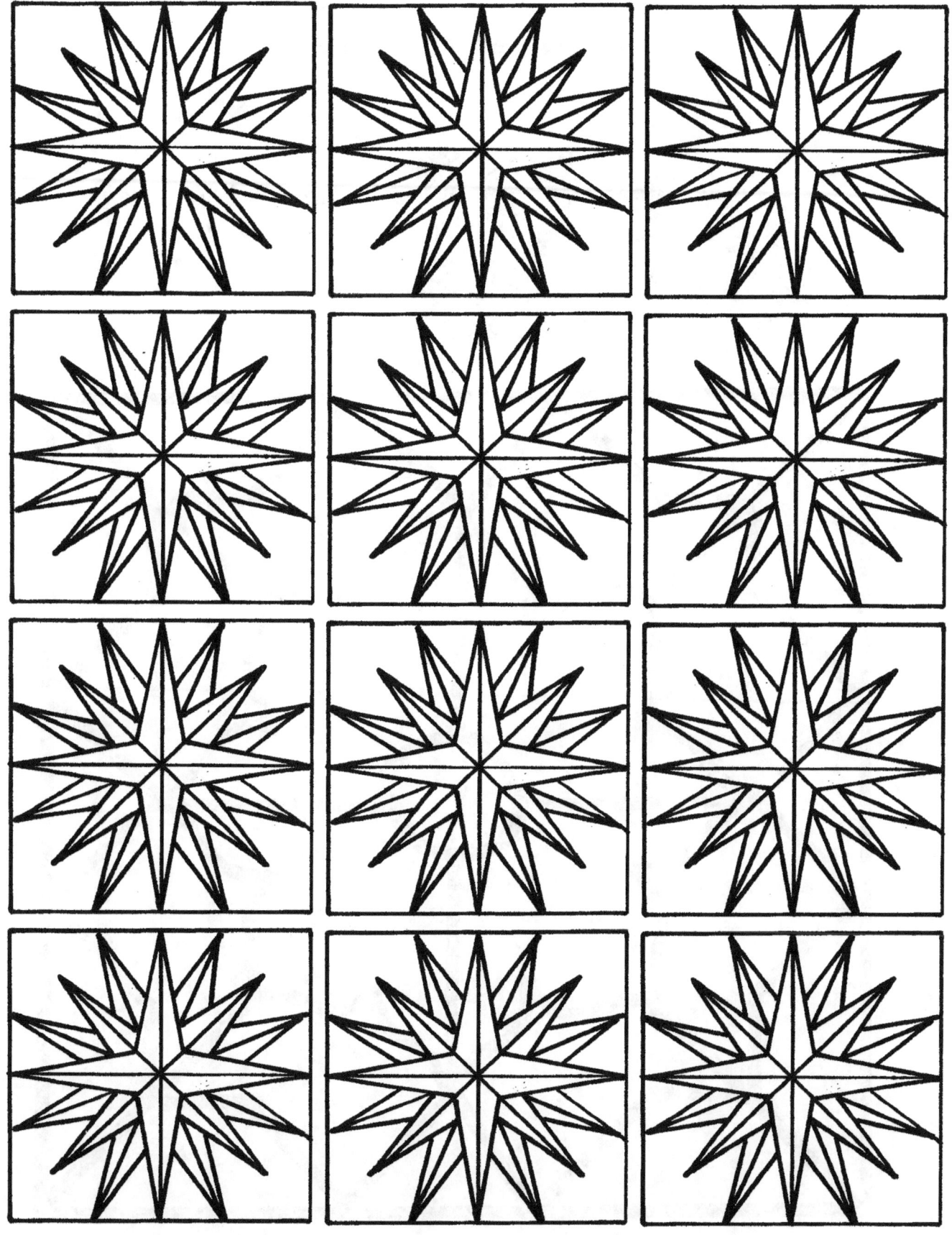

Barn Quilt 9th Infantry Division
Delaware County Iowa

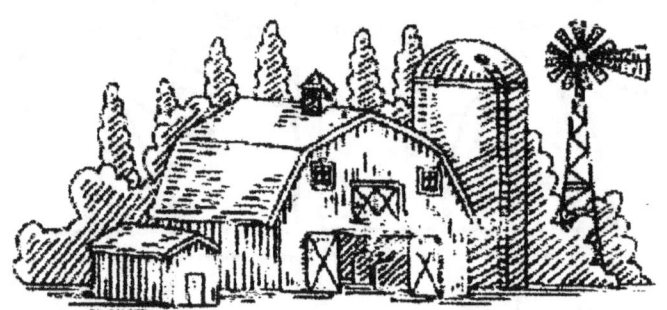

Barn Quilt Location
Hwy 13
Ryan, Iowa

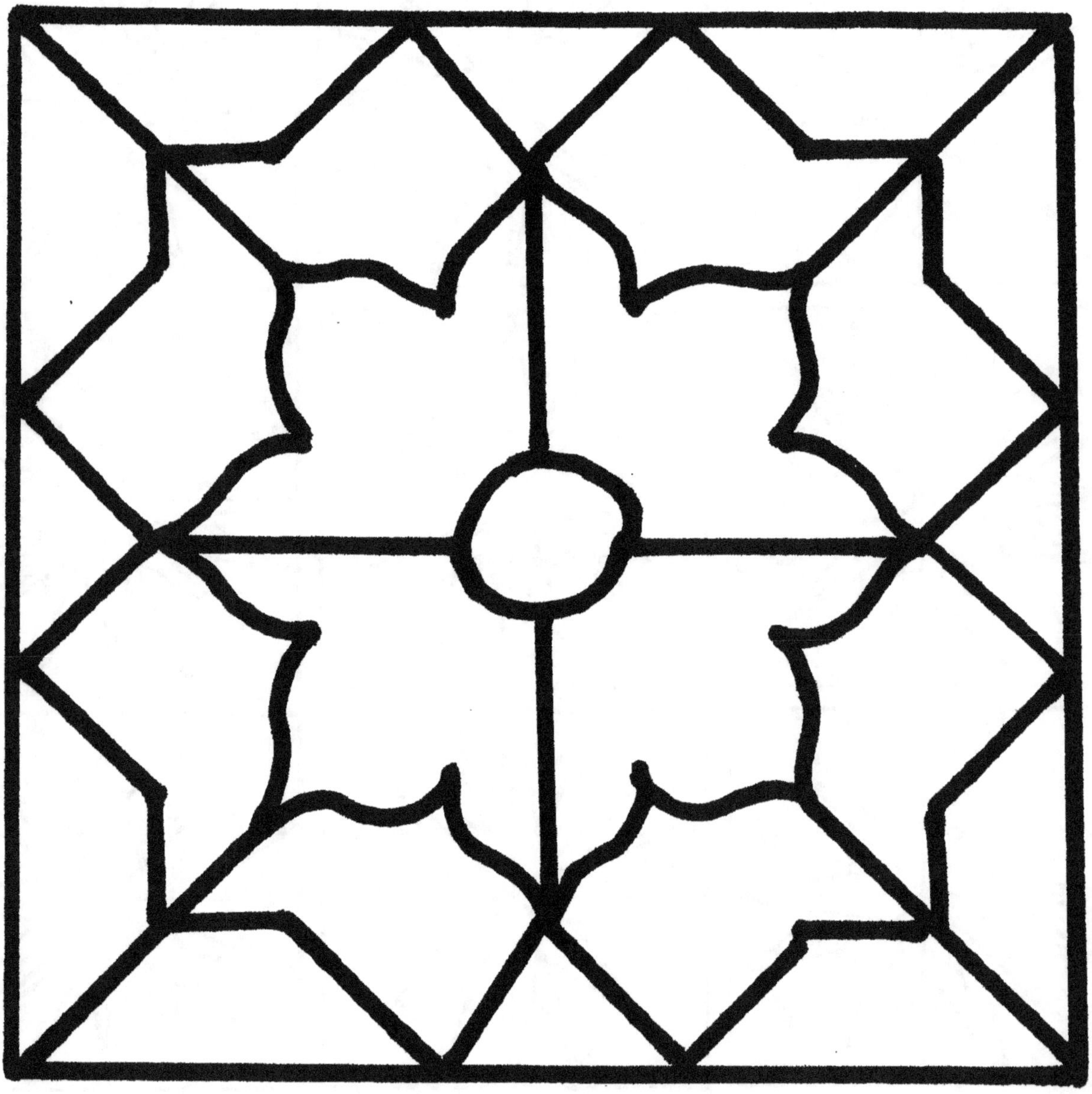

Barn Quilt 9th Infantry Division

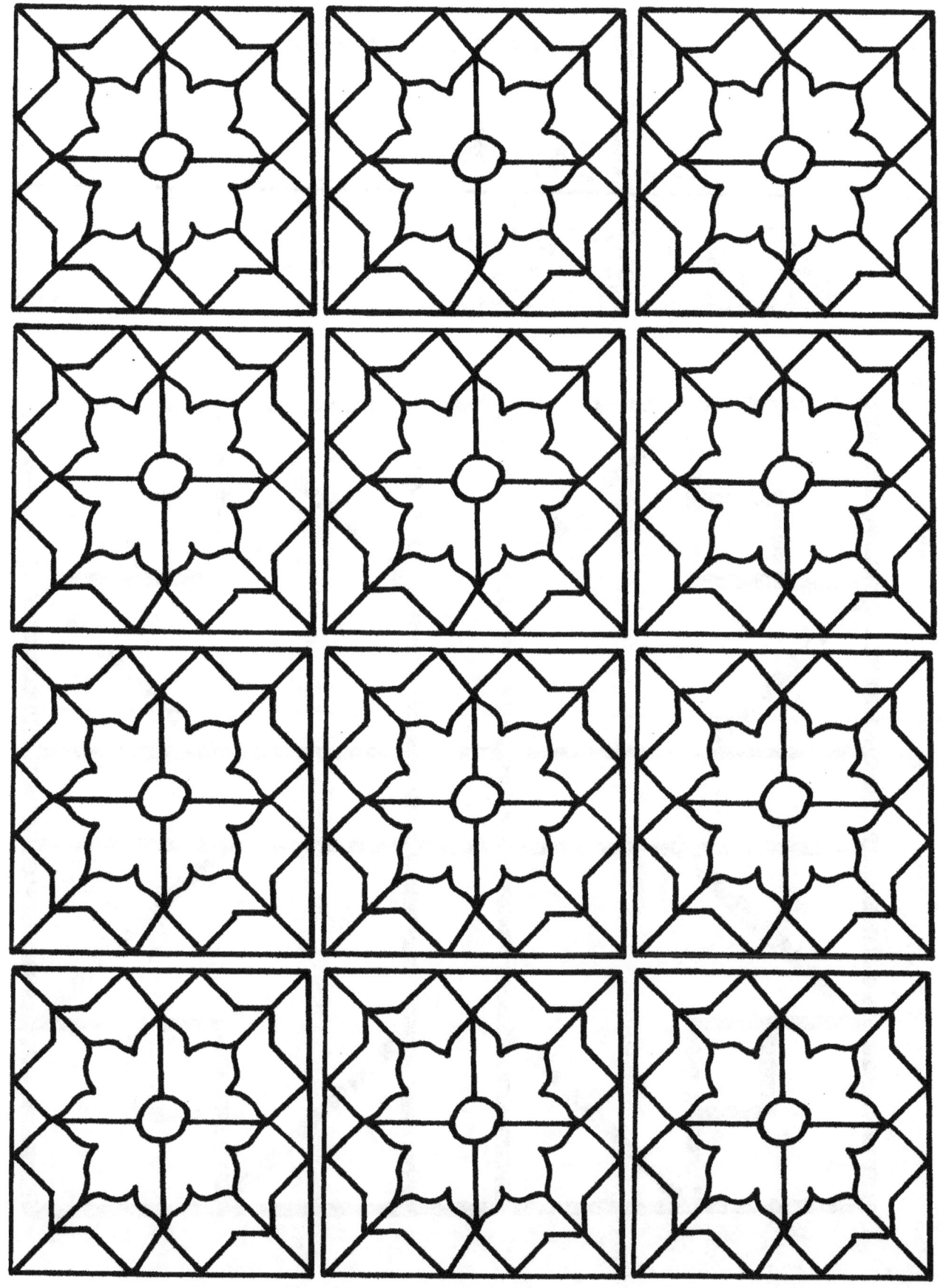

Barn Quilt Four Tulips
Delaware County Iowa

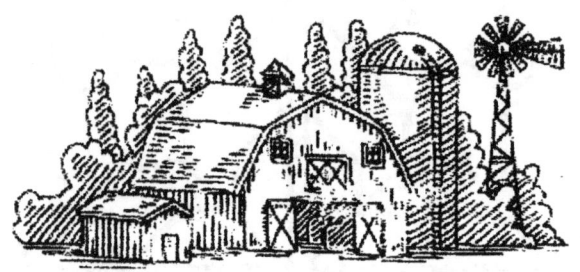

Barn Quilt Location
310 St
Ryan, Iowa

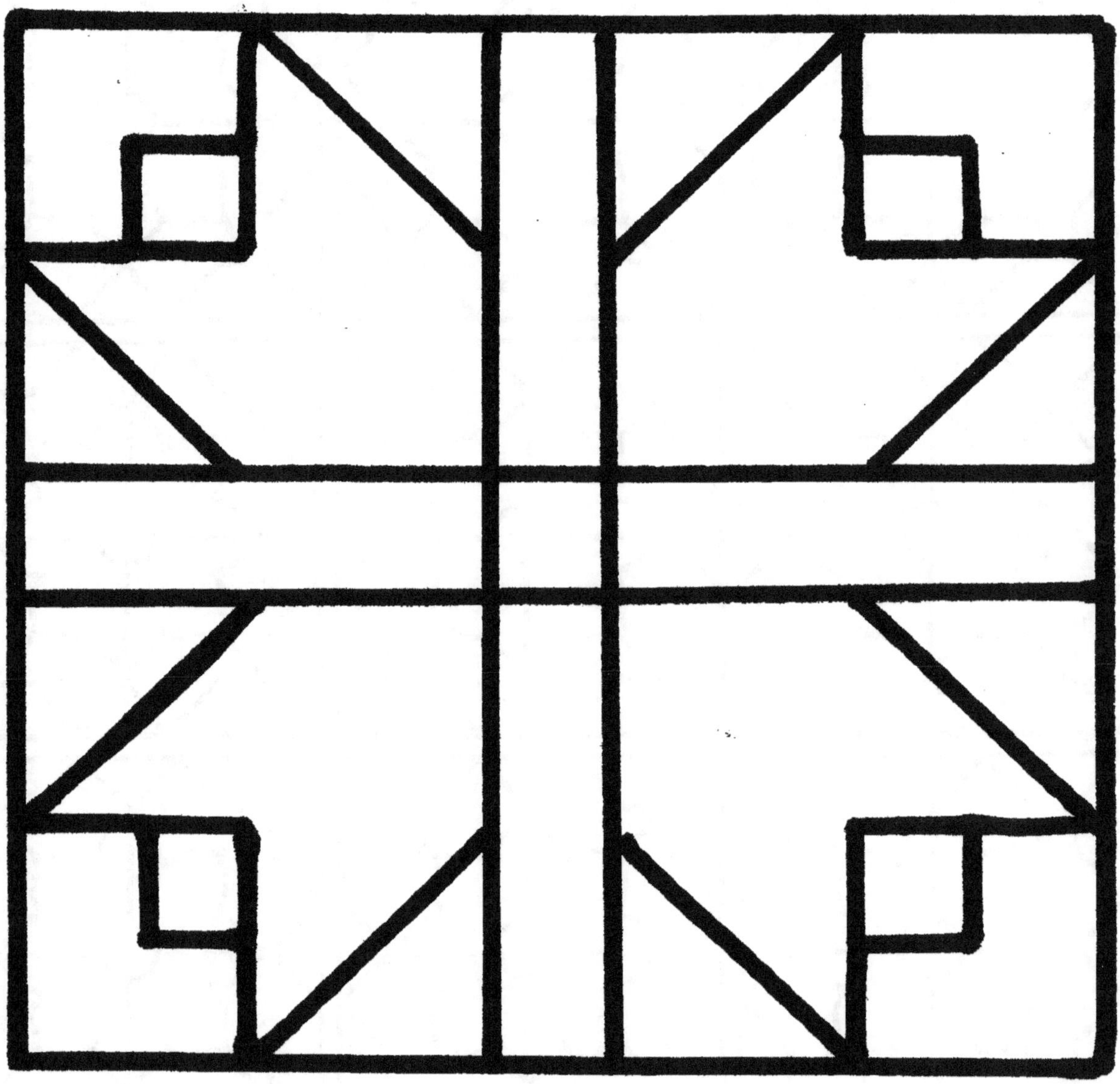

Barn Quilt Four Tulips

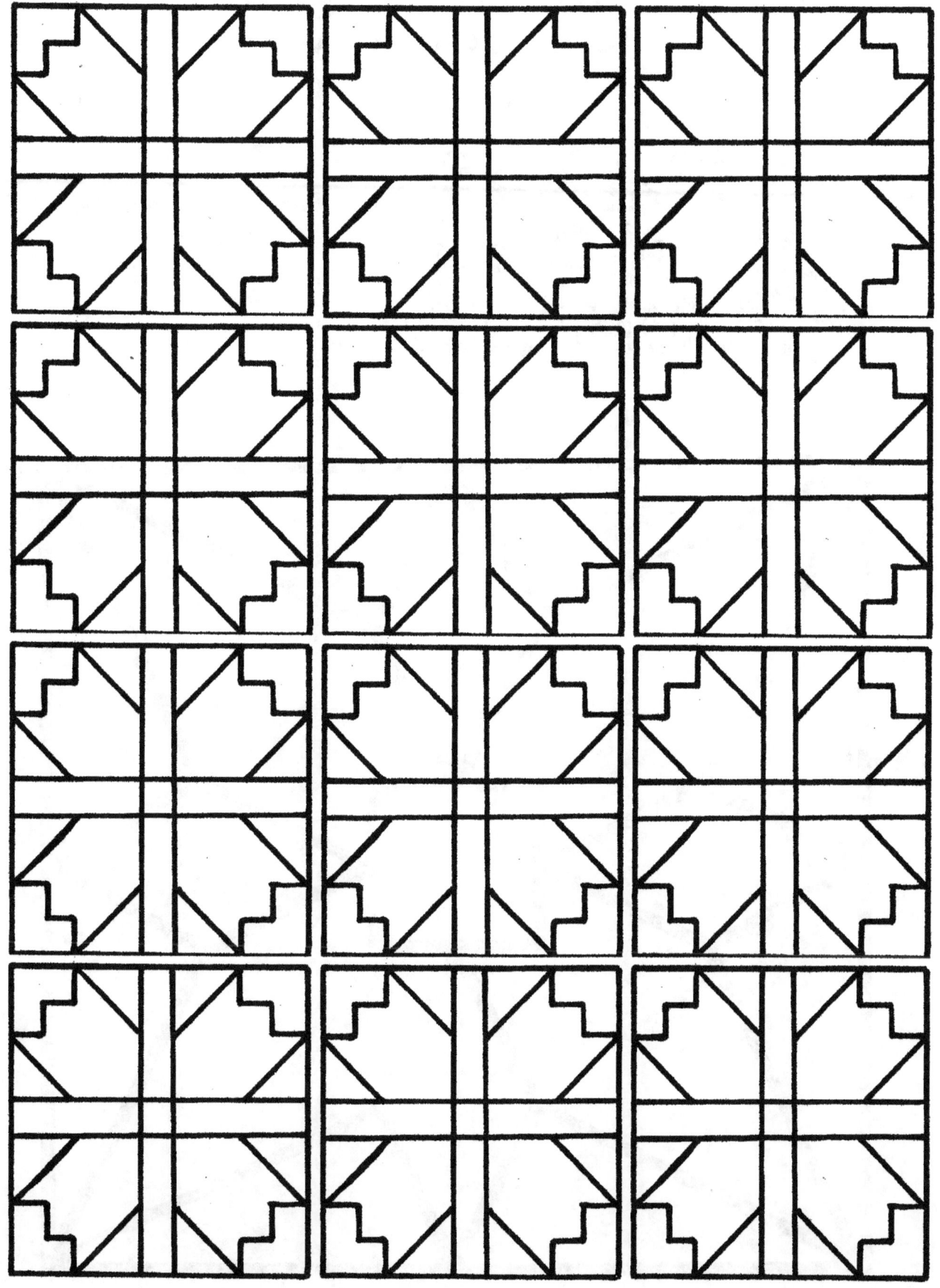

Barn Quilt Lasting Bloom
Delaware County Iowa

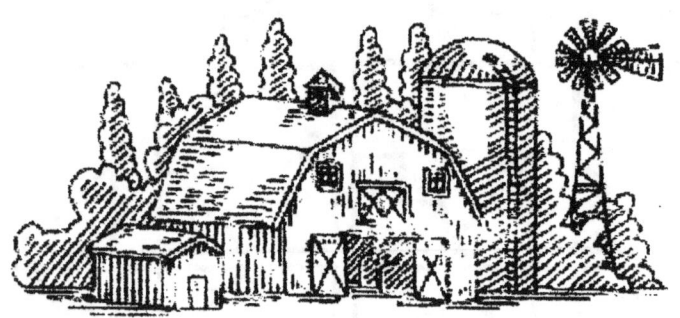

Barn Quilt Location
210th Ave
Manchester, Iowa

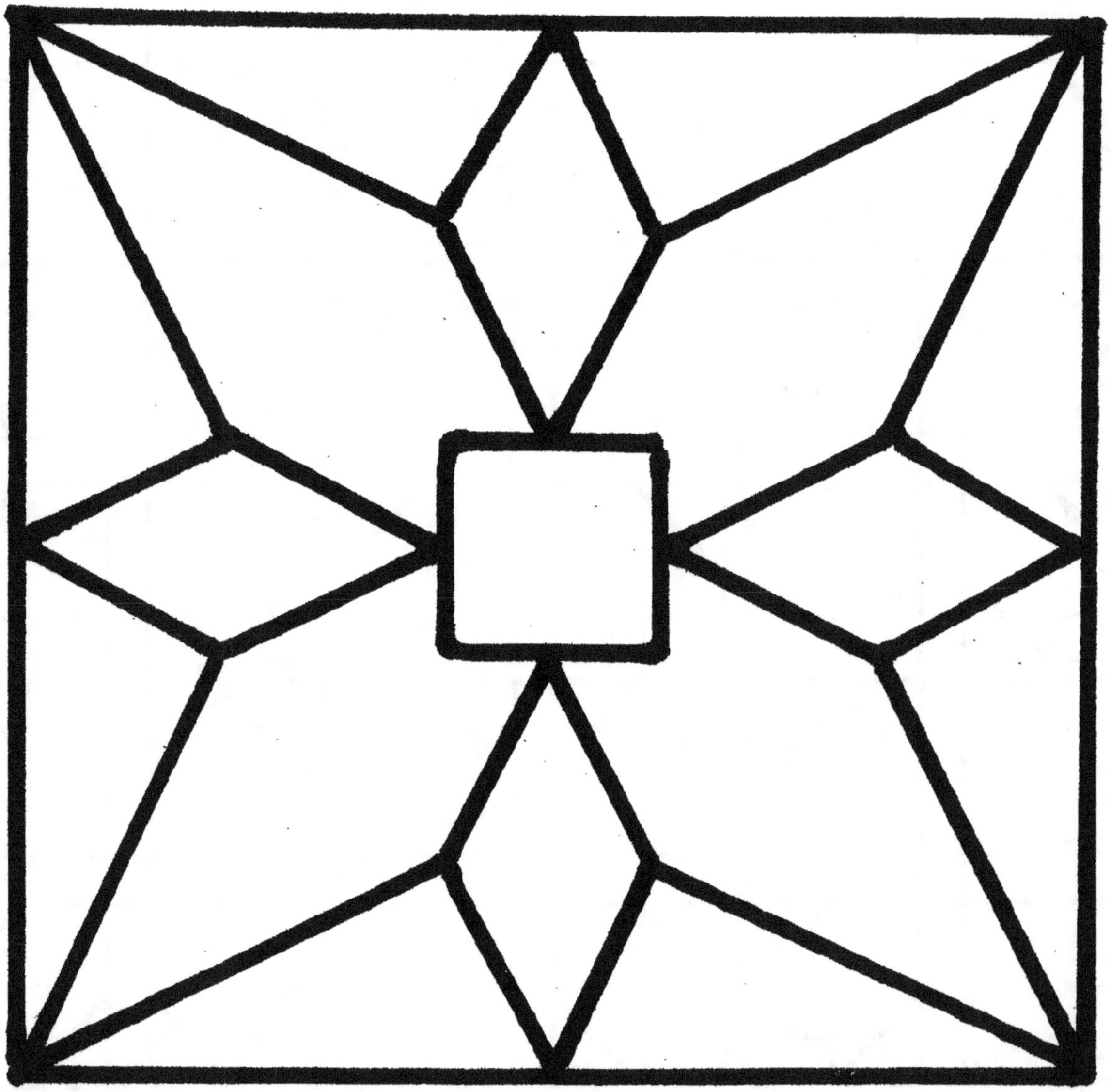

Barn Quilt Lasting Bloom

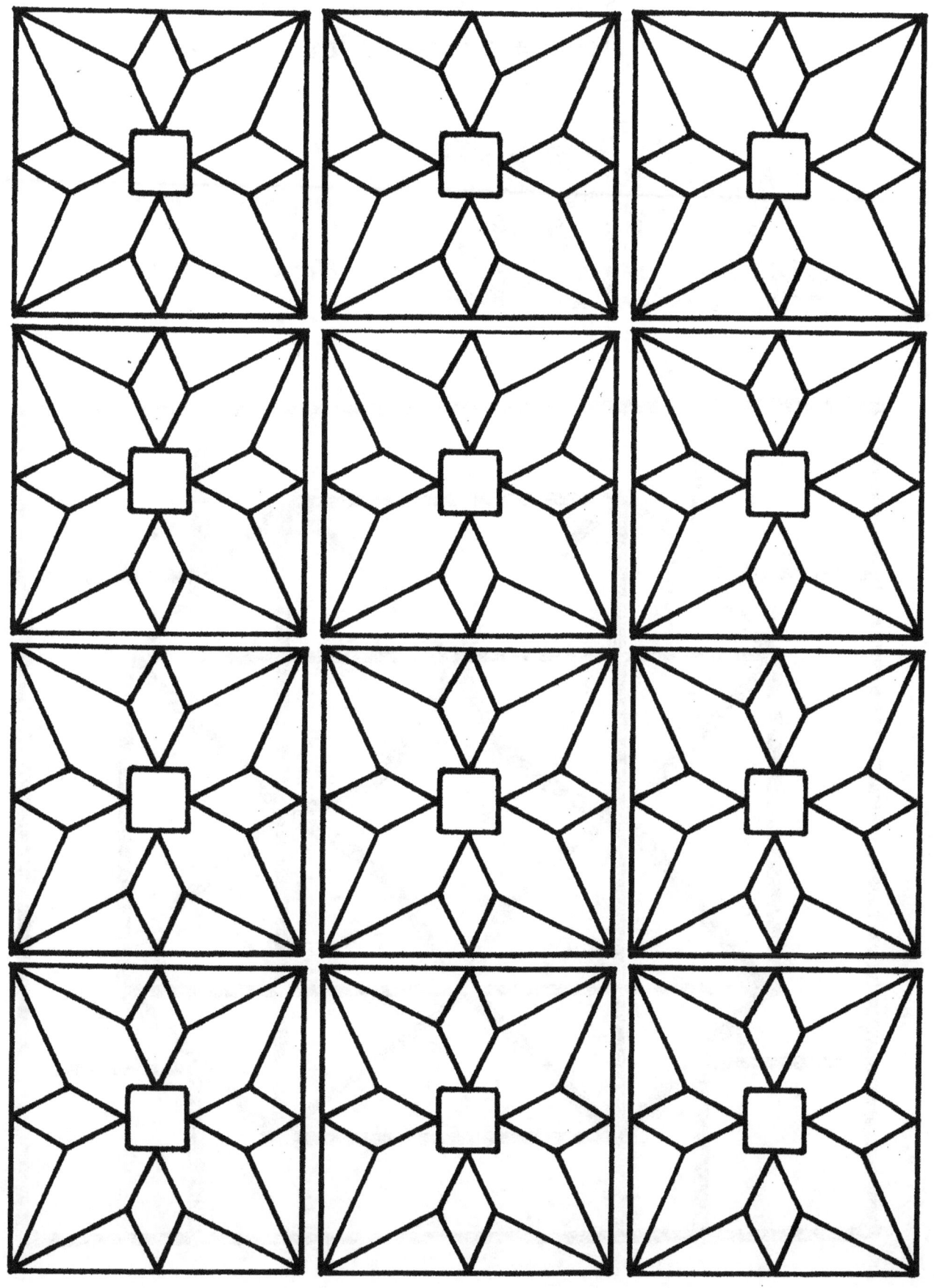

Barn Quilt Star of Lahoma
Delaware County Iowa

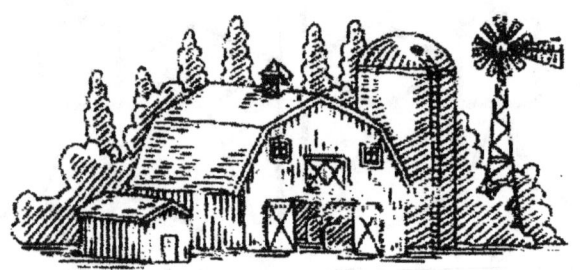

Barn Quilt Location
315th St
Hopkinton, Iowa

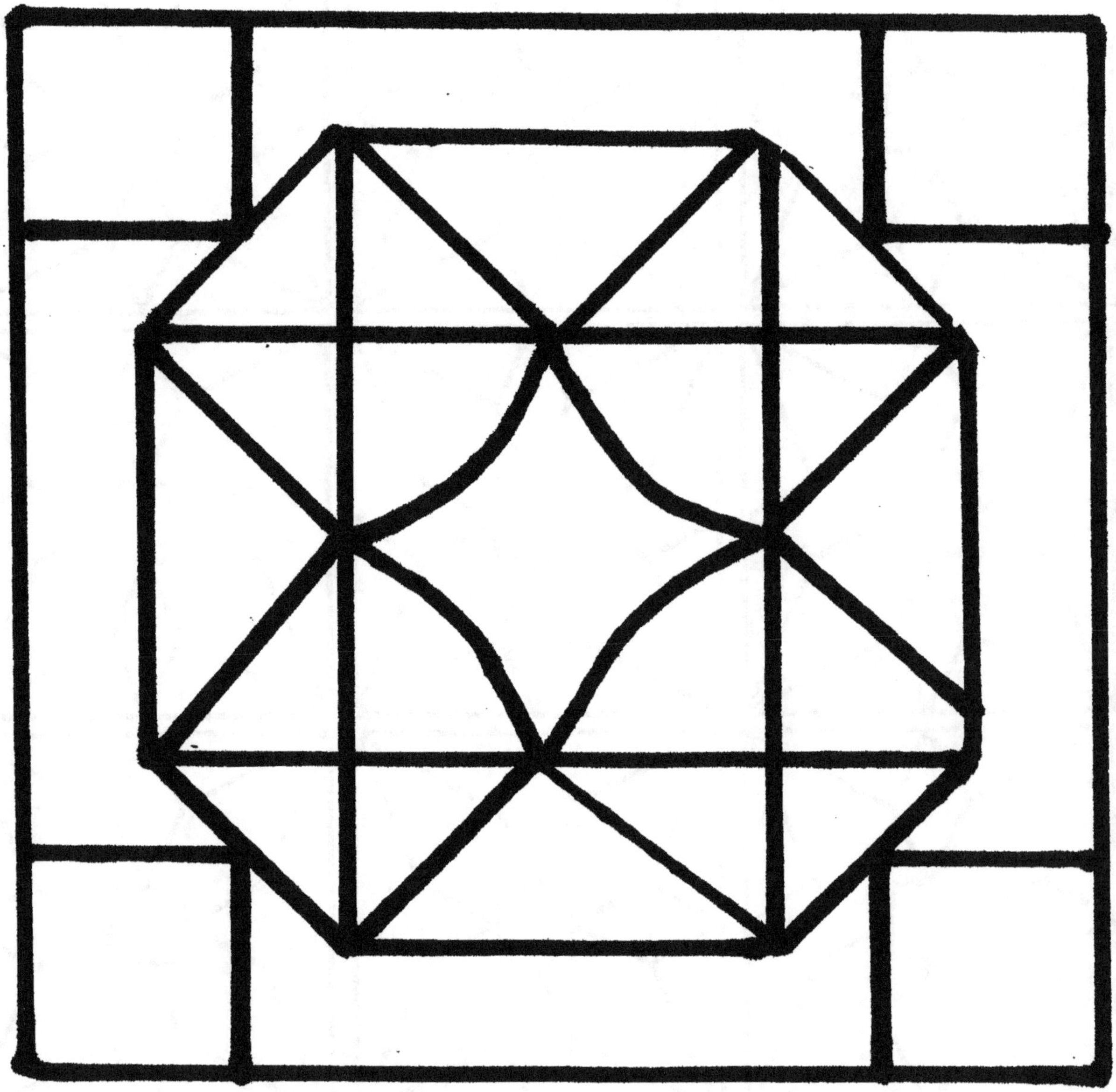

Barn Quilt Star of Lahoma

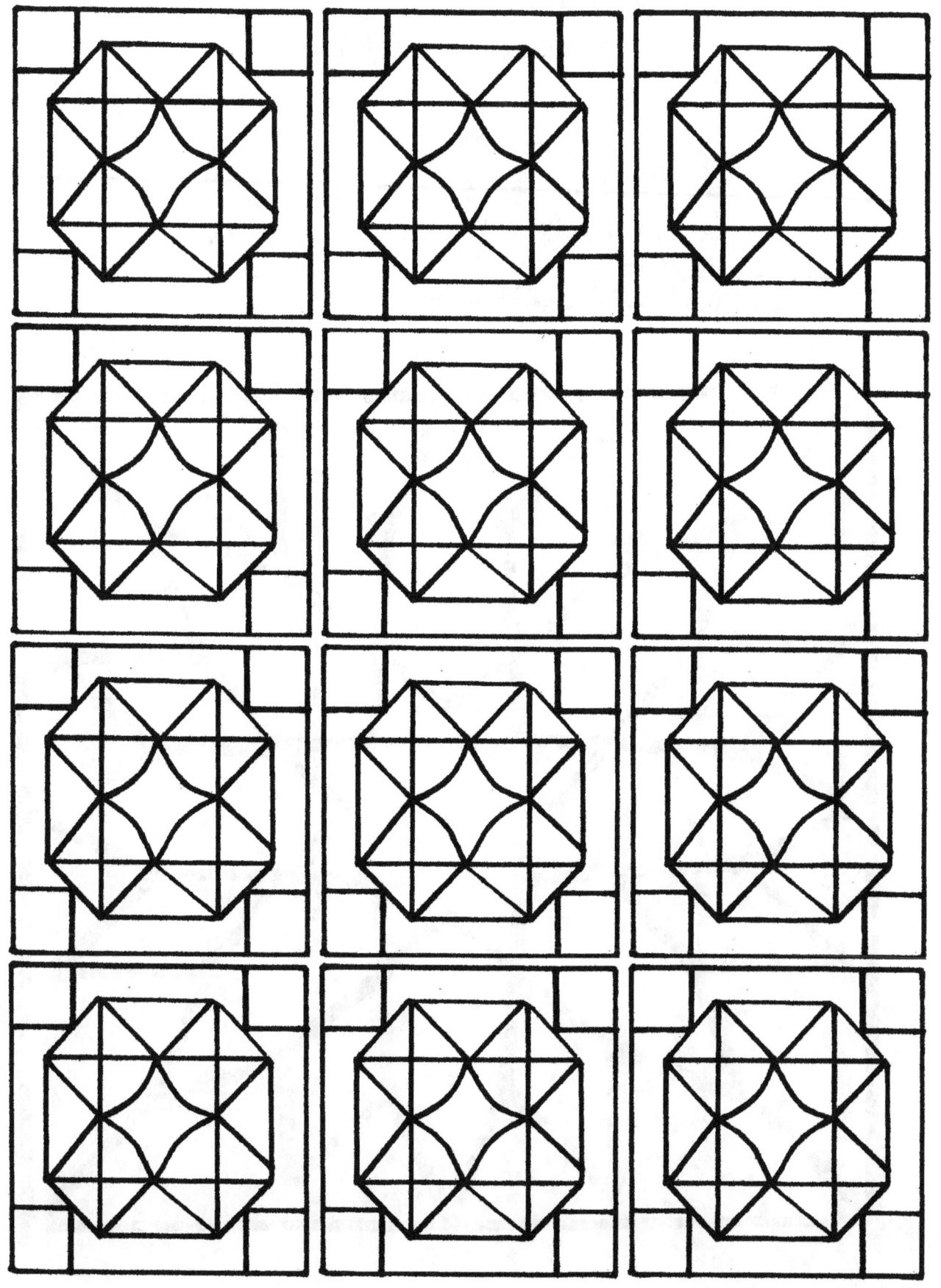

Barn Quilt Starry Compass
Delaware County Iowa

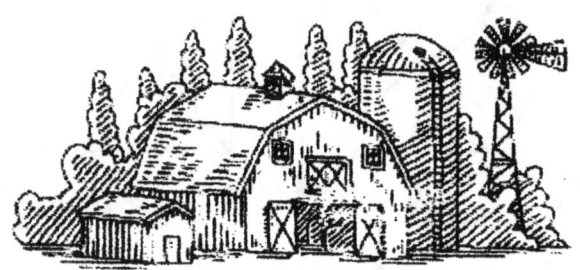

Barn Quilt Location
110th Ave
Dundee, Iowa

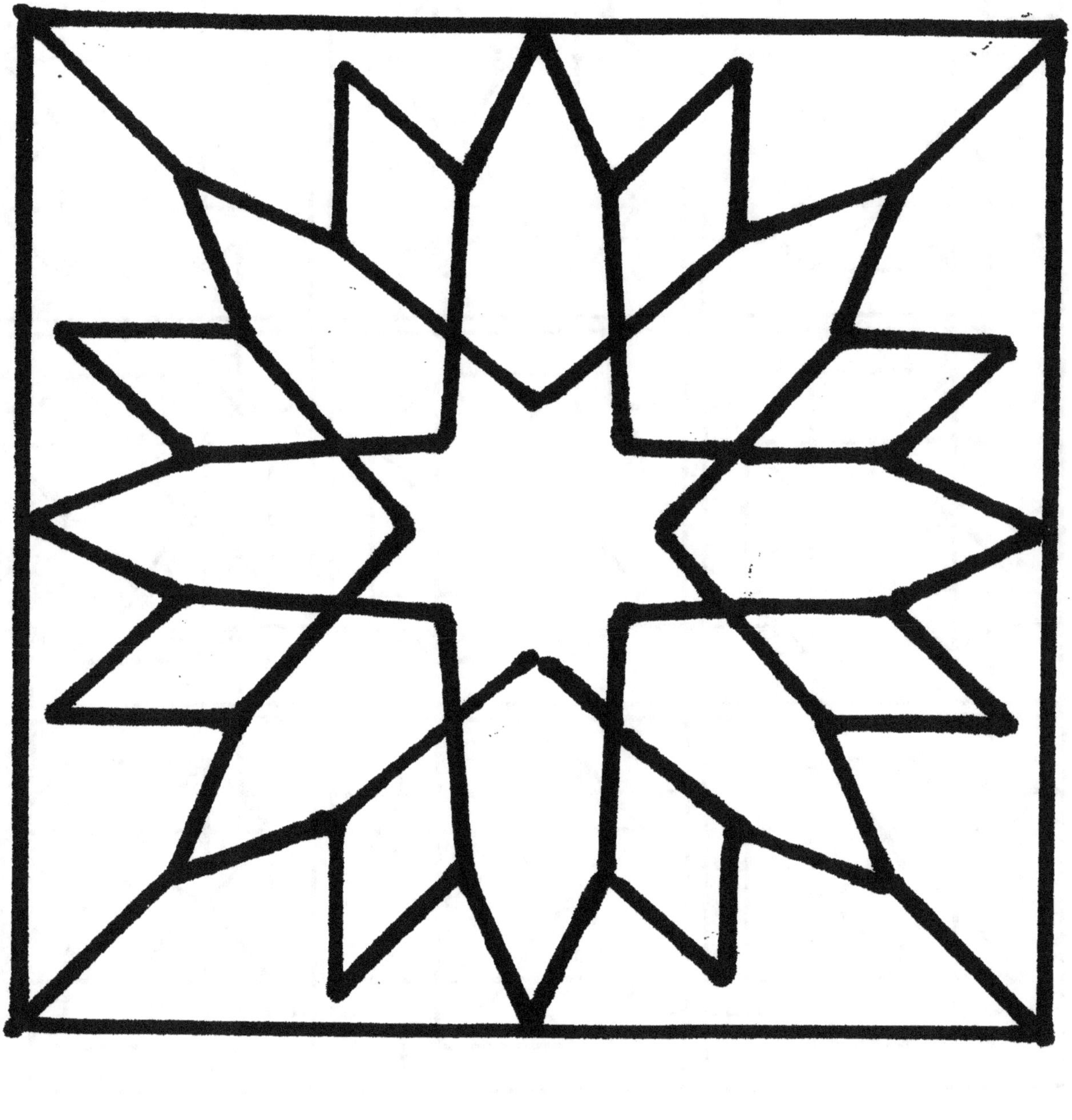

Barn Quilt Starry Compass

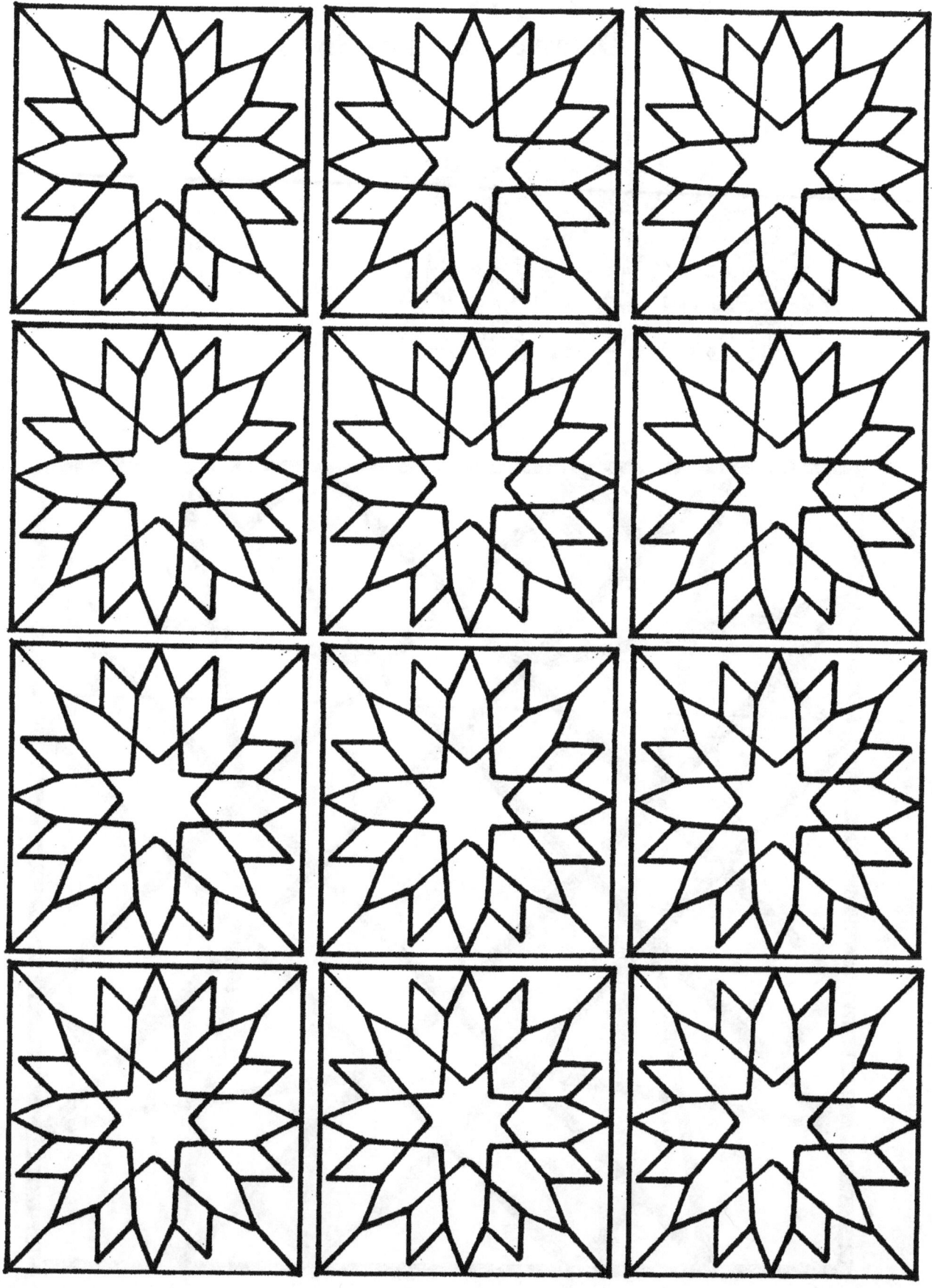

Barn Quilt Bright Side
Delaware County Iowa

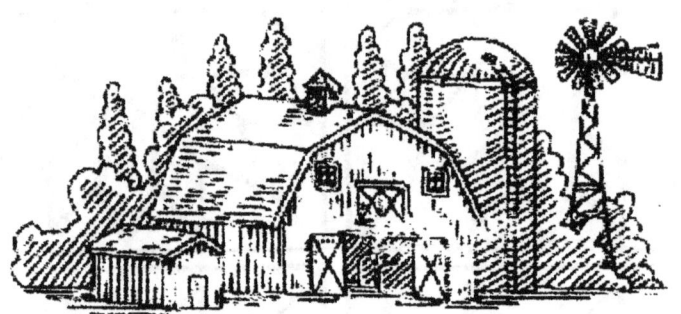

Barn Quilt Location
Thunder Rd
Hopkinton, Iowa

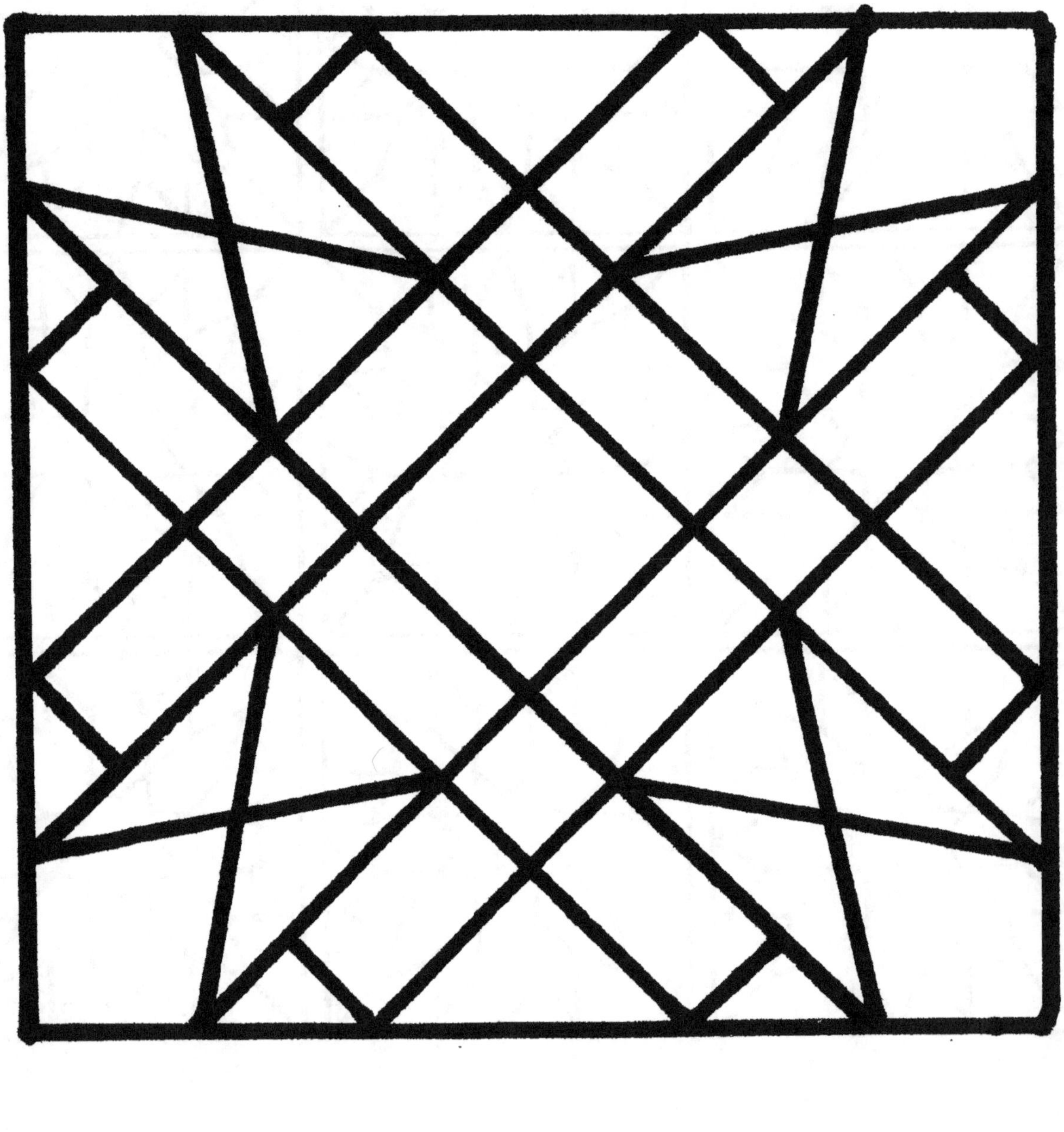

Barn Quilt Bright Side

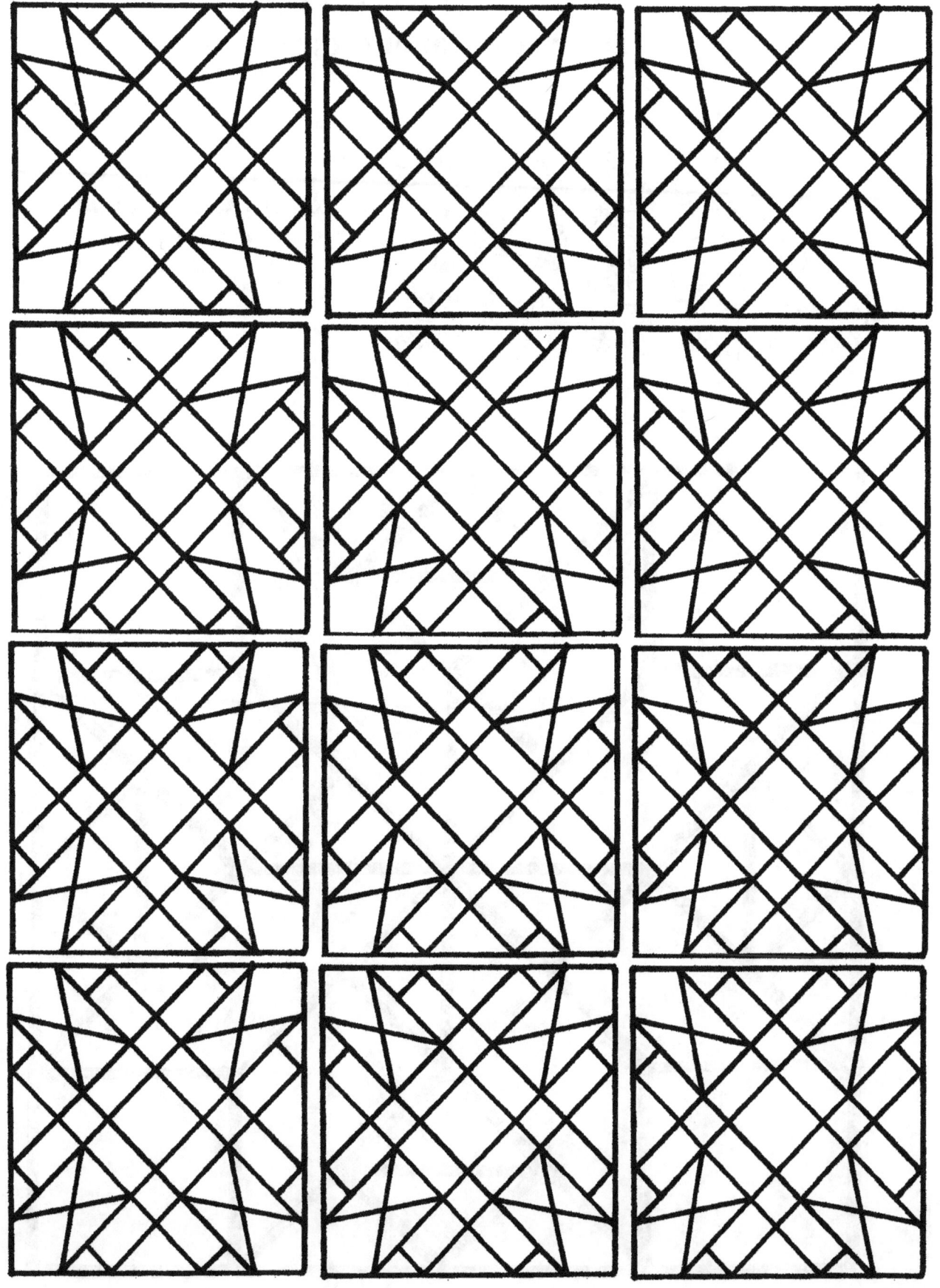

Barn Quilt Turning Star
Delaware County Iowa

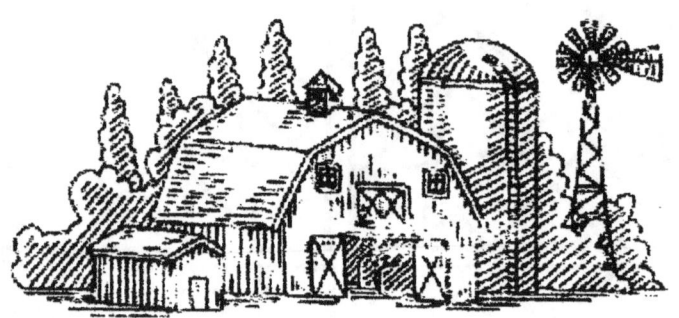

Barn Quilt Location
330th Ave
Coggon, Iowa

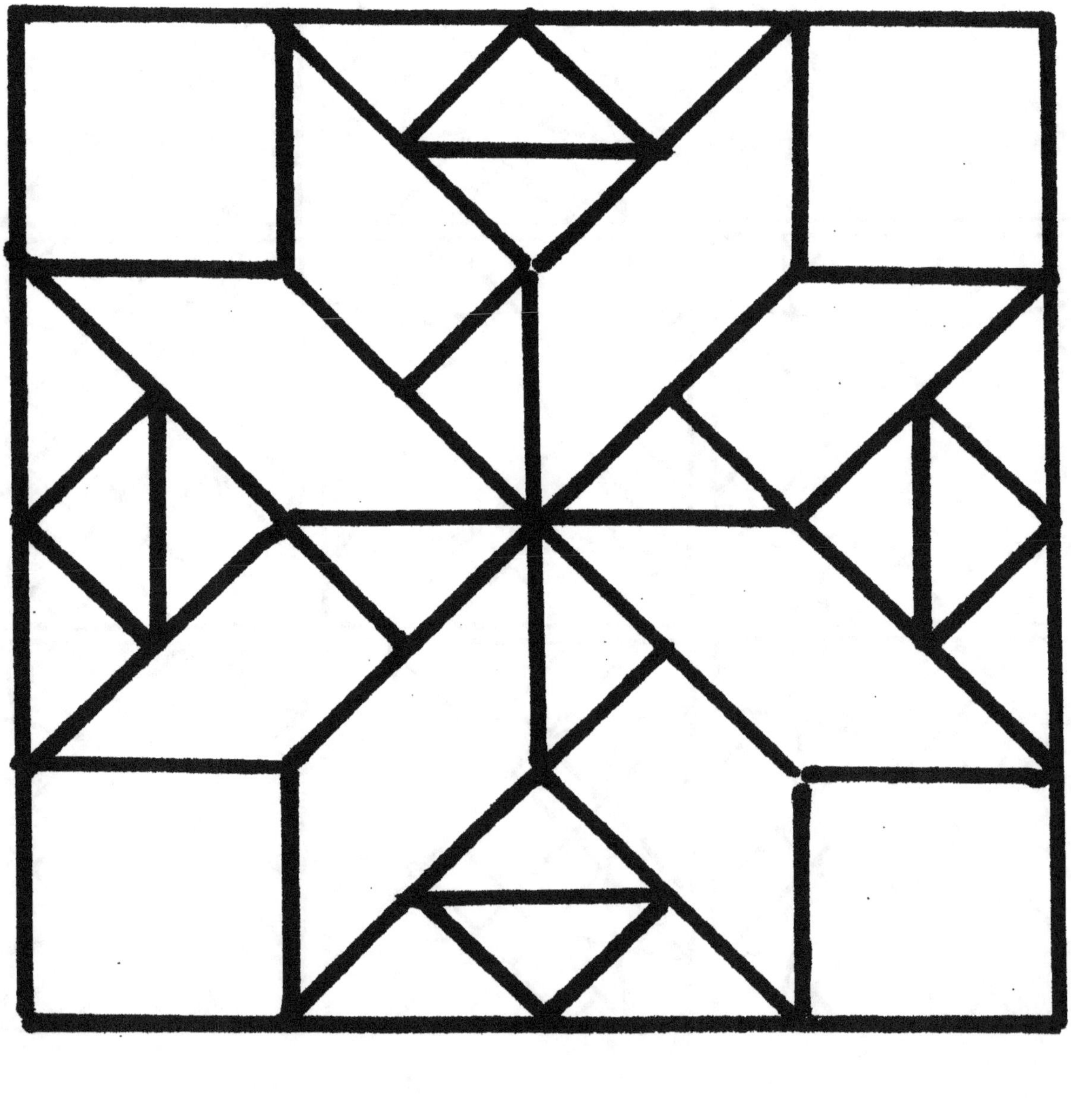

Barn Quilt Turning Star

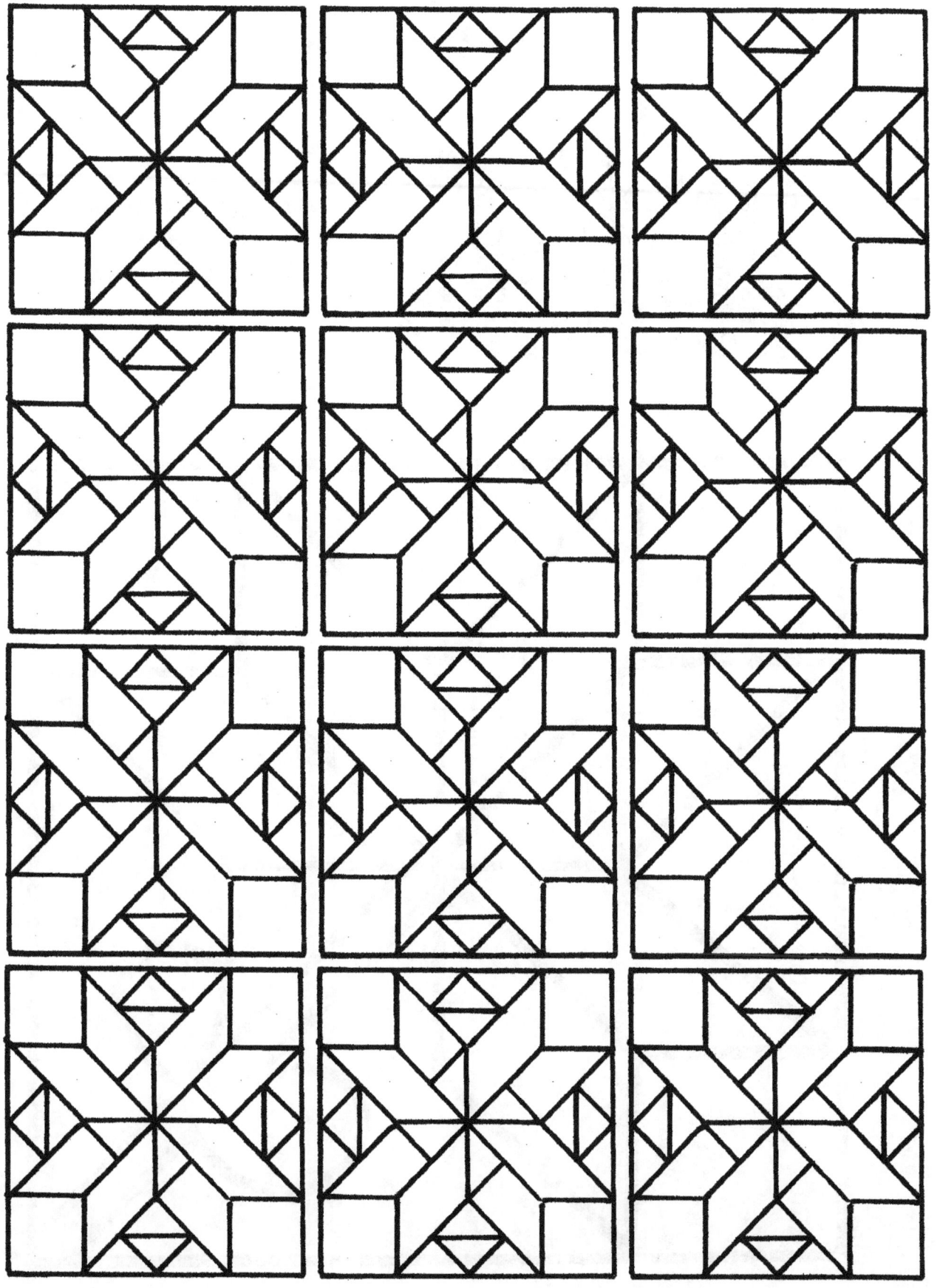

Barn Quilt Single Lily
Delaware County Iowa

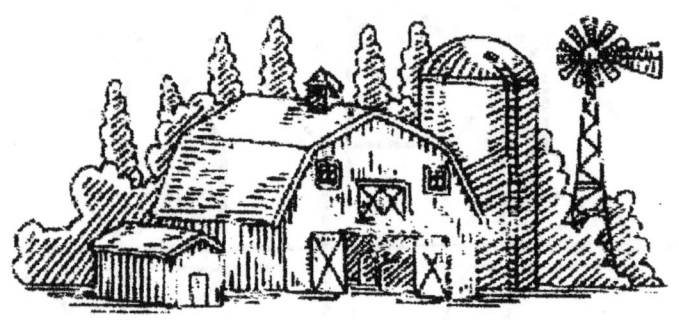

Barn Quilt Location
110th Ave
Masonville, Iowa

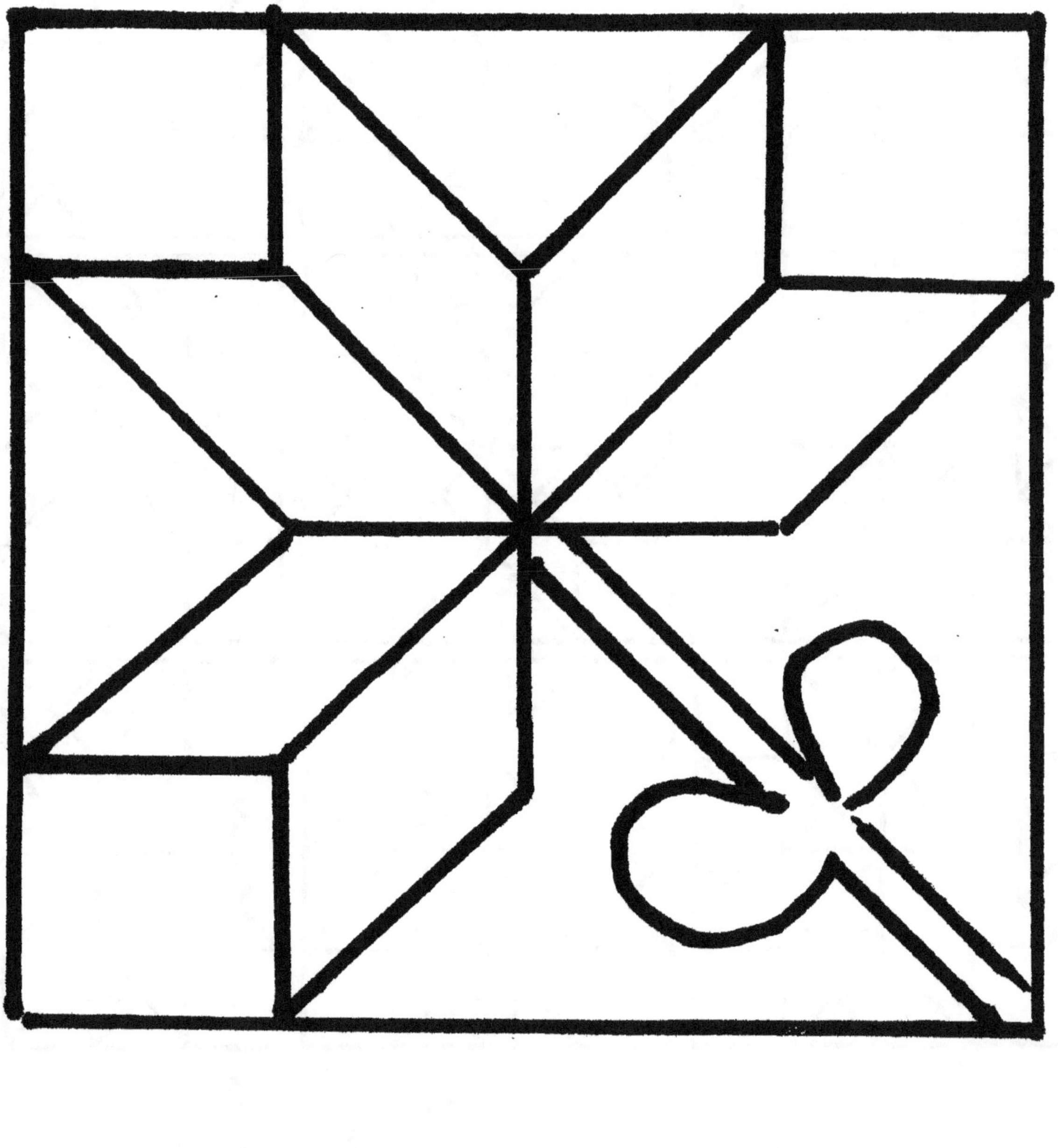

Barn Quilt Single Lily

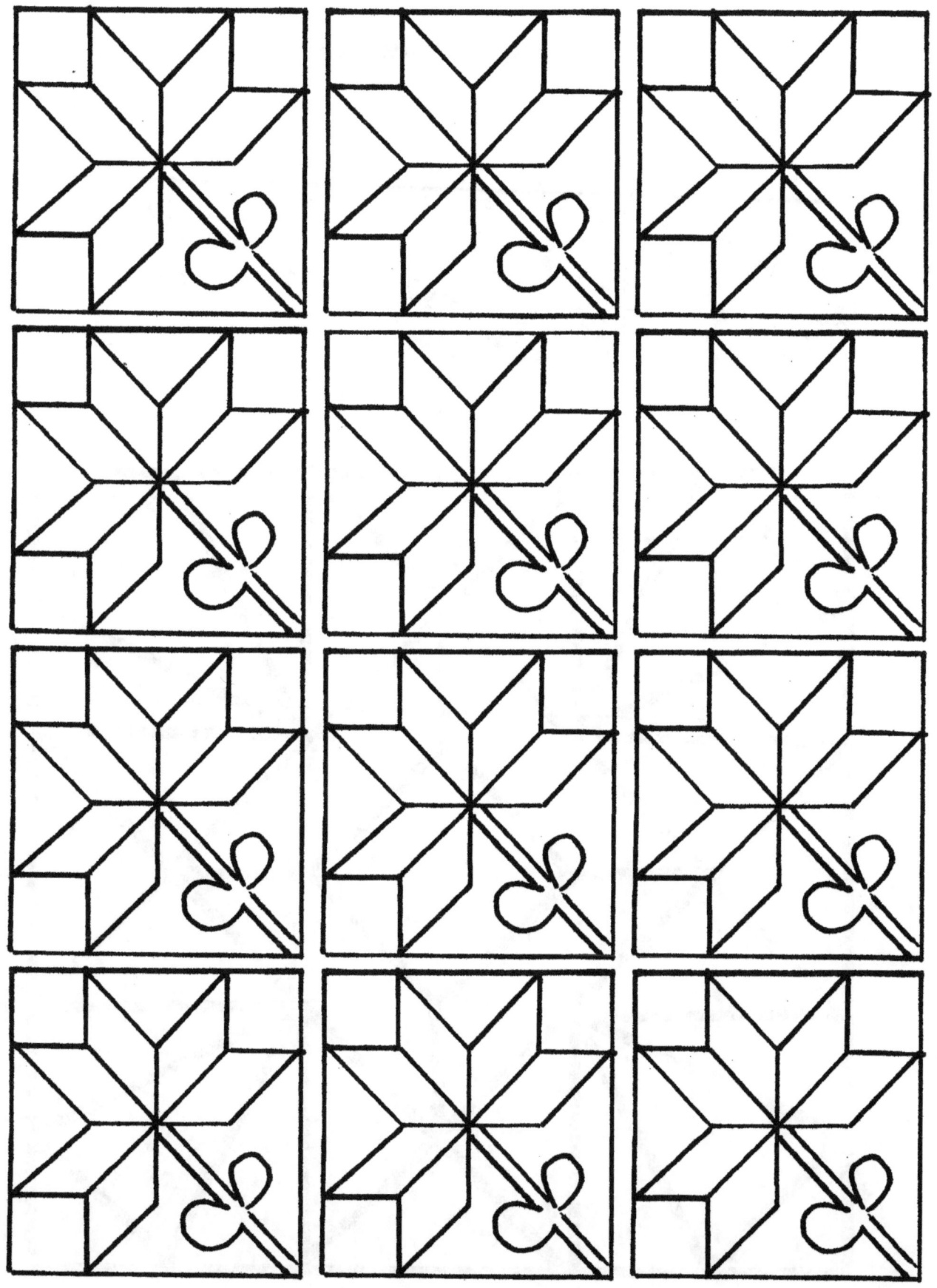

Barn Quilt Homeward Star
Delaware County Iowa

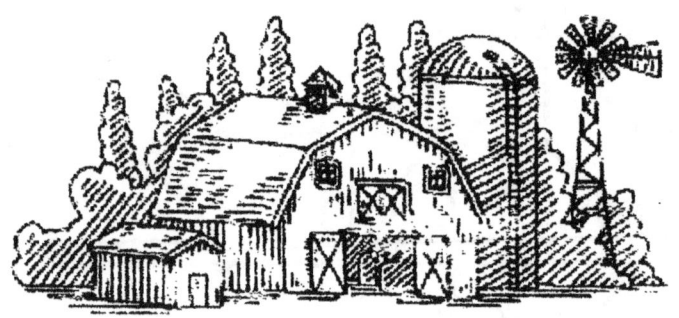

Barn Quilt Location
165th St
Manchester, Iowa

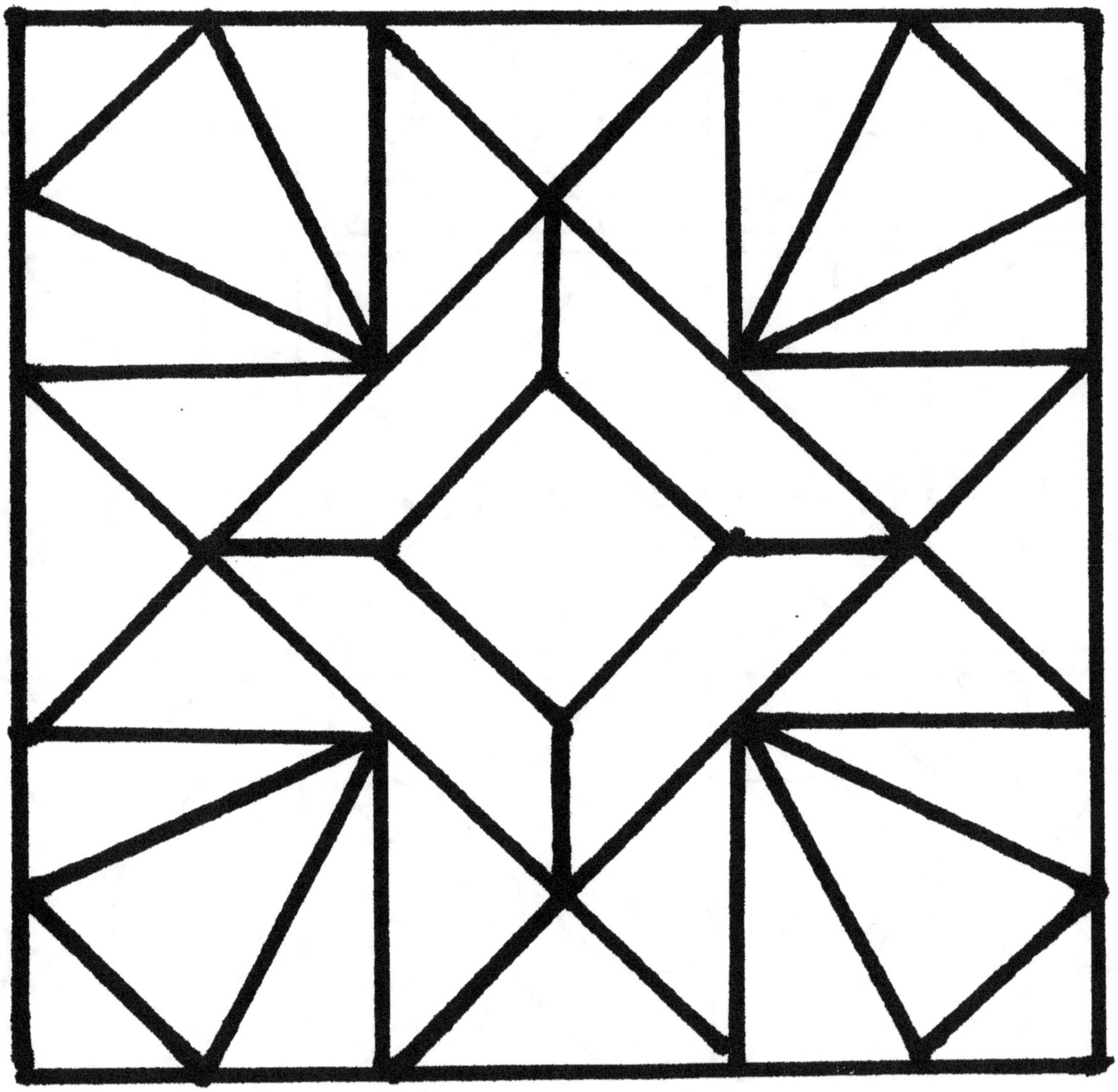

Barn Quilt Homeward Star

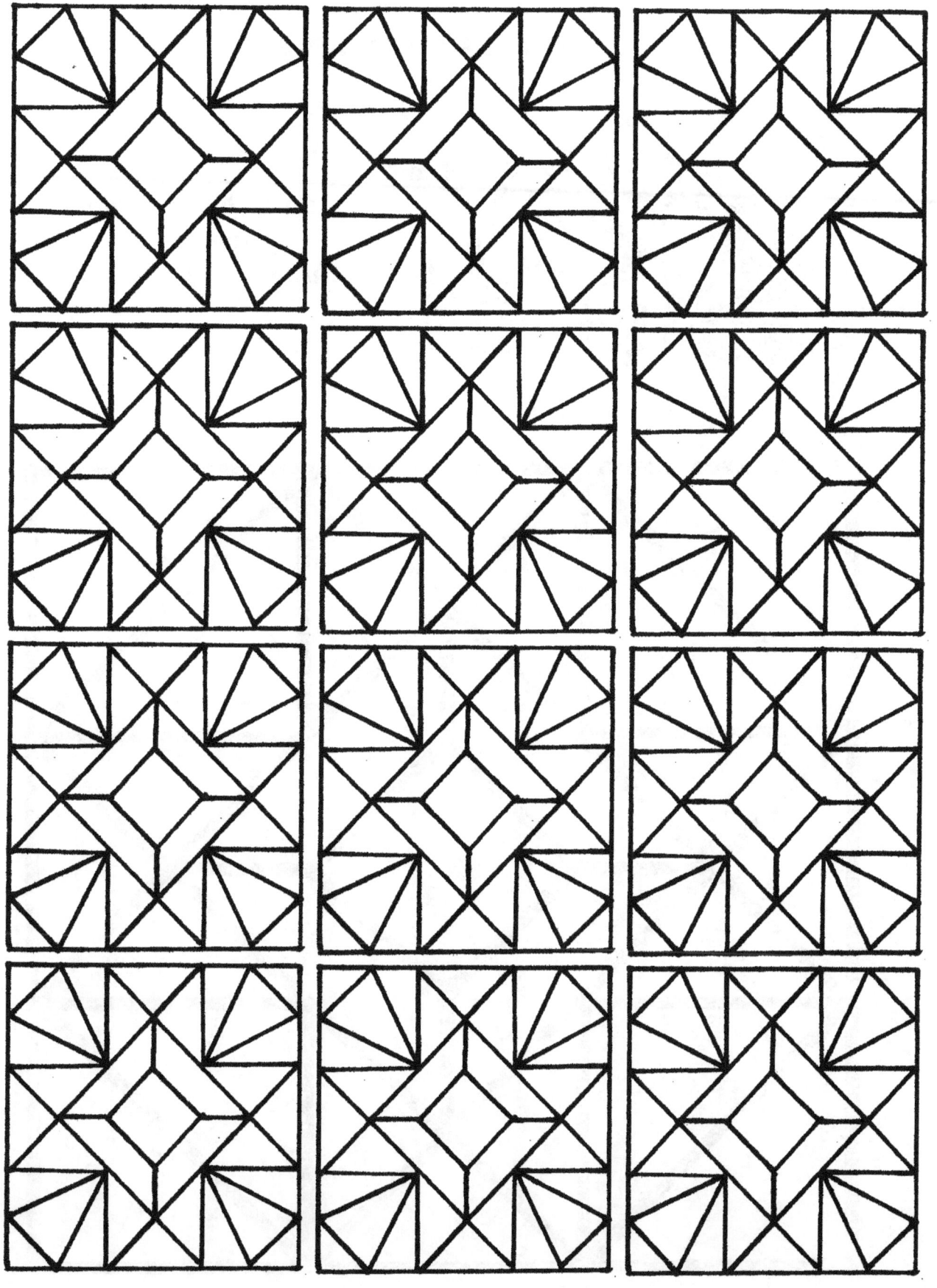

Barn Quilt Card Basket
Delaware County Iowa

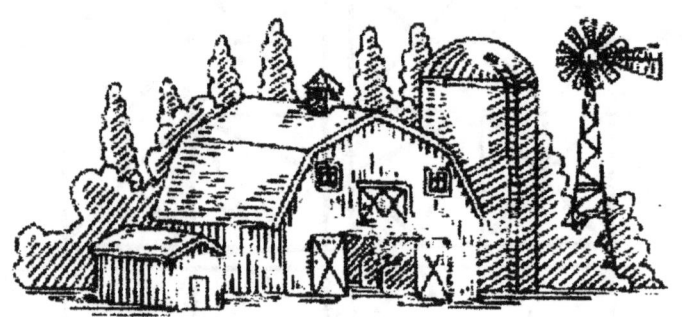

Barn Quilt Location
160th Ave
Strawberry Point, Iowa

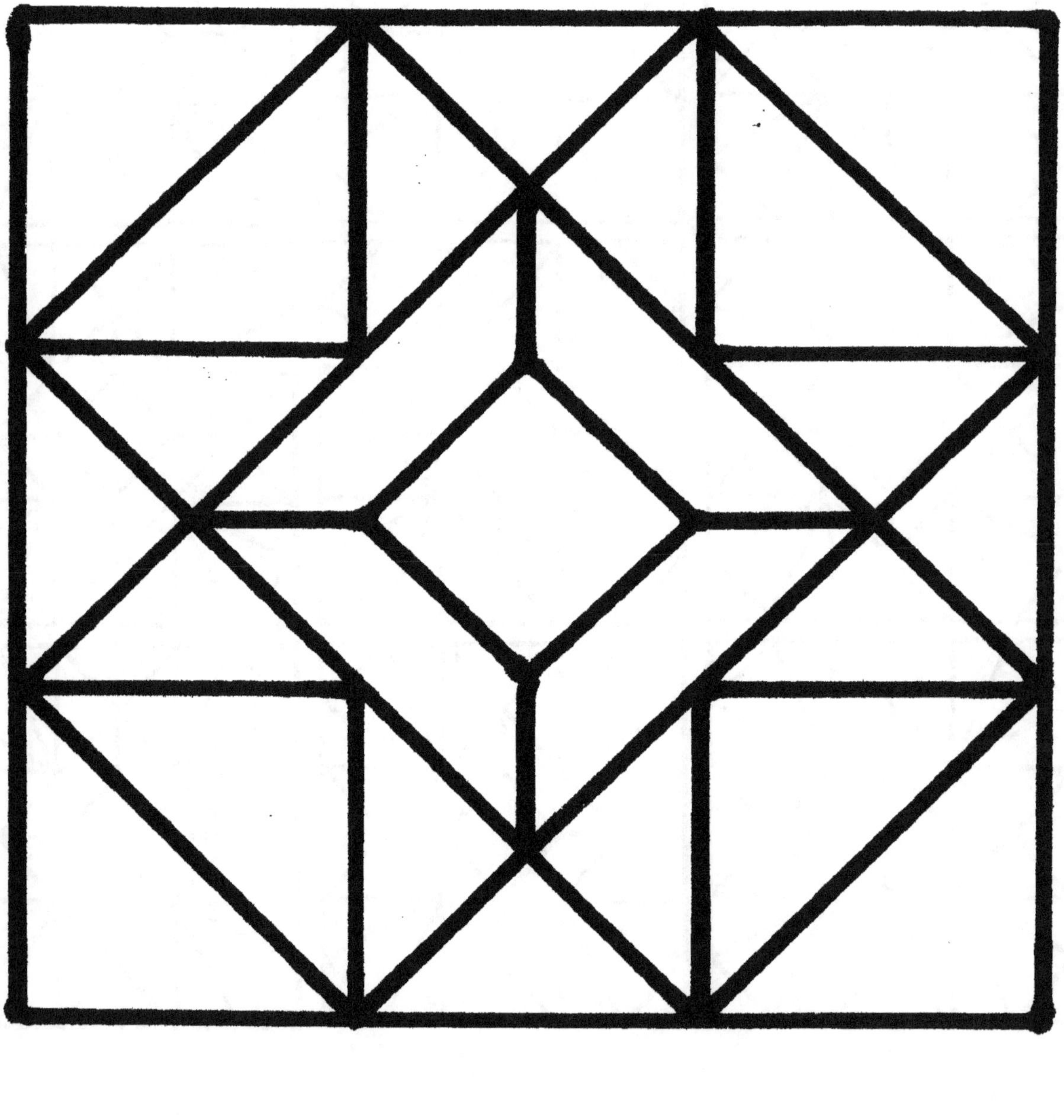

Barn Quilt Card Basket

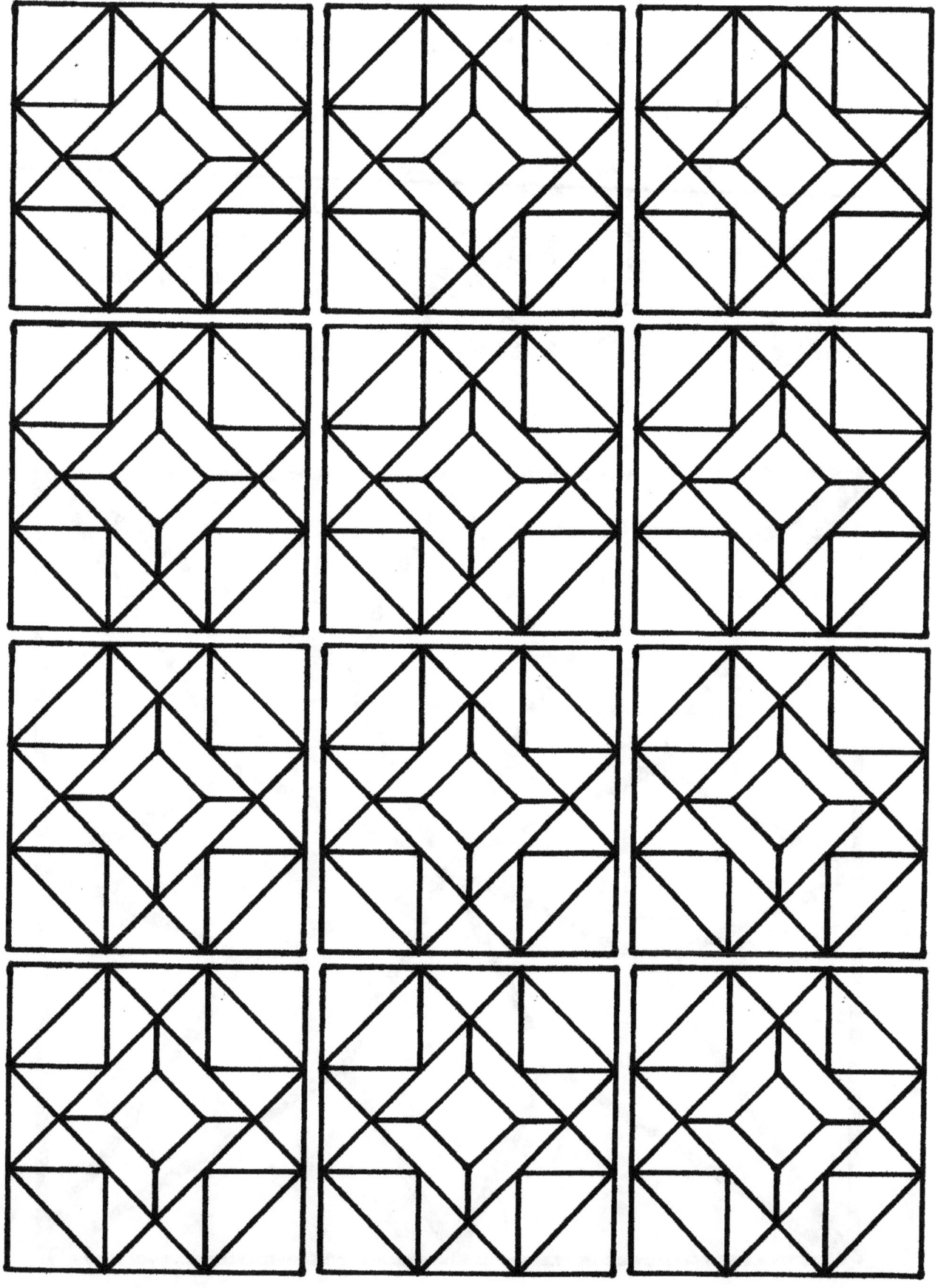

Barn Quilt The Long Pointed Star
Delaware County Iowa

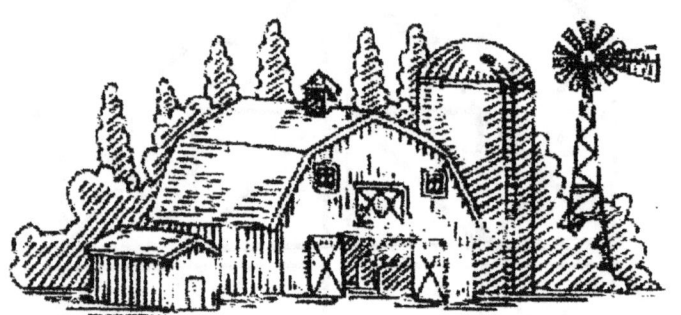

Barn Quilt Location
248th St
Manchester, Iowa

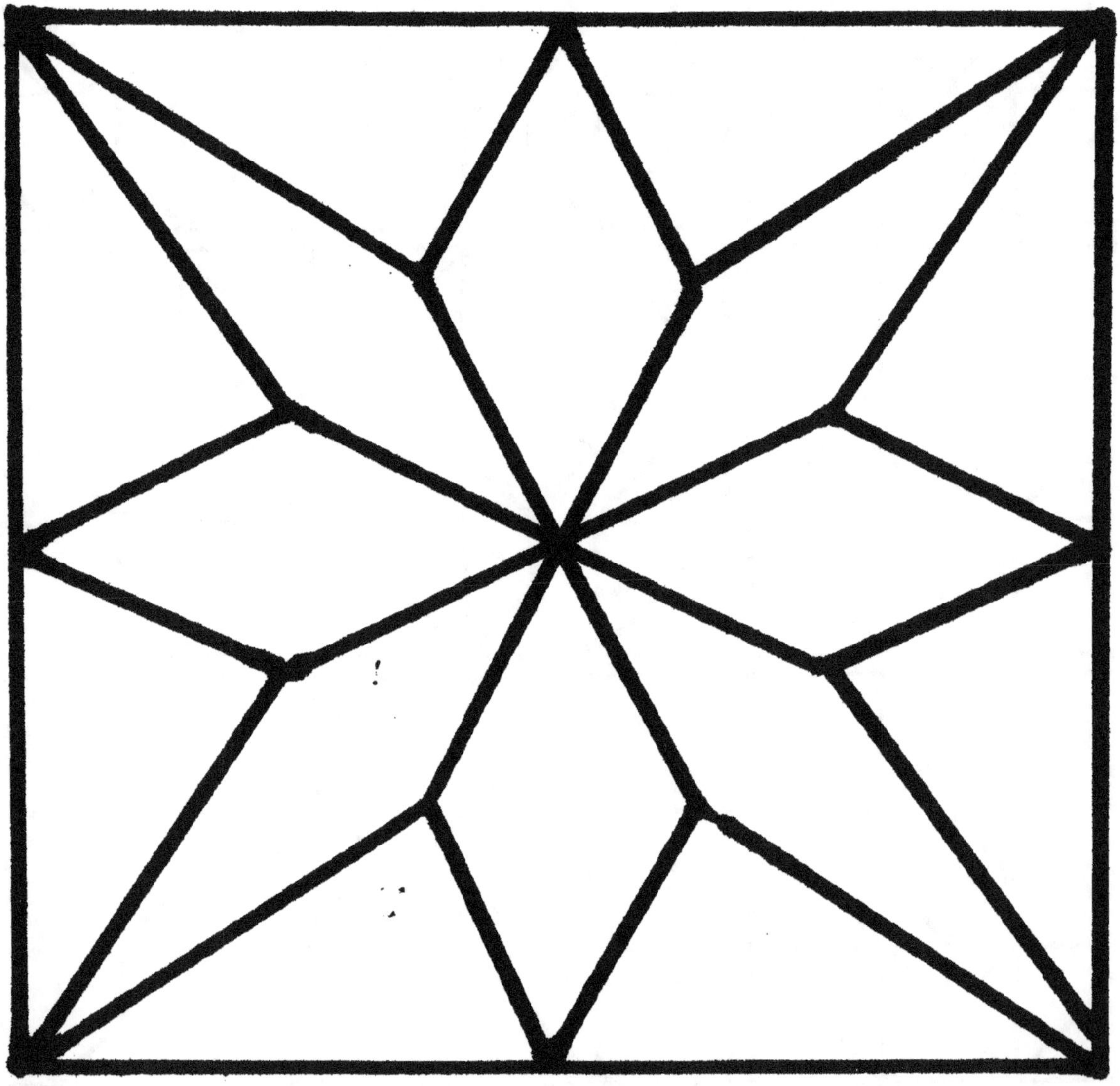

Barn Quilt The Long Pointed Star

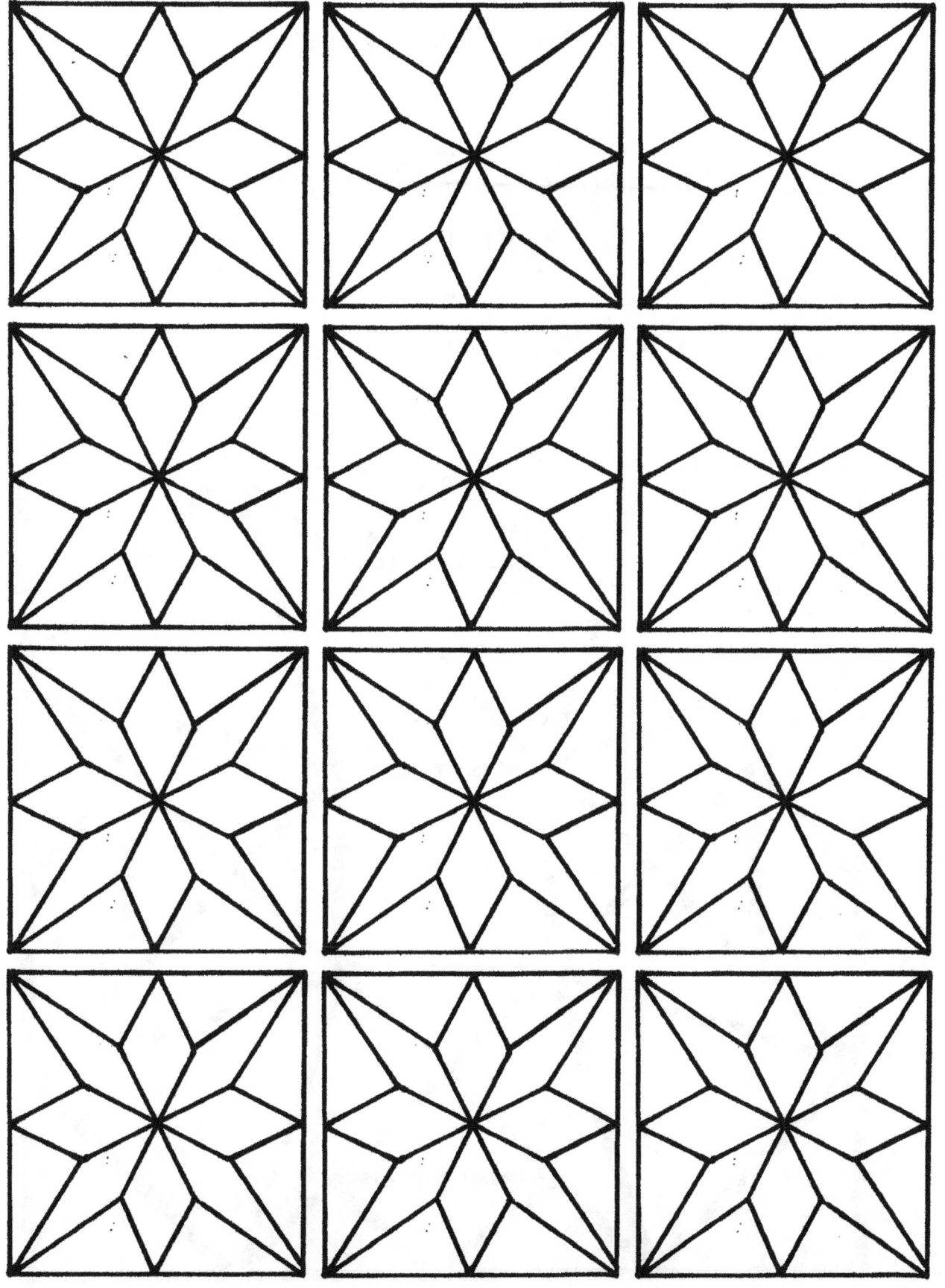

Barn Quilt 1094 Star
Delaware County Iowa

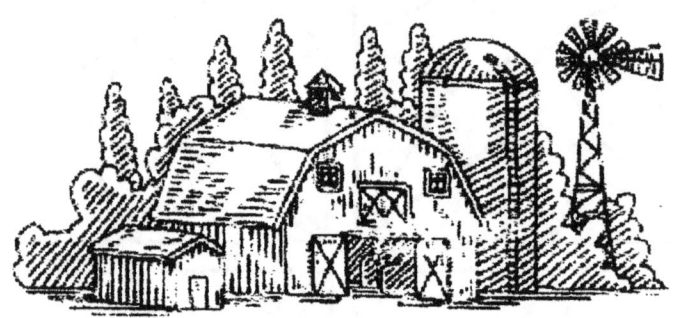

Barn Quilt Location
230ᵗʰ Ave
Hopkinton, Iowa

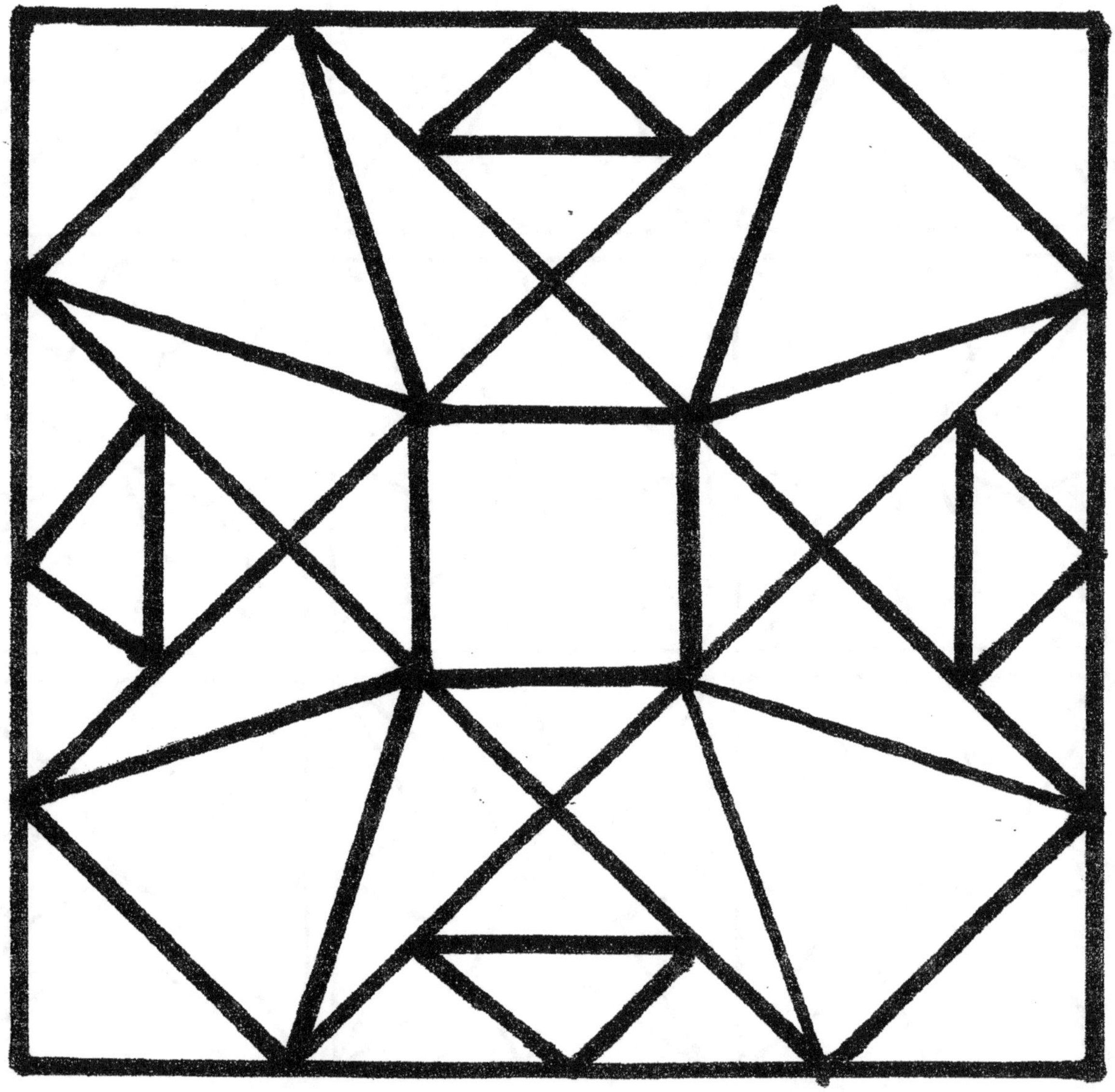

Barn Quilt 1094 Star

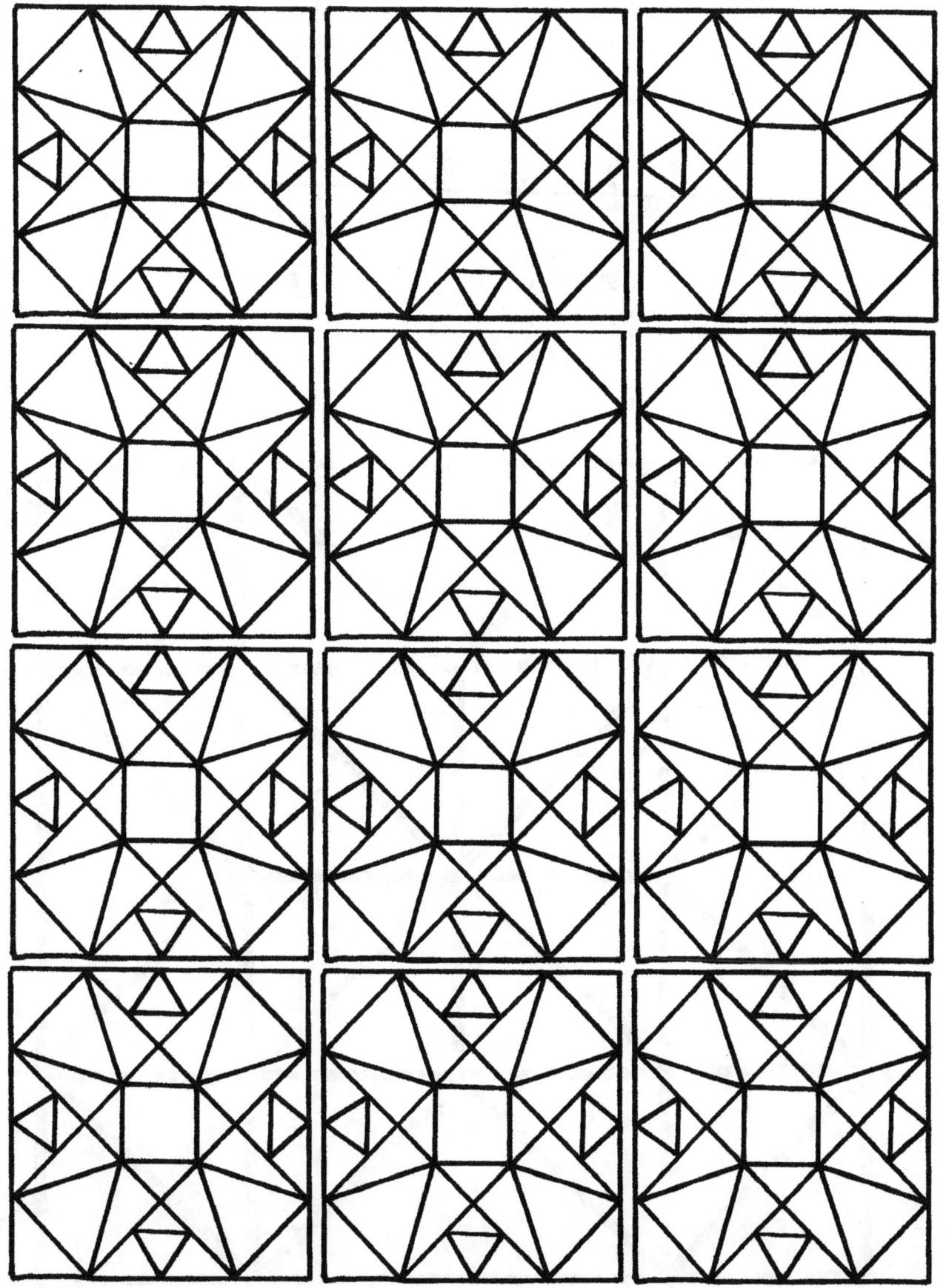

Barn Quilt Old Grey Goose
Delaware County Iowa

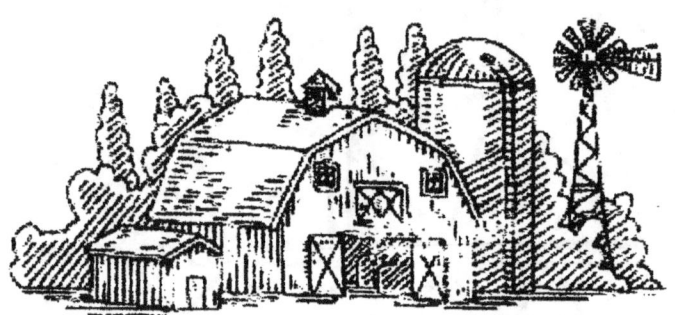

Barn Quilt Location
120th Ave
Dundee, Iowa

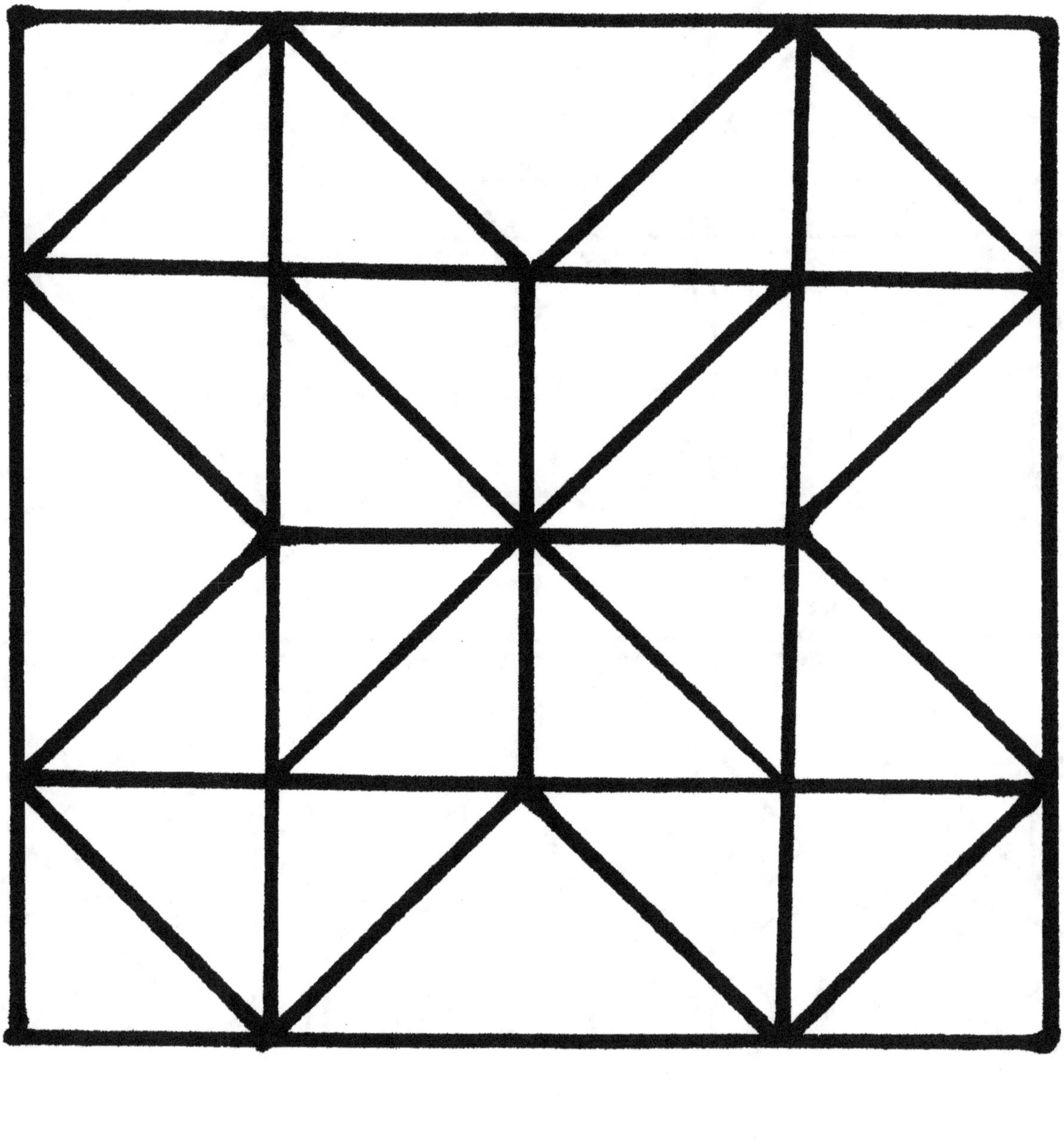

Barn Quilt Old Grey Goose

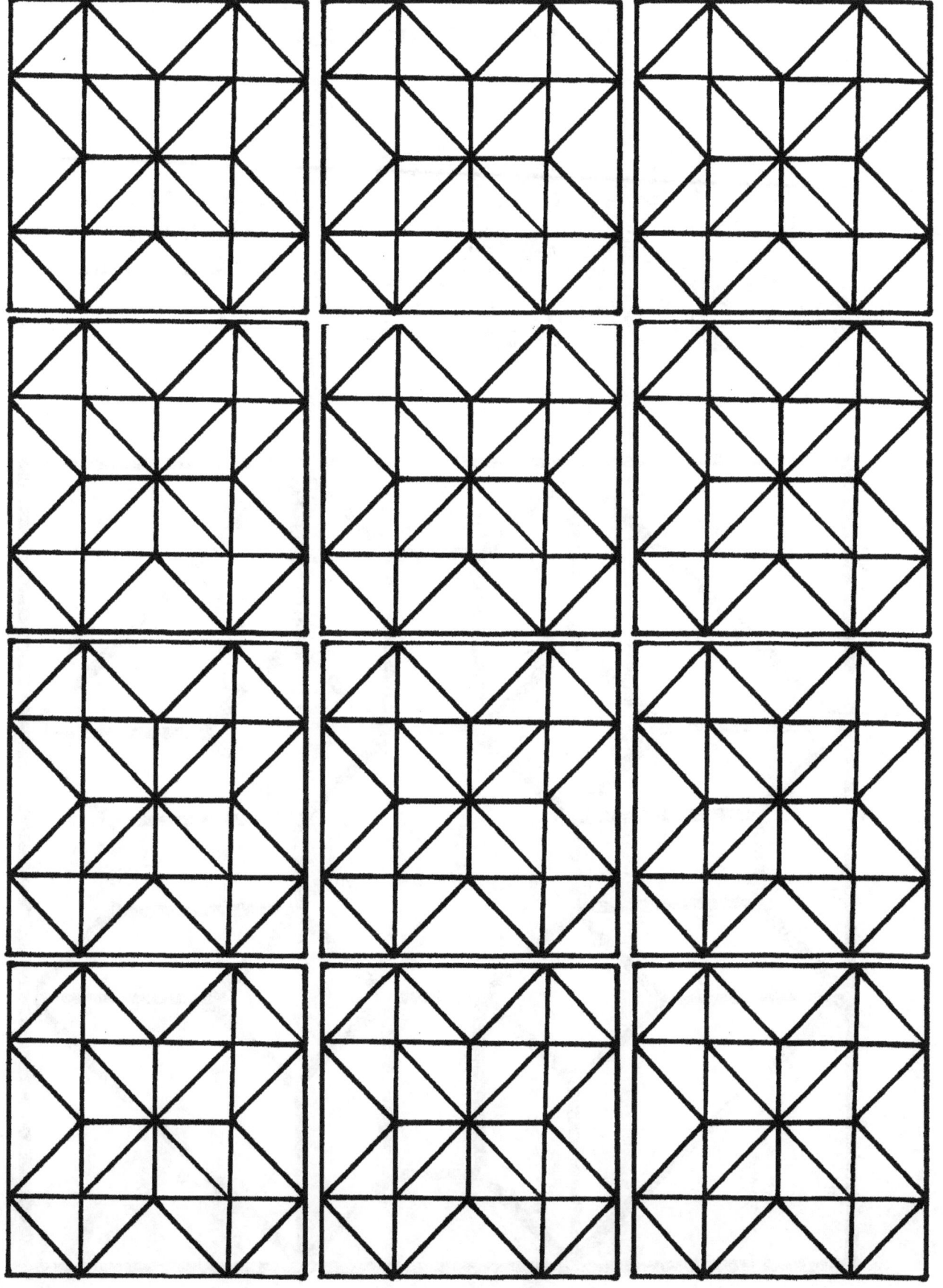

Barn Quilt Prosperity
Delaware County Iowa

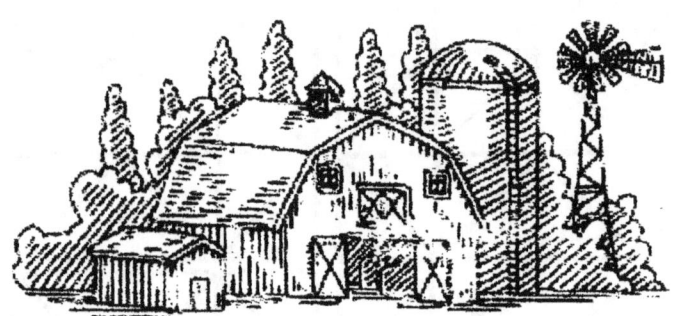

Barn Quilt Location
Quarter Rd
Hopkinton, Iowa

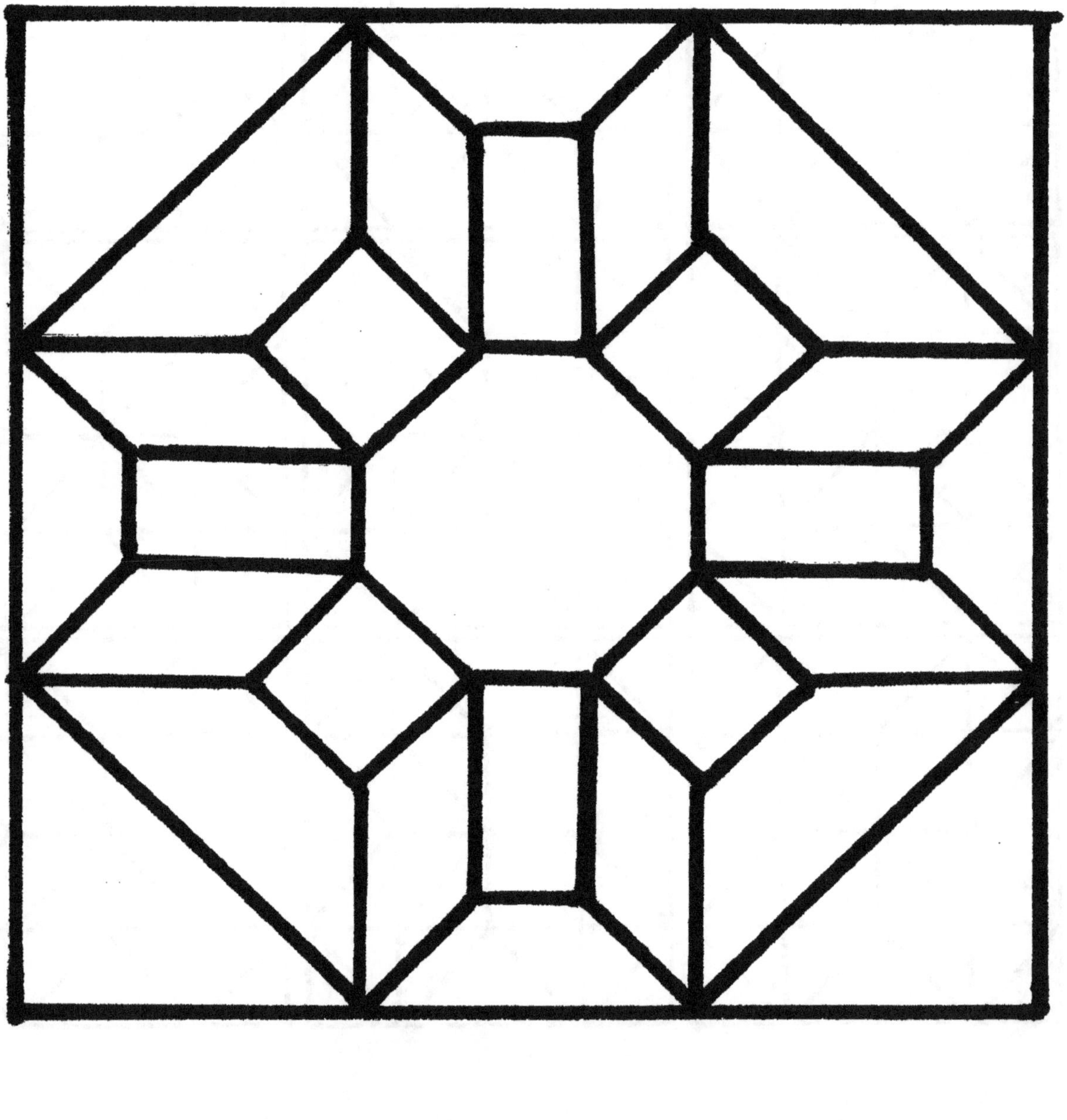

Barn Quilt Prosperity

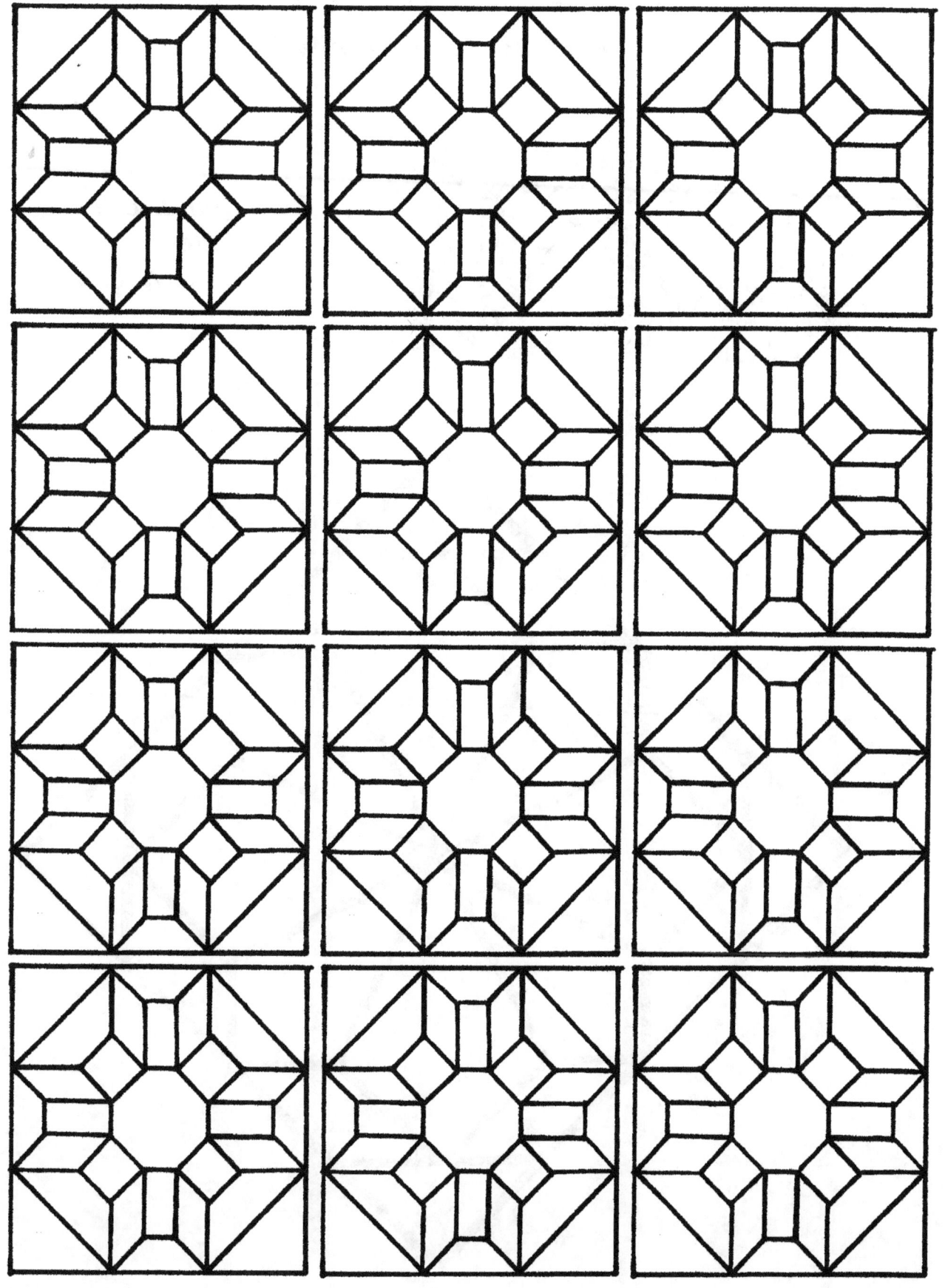

Barn Quilt Home Again
Delaware County Iowa

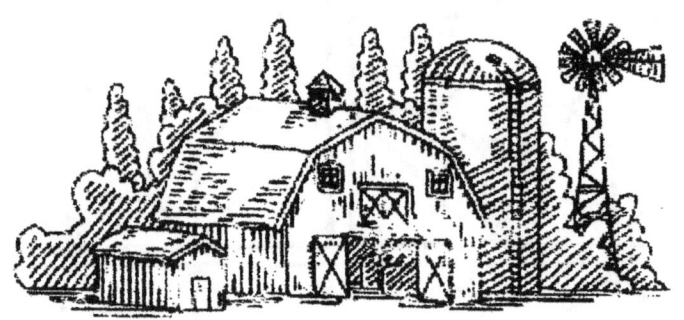

Barn Quilt Location
Stiles
Manchester, Iowa

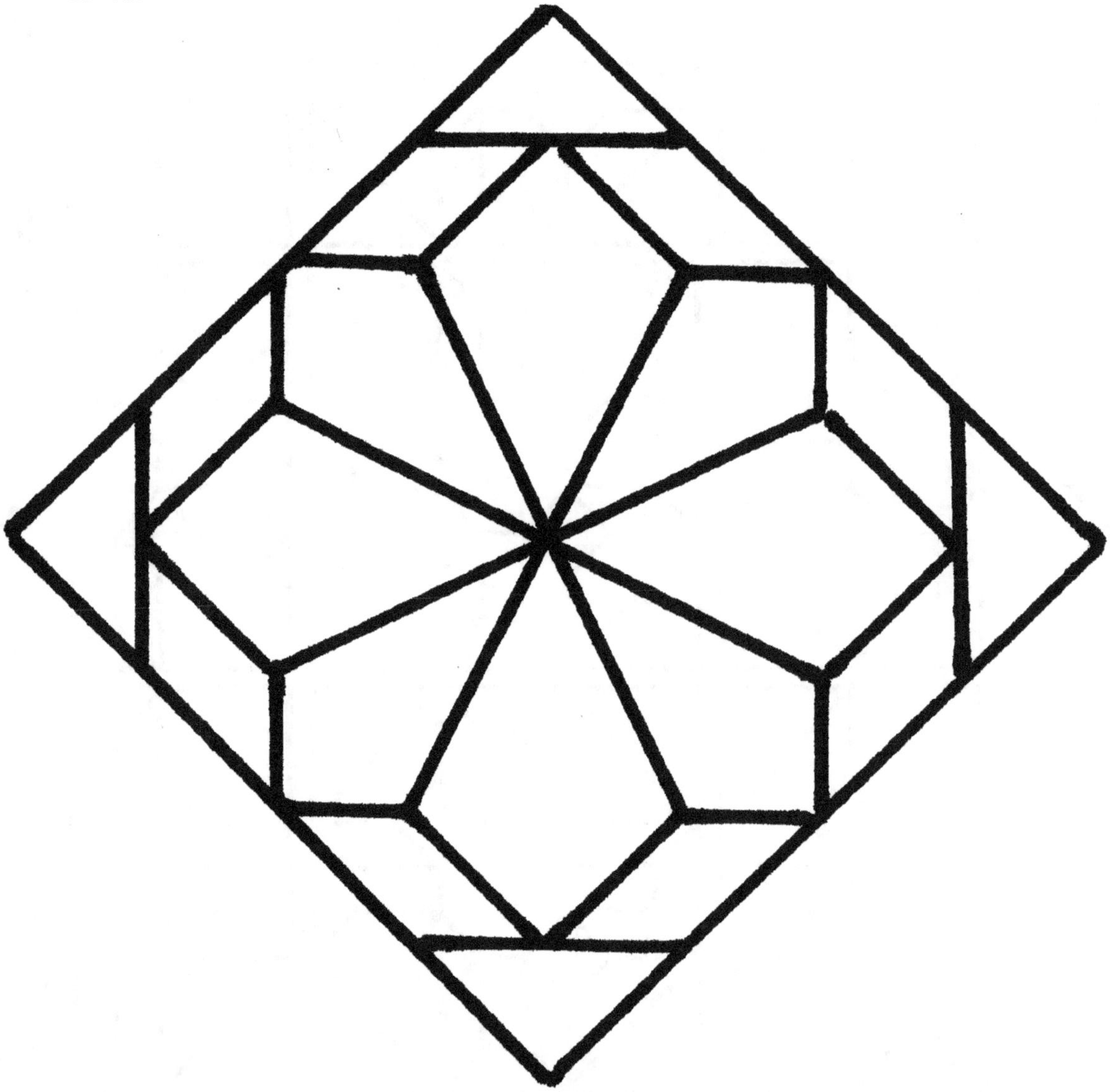

Barn Quilt Home Again

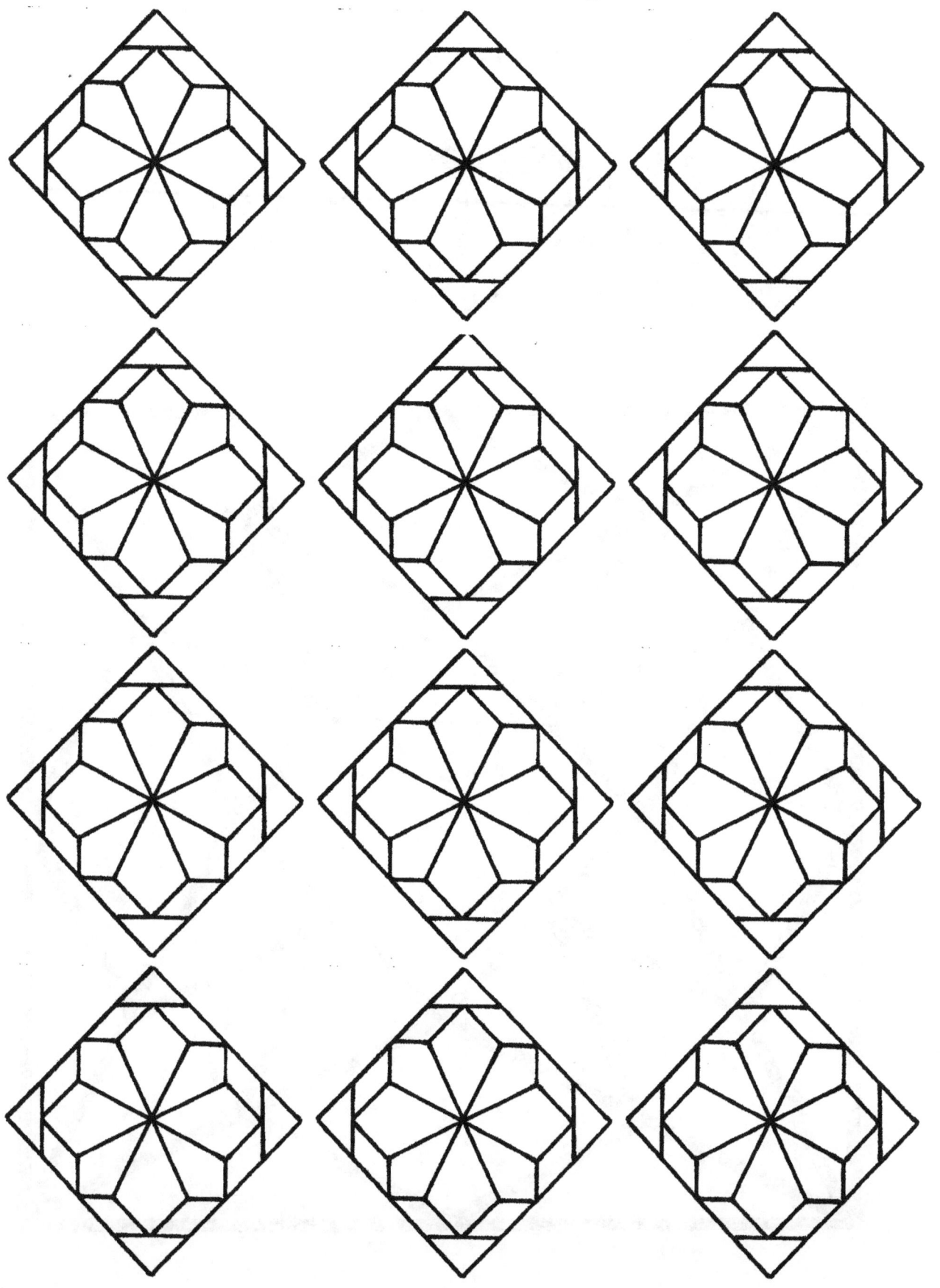

Barn Quilt Lucky Star
Delaware County Iowa

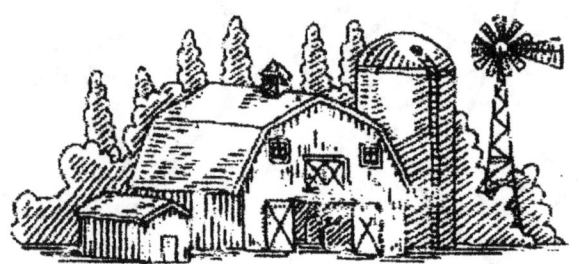

Barn Quilt Location
Hwy 38
Delhi, Iowa

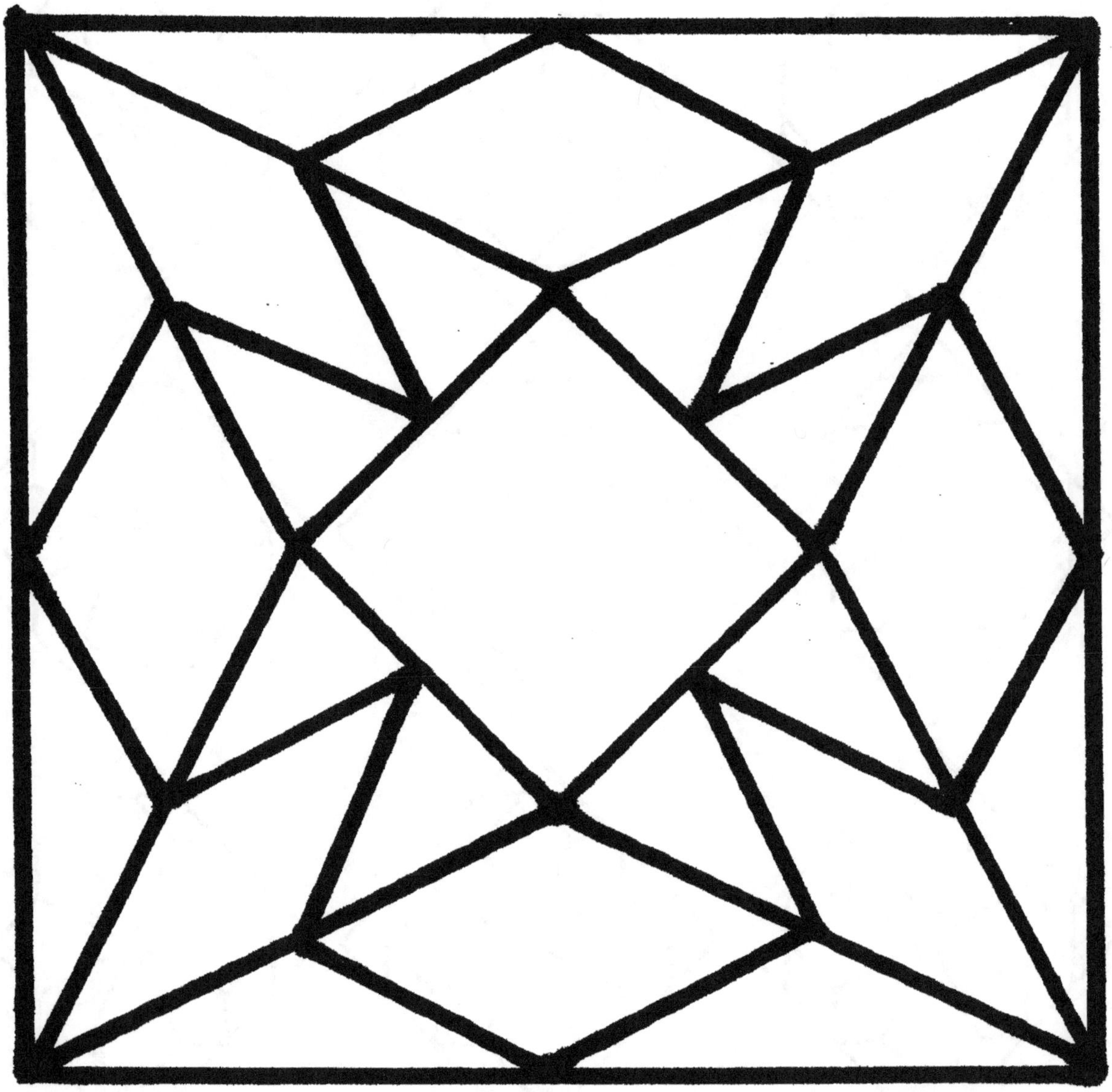

Barn Quilt Lucky Star

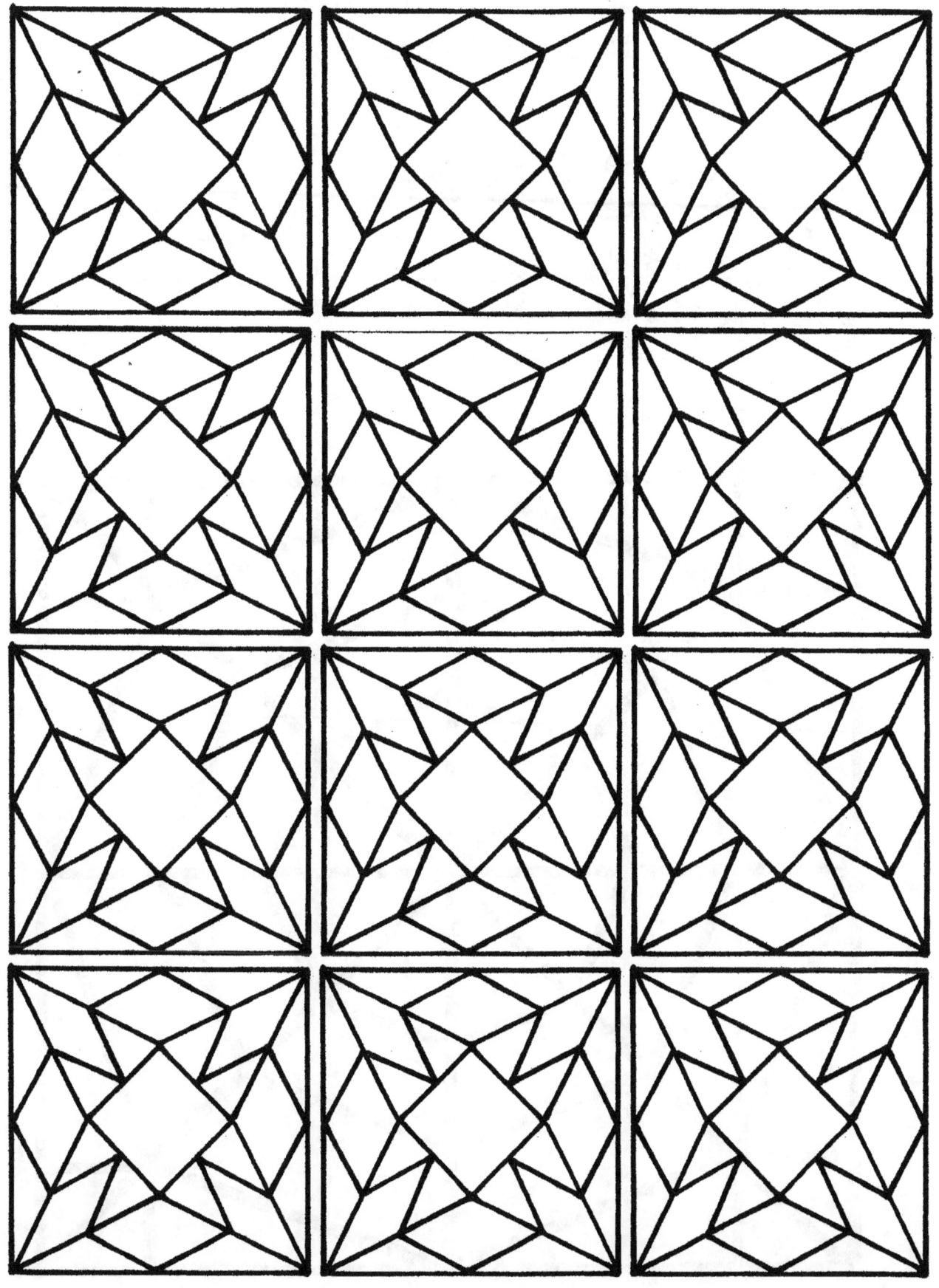

Barn Quilt Homecoming
Delaware County Iowa

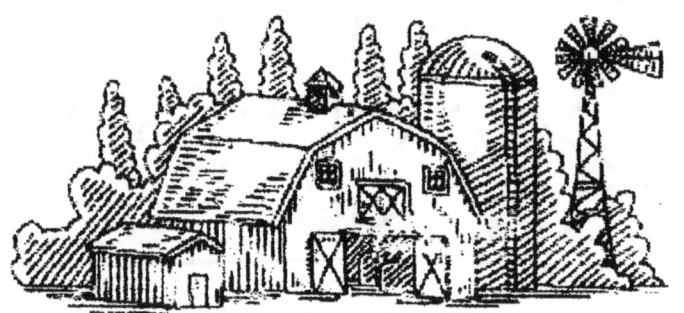

Barn Quilt Location
230th Ave
Delhi, Iowa

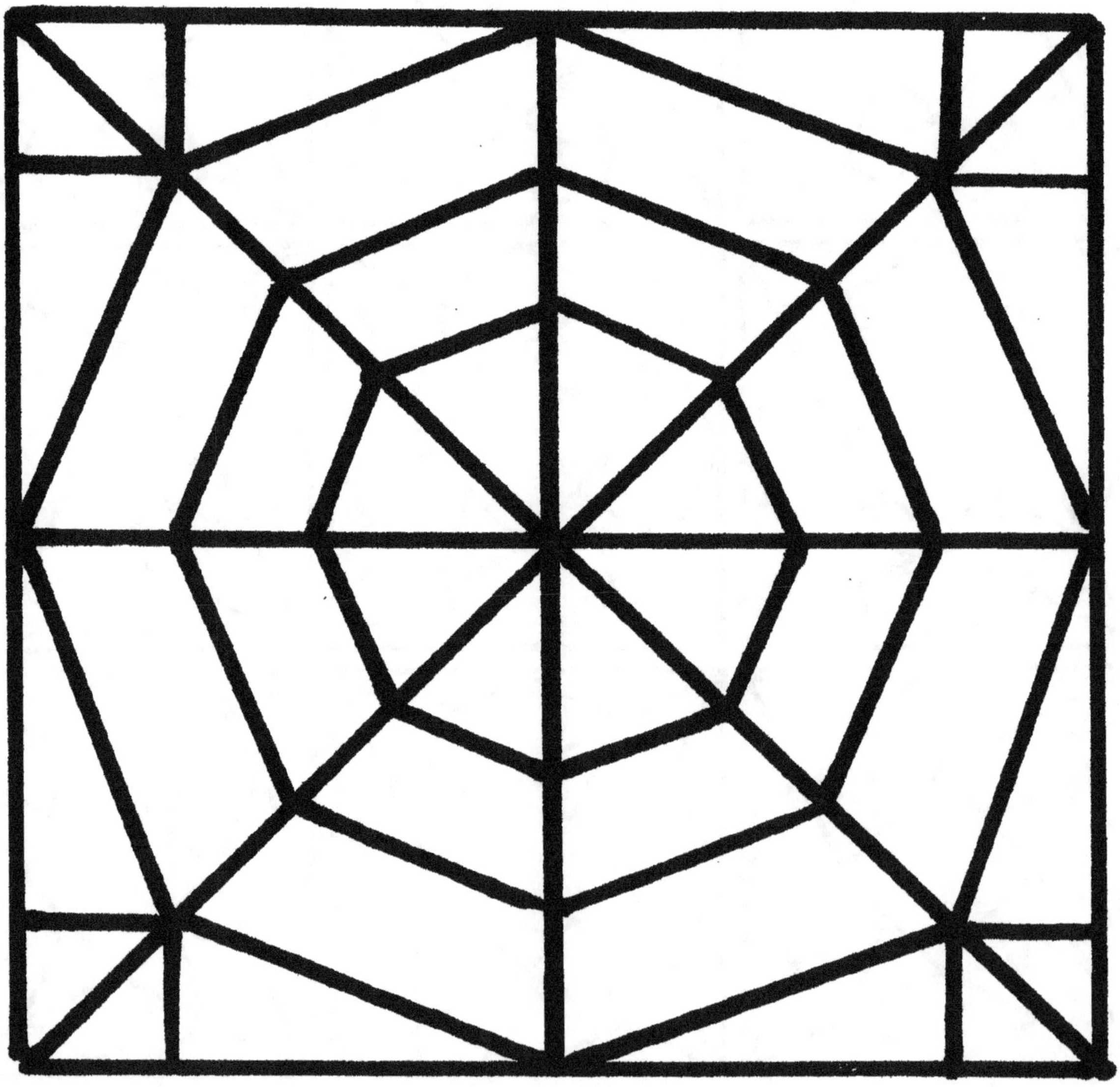

Barn Quilt Homecoming

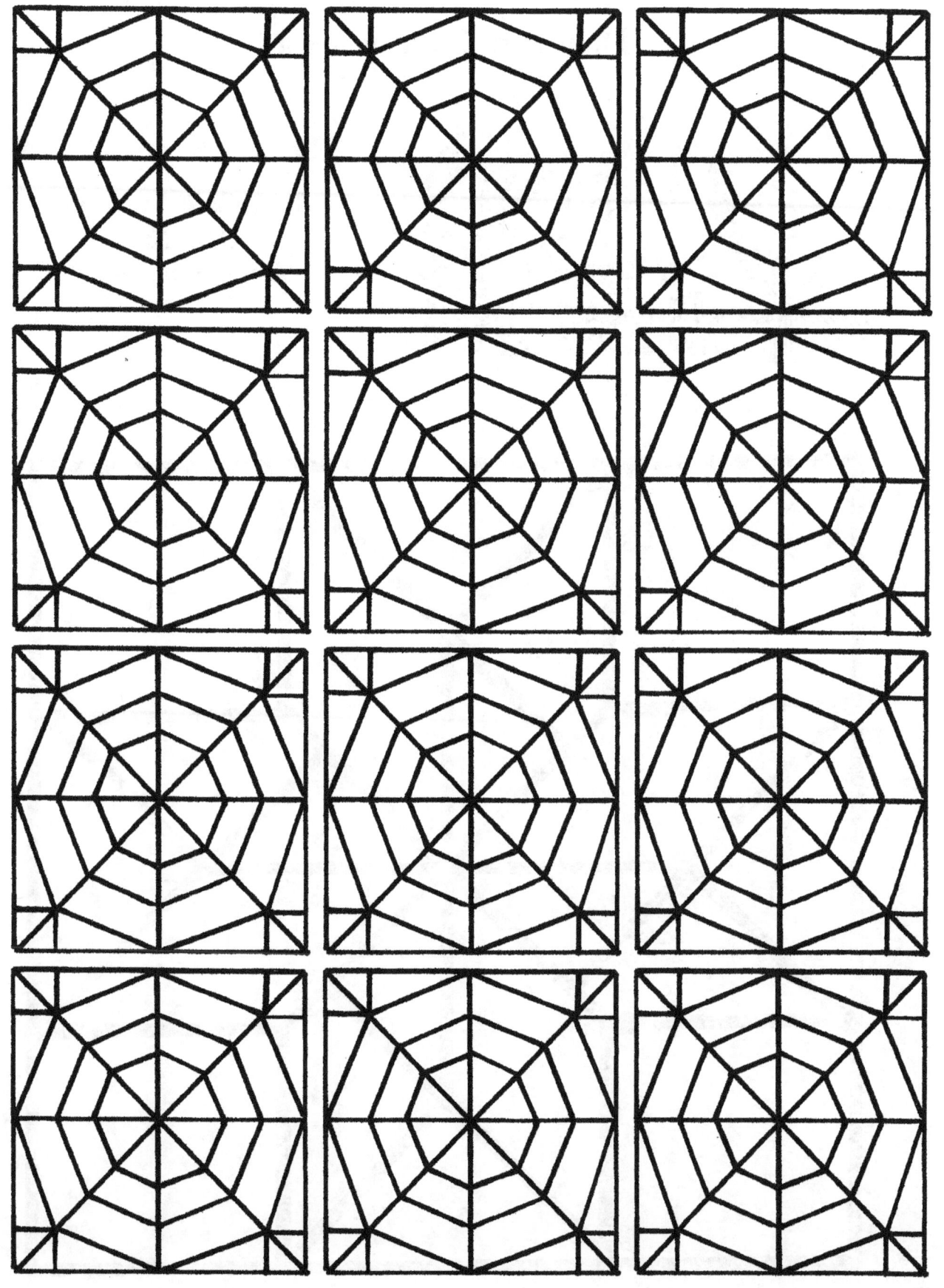

Barn Quilt Eyes of Blue
Delaware County Iowa

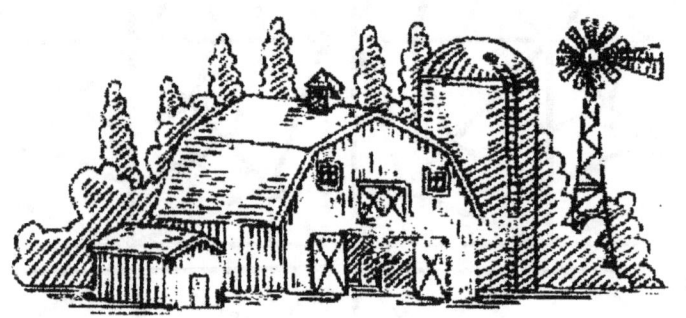

Barn Quilt Location
310th St
Hopkinton, Iowa

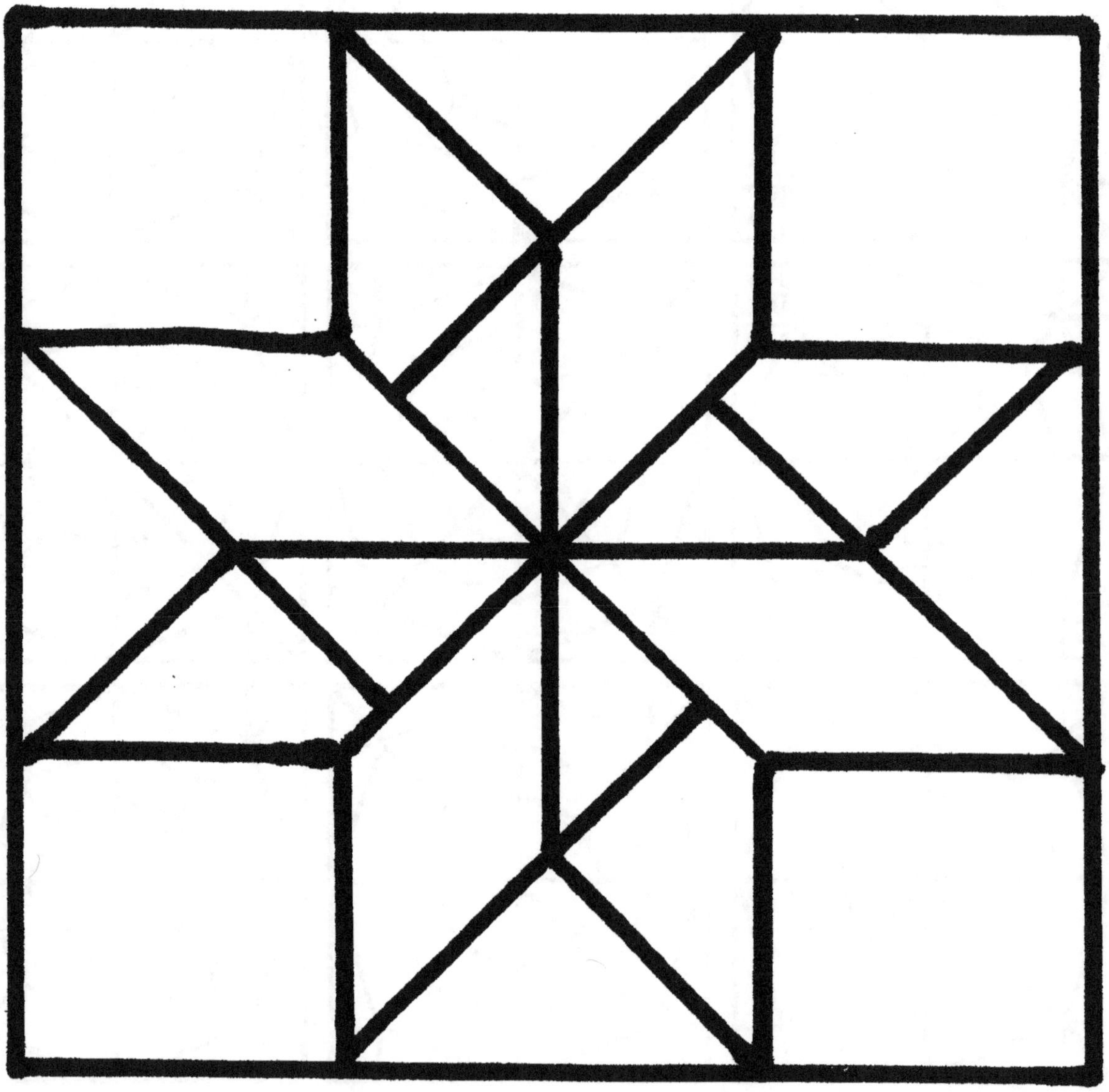

Barn Quilt Eyes of Blue

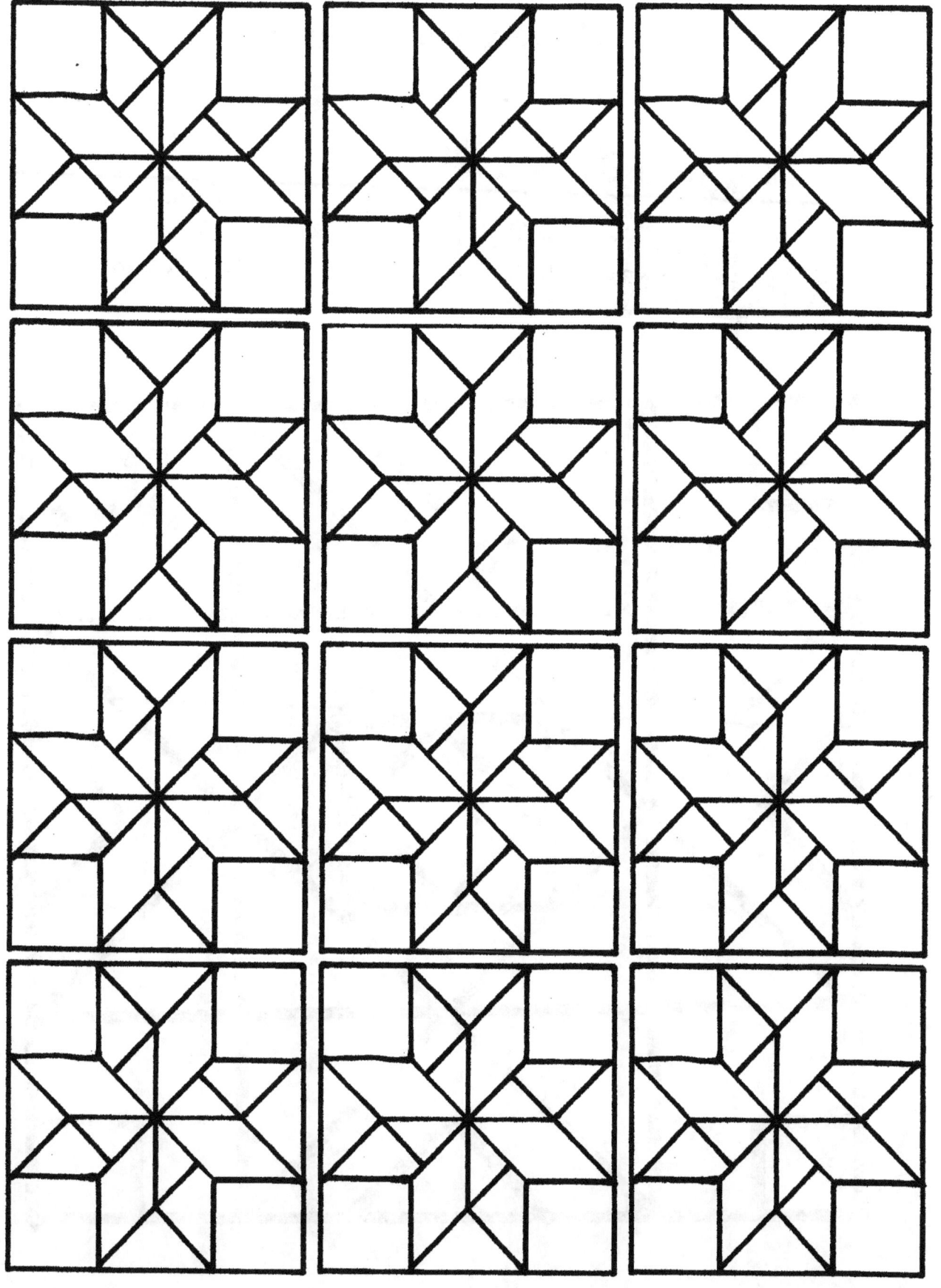

Barn Quilt Country Pride
Delaware Count Iowa

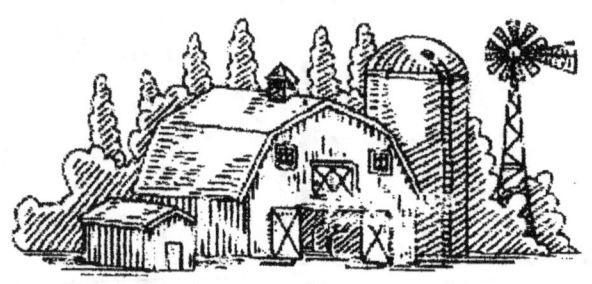

Barn Quilt Location
190th Ave
Manchester, Iowa

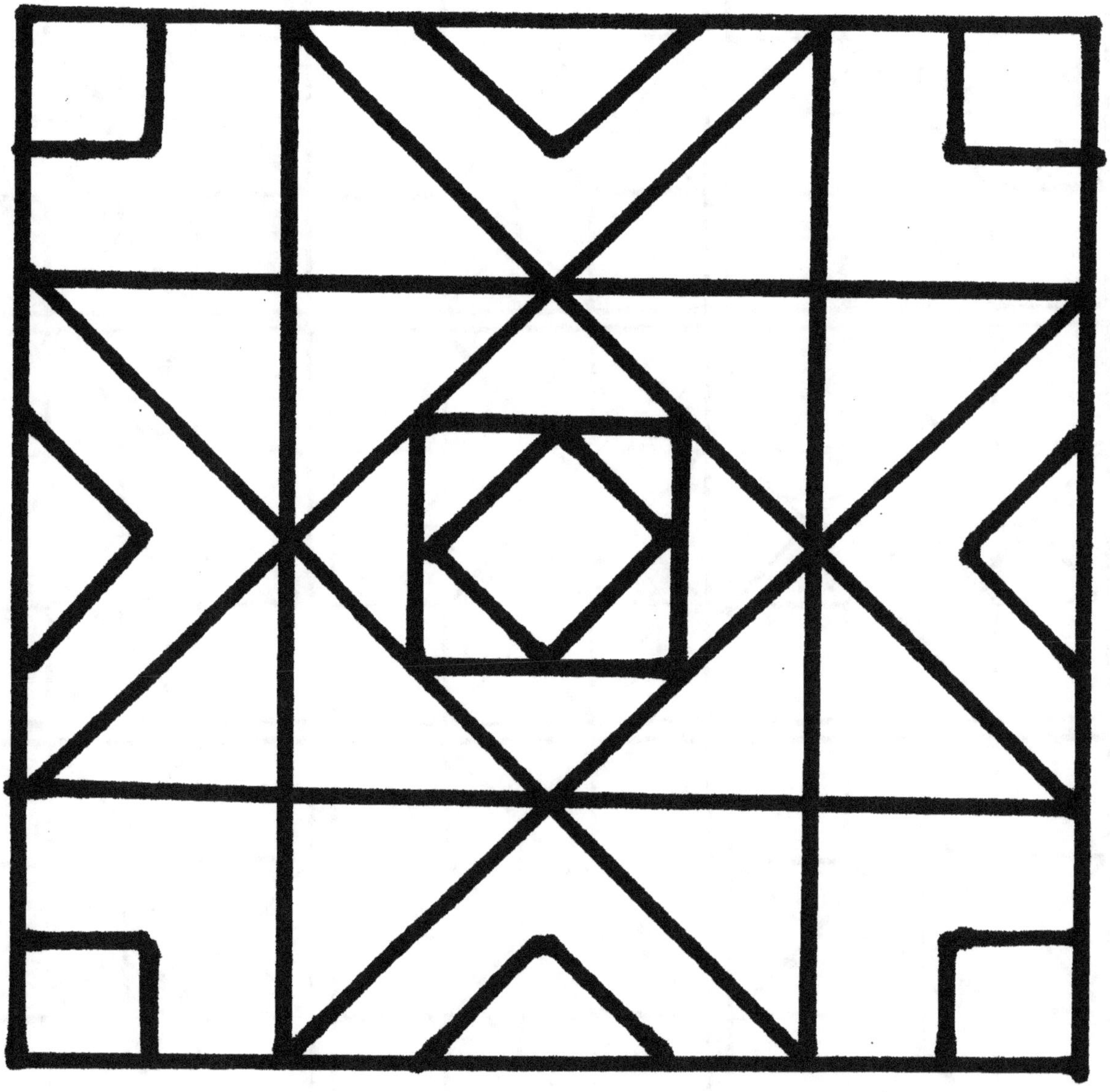

Barn Quilt Country Pride

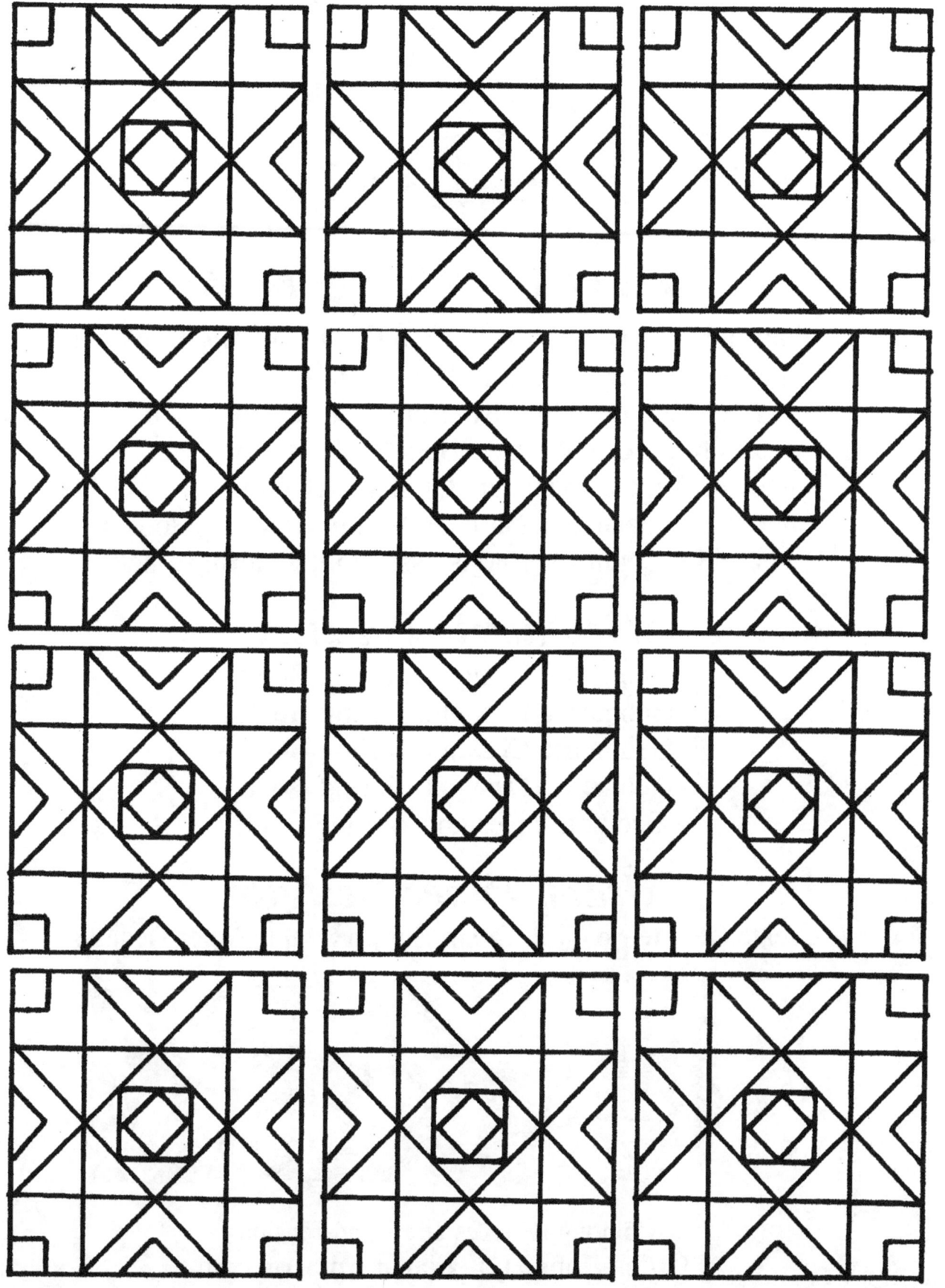

John Lettau Coloring Books

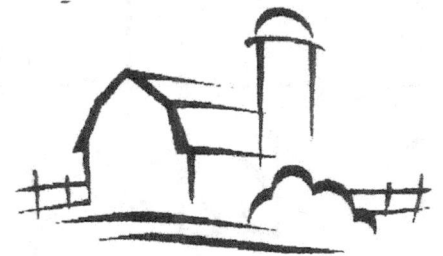

Barn Quilt Coloring Books

Shawano County Wisconsin Barn Quilt Coloring Book One
Shawano County Wisconsin Barn Quilt Coloring Book Two
Green County Wisconsin Barn Quilt Coloring Book
Delaware County Iowa Barn Quilt Coloring Book
Tennessee Appalachian Barn Quilt Trail Coloring Book One
Tennessee Appalachian Barn Quilt Trail Coloring Book Two
Franklin County Vermont Barn Quilt Coloring Book

Geometric Patterns

Geometric Design Coloring Book 1
Geometric Design Coloring Book 2
Geometric Design Coloring Book 3
Geometric Design Coloring Book 4
Geometric Design Coloring Book 5

Graph Paper Designs

Create Geometric Quilt Designs with Graph Paper Designs

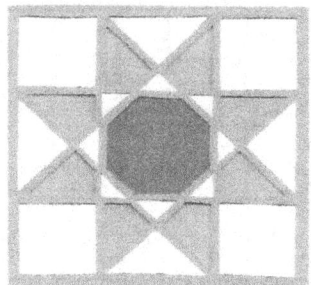 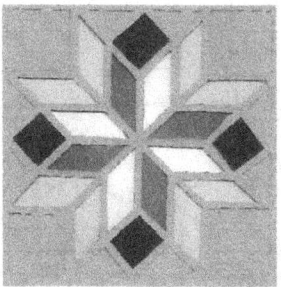 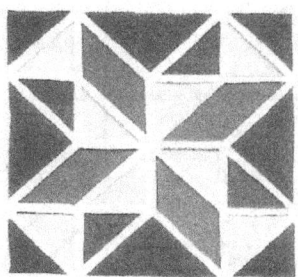

Coloring Relieves Stress and Tension
Order...John H. Lettau at Amazon.com